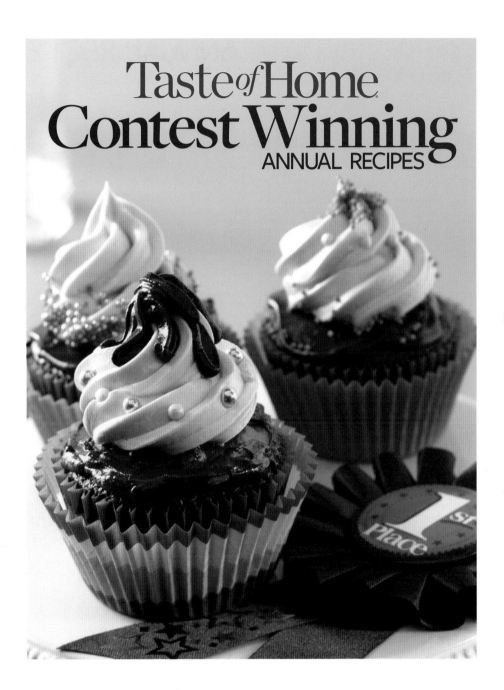

Taste of Home
Contest Winning
ANNUAL RECIPES

Taste of Home
Contest Winning
ANNUAL RECIPES

EDITORIAL
EDITOR-IN-CHIEF Catherine Cassidy
CREATIVE DIRECTOR Howard Greenberg
EDITORIAL OPERATIONS DIRECTOR Kerri Balliet

MANAGING EDITOR/PRINT & DIGITAL BOOKS Mark Hagen
ASSOCIATE CREATIVE DIRECTOR Edwin Robles Jr.

EDITORS Michelle Rozumalski, Christine Rukavena, Amy Glander
ART DIRECTOR Jessie Sharon
LAYOUT DESIGNER Nancy Novak
EDITORIAL PRODUCTION MANAGER Dena Ahlers
COPY CHIEF Deb Warlaumont Mulvey
COPY EDITOR Kaitlin Stainbrook
CONTRIBUTING COPY EDITOR Valerie Phillips

CHIEF FOOD EDITOR Karen Berner
FOOD EDITORS James Schend; Peggy Woodward, RD
RECIPE EDITORS Mary King; Jenni Sharp, RD; Irene Yeh
CONTENT OPERATIONS MANAGER Colleen King
CONTENT OPERATIONS ASSISTANT Shannon Stroud
EXECUTIVE ASSISTANT Marie Brannon

TEST KITCHEN & FOOD STYLING MANAGER Sarah Thompson
TEST COOKS Nicholas Iverson (lead), Matthew Hass, Lauren Knoelke
FOOD STYLISTS Kathryn Conrad (senior), Shannon Roum, Leah Rekau
PREP COOKS Megumi Garcia, Melissa Hansen, Bethany Van Jacobson, Sara Wirtz

PHOTOGRAPHY DIRECTOR Stephanie Marchese
PHOTOGRAPHERS Dan Roberts, Jim Wieland
PHOTOGRAPHER/SET STYLIST Grace Natoli Sheldon
SET STYLISTS Stacey Genaw, Melissa Haberman, Dee Dee Jacq
PHOTO STUDIO ASSISTANT Ester Robards

EDITORIAL BUSINESS MANAGER Kristy Martin
EDITORIAL BUSINESS ASSOCIATE Samantha Lea Stoeger

EDITOR, *TASTE OF HOME* Jeanne Ambrose
ASSOCIATE CREATIVE DIRECTOR, *TASTE OF HOME* Erin Burns
ART DIRECTOR, *TASTE OF HOME* Kristin Bowker

BUSINESS
VICE PRESIDENT, CHIEF SALES OFFICER Mark S. Josephson
GENERAL MANAGER, TASTE OF HOME COOKING SCHOOL Erin Puariea

THE READER'S DIGEST ASSOCIATION, INC.
PRESIDENT AND CHIEF EXECUTIVE OFFICER Bonnie Kintzer
CHIEF FINANCIAL OFFICER Colette Chestnut
VICE PRESIDENT, CHIEF OPERATING OFFICER, NORTH AMERICA Howard Halligan
VICE PRESIDENT, ENTHUSIAST BRANDS, BOOKS & RETAIL Harold Clarke
CHIEF MARKETING OFFICER Leslie Dukker Doty
VICE PRESIDENT, NORTH AMERICAN HUMAN RESOURCES Phyllis E. Gebhardt, SPHR
VICE PRESIDENT, BRAND MARKETING Beth Gorry
VICE PRESIDENT, GLOBAL COMMUNICATIONS Susan Russ
VICE PRESIDENT, CHIEF TECHNOLOGY OFFICER Aneel Tejwaney
VICE PRESIDENT, CONSUMER MARKETING PLANNING Jim Woods

COVER PHOTOGRAPHY
PHOTOGRAPHER Rob Hagen
FOOD STYLIST Ronne Day
SET STYLIST Dee Dee Jacq

PICTURED ON THE FRONT COVER: Chocolate Peanut Butter Cupcakes, page 193.
PICTURED ON THE BACK COVER: Caribbean Four-Fruit Salsa, page 154; Berry-Apple-Rhubarb Pie, page 194; Seafood Pasta Alfredo, page 147; Never-Miss Apple Cake, page 207.

TABLE OF CONTENTS

MORE THAN 350 PRIZEWINNING RECIPES & TIPS!

You know a recipe is special when it comes out on top of thousands of tasty entrees in a national competition. In *Contest Winning Annual Recipes*, you'll find hundreds of prizewinning dishes—all in one convenient collection. Each first-rate favorite comes straight from the kitchen files of a home cook like you, making it a tried-and-true dish that proved to be a winner again and again.

Our *Taste of Home* judges loved sampling all the creative submissions they received in each contest. After tasting and reviewing the appetizing entries, our judges selected the very best. This 12th edition of *Contest Winning Annual Recipes* features more than two dozen Grand Prize winners and hundreds of runners-up, so you can rest assured that every dish was a scrumptious standout.

The #1 food magazine in the world, *Taste of Home* always makes it easy to fix delicious, memorable dishes that use everyday ingredients and simple techniques. Thanks to *Contest Winning Annual Recipes*, you can serve fuss-free meals your family and friends will find truly exceptional. So gather loved ones around the table and discover a new favorite today. When you cook from this special treasury of best-loved recipes, everybody wins!

Teriyaki Chicken Salad with Poppy Seed Dressing, page 28

Winners from Dozens of Contests

The national recipe contests showcased in this cookbook cover a wide range of dishes—classic main courses, skillet entrees, hearty casseroles, slow-cooked suppers, healthier foods, five-ingredient fare, delectable desserts and more. No matter what type of recipe you're looking for or what kind of meal you're planning, you're sure to find the perfect choice in this big collection. For a complete list of chapters, see the Table of Contents on page 3.

Here's a quick preview of the Grand Prize winning recipes in this cookbook (each listed underneath the name of the national recipe contest it won):

TANTALIZING TENDERLOIN
Sink your teeth into Grand Prize winner Peppered Filets with Cherry Port Sauce for 2 (page 81) when you're craving hearty food that has stick-to-your-ribs appeal. A timeless classic with a fruity twist, this mouthwatering beef entree was a cut above the rest.

SLOW-COOKED WINNERS
Don't let hectic weekdays or activity-packed weekends keep you from sitting down to a wholesome, home-cooked dinner. An effortless, all-in-one meal is yours for the taking when you fix Slow Cooker Tamale Pie (page 88)—or any of the slow-simmered sensations in this cookbook.

EASY, HEALTHY DINNERS
Eating right doesn't have to mean giving up the foods you love most. Fuss-free creations like Slow-Cooked Caribbean Pot Roast (page 79) make it simple to prepare lighter fare that will leave you and your family satisfied.

GROUND BEEF
Versatile and economical, ground beef is always a popular ingredient for today's time-crunched cooks. Discover just how easy it is to "beef up" your weeknight routine with zesty Tacoritos (page 84), an unforgettable main course loaded with south-of-the-border spice.

EXCEPTIONAL EGGS
Rise and shine with an assortment of farm-fresh egg dishes our judging panel considered top-notch, including Diana Neves' first-place Sunny-Side-Up Herbed Tart (page 72). What an amazing way to start the day!

HEALTHY FALL CASSEROLES
For a comforting casserole without all the fat and calories, pick Danna Rogers' award-winning Vegetarian Egg Strata (page 65). Scrumptious one-pan meals like this won't throw a healthy eating plan off track...and the tantalizing layers will have you savoring every bite.

CAKES & TORTES

No matter how full you are, there's always room for a prizewinning dessert! Surrender to temptation and indulge in a big slice of JoAnn Koerkenmeier's Chocolate Truffle Cake (page 200). Covered with a rich and velvety ganache, this honored dessert is worth the splurge.

PIE RECIPES

Get ready to roll out some of the best pies from around the country—including Martha Sorensen's Sour-Cream Lemon Pie (page 209). From fruit-filled wonders to silky cream delights, our collection makes it easy as pie to end lunch or dinner on a sweet note.

COOKIE JAR STARS

You'll want to give in to your biggest cookie cravings when you see these first-place goodies. Extra-Special Cashew Crescents (page 187) were tops in our contest—and are sure to earn a prominent spot in your recipe box, too!

BEST-EVER BROWNIES

When it comes to crowd-pleasers, brownies are always a winning bet. Carol Prewett's Ultimate Double Chocolate Brownies recipe (page 182) and the other bars in this book will give you a finger-licking panful every time.

BERRY BONANZA

What can brighten your day like a bounty of berries? Juicy and colorful, these tongue-tingling fruits make recipes like Over-the-Top Blueberry Bread Pudding (page 220) ripe for the picking when you're looking for an impressive treat.

FRESH HERBS

From the garden to the table, fresh herbs are the secret to transforming a ho-hum dish into something extraordinary. Grilled Shrimp with Cilantro Dipping Sauce (page 145) was awarded the biggest prize among entries dressed up with these unbeatable ingredients.

CLASSIC COUNTRY CASSEROLES

For a taste of traditional country cooking, dig in to simple and satisfying bakes that boast home-style flavor. Donetta Brunner's Ham and Asparagus Casserole (page 105) is a favorite you'll get requests for over and over again.

SUPER STOVETOP ENTREES

Are jam-packed workdays making it difficult to get a handle on dinner? You don't need to rush to the drive-thru! Simply grab a skillet, turn on the stove and stir up mouthwatering Bacon & Rosemary Chicken (page 127). It's a speedy entree that looks and tastes extra-special.

COMFORTING CASSEROLES

Casseroles are comfort food at its very best. Your family will clamor for the oven-baked goodness inside Michele Sheppard's Chicken Alfredo Stuffed Shells (page 120) and the other piping-hot creations in this book—all guaranteed to warm the heart and soul.

LIGHTEN UP

Get the skinny on eating healthier with our judging panel's top-rated selections that are trimmed down but delicious. Once you sample Chicken Florentine Meatballs (page 114) and other guilt-free specialties, you'll agree that eating on the lighter side has never tasted so good.

CRAZY ABOUT CRANBERRIES

Get on a cranberry kick with outstanding foods full of sweet-tart flavor. Susan Cortesi's fantastic Chicken with Cranberry-Balsamic Sauce (page 132) was the cream of this contest crop featuring ruby-red gems.

EASY-AS-PIE PIZZA

Take your local pizza place off speed dial—your kitchen is about to become your go-to pizzeria! Readily available convenience items such as refrigerated dough and string cheese make short work of Stuffed-Crust Chicken Pizza (page 130) and other homemade pies.

SENSATIONAL SPUDS

Round out tonight's dinner with Cathy Hall's incredible Au Gratin Potato Pancakes (page 164), our contest judges' number one choice among spud-filled entries. The fried herbed patties will have 'em begging for seconds!

SAY CHEESE!

A dish loaded with golden ooey-gooey goodness always gets smiles. Pepper Jack Mac (page 160) emerged as the big cheese in our contest celebrating cheddar, mozzarella, Swiss and many more varieties.

5-INGREDIENT FAVORITES

Recipes that require only five or fewer ingredients can be lifesavers to short-on-time cooks. Beat the clock and slash your grocery bill, too, with surprisingly easy recipes like Chipotle Sliders (page 15), ready in just 30 minutes.

GARLIC & ONIONS

Whether used to season or garnish, onions and garlic take the flavor factor up a notch. You're sure to agree that the signature taste of Charlene Chambers' Champion Lamb Burgers (page 54) is worthy of first prize.

MEATLESS DISHES

Want to skip the meat? Your family won't mind when they dive in to a big bowlful of Sweet Potato & Black Bean Chili (page 42). Chunky and filling, this dish is likely to become a mainstay on your menus.

HEALTHY WHOLE GRAINS

Whether you're sticking to a special diet or just want to eat healthier, incorporating whole grains into meals can help. Grand Prize winning Bulgur Greek Salad (page 36) stood out as a low-calorie but satisfying option.

BEST SPRING PRODUCE

Celebrate the return of spring with dishes that call for the season's freshest produce. You'll harvest compliments by the bushel when you serve highly rated Teriyaki Chicken Salad with Poppy Seed Dressing (page 28).

When you choose from the celebrated favorites in *Contest Winning Annual Recipes*, your meals just can't miss. So go ahead and select any of this book's sensational specialties to put on your family menus. One thing is for certain—no matter what the occasion, every dish you prepare will be a true, honest-to-goodness winner!

Mango Guacamole, page 13

10
13
20

Snacks & Appetizers

For **small-bite standouts**, rely on this chapter packed with popular finger foods, fun munchies and special party starters. You're sure to agree—they're **anything but ordinary.**

Triple Cranberry Chicken Lettuce Wraps

If you like cranberries, this is the recipe for you! It uses dried berries, sauce and juice to give chicken lettuce wraps a burst of tongue-tingling fruit flavor.

—**PRISCILLA YEE** CONCORD, CA

PREP: 20 MIN. • **COOK:** 15 MIN.
MAKES: 1 DOZEN

- 1 cup whole-berry cranberry sauce
- ½ cup cranberry juice
- ¼ cup reduced-sodium soy sauce
- 2 tablespoons sugar
- 1 tablespoon minced fresh gingerroot
- 2 teaspoons chili garlic sauce
- 2 garlic cloves, minced
- 2 tablespoons lime juice
- 1 tablespoon grated lime peel
- 1½ cups shredded cooked chicken breast
- 1 cup dried cranberries
- ½ cup shredded carrot
- ⅓ cup thinly sliced green onions
- ¼ cup minced fresh mint
- ¼ cup minced fresh basil
- 12 Bibb or Boston lettuce leaves
- ½ cup chopped salted peanuts

1. In a small saucepan, combine the first seven ingredients. Bring to a boil. Reduce the heat; simmer, uncovered, for 5 minutes. Remove from the heat; stir in the lime juice and peel; set aside.
2. In a small bowl, combine chicken, dried cranberries, carrot, onions, mint and basil. Place about 3 tablespoons chicken mixture on each lettuce leaf. Top with 1 tablespoon cranberry sauce mixture and 2 teaspoons peanuts. Fold the lettuce over the filling. Serve with the remaining sauce.

CRUMB CLUE

Soft (fresh) bread crumbs are easy to make in a food processor or blender. Tear a few slices of bread into 1½-in. pieces and place them in the food processor or blender container. Cover and pulse (short on/off actions) until you have crumbs. The more you pulse, the finer they will be.

Tapas Meatballs with Orange Glaze

Crisp on the outside and moist on the inside, these cheese-stuffed baked bites in a sweet-sour glaze are sure to impress.

—**BONNIE STALLINGS** MARTINSBURG, WV

PREP: 25 MIN. • **BAKE:** 20 MIN.
MAKES: 16 MEATBALLS

- 1 egg, lightly beaten
- ¼ cup ketchup
- 1 small onion, finely chopped
- ½ cup soft bread crumbs
- ¼ cup minced fresh parsley
- 3 teaspoons paprika
- 2 garlic cloves, minced
- ½ teaspoon salt
- ½ teaspoon pepper
- 1 pound lean ground beef (90% lean)
- 2½ ounces feta cheese, cut into sixteen ½-in. cubes

GLAZE
- 1 jar (12 ounces) orange marmalade
- ¼ cup orange juice
- 3 green onions, chopped, divided
- 1 jalapeno pepper, seeded and chopped

1. In a large bowl, combine the first nine ingredients. Crumble the beef over the mixture and mix well. Divide into 16 portions; flatten. Top each with a cheese cube; form the beef mixture around cheese into meatballs.
2. Place on a greased rack in a shallow baking pan. Bake, uncovered, at 400° for 20-25 minutes or until no longer pink. In a small saucepan, heat the marmalade, orange juice, half of the green onions and the jalapeno.
3. Place the meatballs in a serving dish; pour the glaze over the top and gently stir to coat. Garnish with the remaining green onions.

FREEZE OPTION *Freeze the cooled meatballs in freezer containers. To use, partially thaw meatballs in refrigerator overnight. Microwave, covered, on high in a microwave-safe dish until heated through, gently stirring and adding a little water if necessary. Meanwhile, combine and heat glaze ingredients as directed. Serve over meatballs.*

NOTE *Wear disposable gloves when cutting hot peppers; the oils can burn skin. Avoid touching your face.*

Lick-the-Bowl-Clean Hummus

As a fan of hummus that features garlic and onion, I came up with a homemade version that really lets those ingredients shine. I serve it with a basket of pita chips or a platter of fresh vegetables.
—**SARAH GILBERT** BEAVERTON, OR

PREP: 10 MIN. • **COOK:** 35 MIN.
MAKES: 2½ CUPS

- 2 large sweet onions, thinly sliced
- ¼ cup plus ⅓ cup olive oil, divided
- 1 can (15 ounces) garbanzo beans or chickpeas, rinsed and drained
- ¼ cup plus 2 tablespoons lemon juice
- ¼ cup tahini
- 4 garlic cloves, minced
- ⅛ teaspoon salt
- ⅛ teaspoon pepper
  Baked pita chips or assorted fresh vegetables

1. In a large skillet, saute sweet onions in ¼ cup oil until softened. Reduce the heat to medium-low; cook, stirring occasionally, for 30 minutes or until deep golden brown.
2. Transfer to a food processor; add the beans, lemon juice, tahini, garlic, salt, pepper and remaining oil. Cover and process for 30 seconds or until smooth. Serve with baked pita chips or fresh vegetables.

Stuffed Cherry Tomatoes

I've made stuffed mushrooms for years and decided to adapt that idea for cherry tomatoes. They're perfect for potlucks, parties and luncheons. Chopped walnuts and water chestnuts add a bit of crunch to the rich cream-cheese filling.
—**DONNA SMITH** GREY CLIFF, MT

START TO FINISH: 30 MIN.
MAKES: ABOUT 2 DOZEN

- 1 pint small cherry tomatoes
FILLING
- 1 package (3 ounces) cream cheese, softened
- ¼ cup ranch-style dressing
- 2 tablespoons thinly sliced green onions
- 2 tablespoons finely chopped water chestnuts
- 2 tablespoons finely chopped walnuts

1. Slice off the tops of the cherry tomatoes. Scoop out the pulp with a small melon ball cutter, reserving the pulp to use as necessary to thin the filling. Drain the cherry tomatoes, upside-down, on paper towel.
2. Combine the filling ingredients in a small bowl. Stuff the tomatoes with the filling. Keep refrigerated until serving time.

Presto Black Bean & Corn Salsa

Salsa is one of my favorite foods to tinker with in the kitchen. Dress up the jarred kind with black beans, corn, cilantro and more for a big batch everyone will love.
—**JANICE DANIELS** ROCHESTER, MN

START TO FINISH: 25 MIN.
MAKES: 28 SERVINGS (¼ CUP EACH)

- 1 can (15 ounces) black beans, rinsed and drained
- 2 cups fresh or frozen corn, thawed
- 5 plum tomatoes, chopped
- 1 large sweet red pepper, chopped
- 1 small green pepper, chopped
- 1 can (4 ounces) chopped green chilies
- ¼ cup chopped red onion
- ¼ cup minced fresh cilantro
- 2 tablespoons lime juice
- 2 garlic cloves, minced
- 1 teaspoon sugar
- 1 teaspoon salt
- ½ teaspoon ground cumin
- 1 jar (16 ounces) salsa
  Tortilla chips

In a large bowl, combine the black beans, corn, plum tomatoes, peppers, chilies, red onion, cilantro, lime juice, garlic, sugar, salt and cumin. Stir in the salsa until blended. Serve with chips.

Three-Cheese Fondue

My youngest daughter, who lives in France, shared this recipe. I make sure to prepare it when my oldest daughter and her family visit my husband and me. They love it just as much as we do!

—BETTY MANGAS TOLEDO, OH

START TO FINISH: 30 MIN. **• MAKES:** 4 CUPS

- ½ pound each Emmenthaler, Gruyere and Jarlsberg cheeses, shredded
- 2 tablespoons cornstarch, divided
- 4 teaspoons cherry brandy
- 2 cups dry white wine
- ⅛ teaspoon ground nutmeg
- ⅛ teaspoon paprika
  Dash cayenne pepper
  Cubed French bread baguette, boiled red potatoes and/or tiny whole pickles

1. In a large bowl, combine the cheeses and 1 tablespoon cornstarch. In a small bowl, combine remaining cornstarch and cherry brandy; set aside. In a large saucepan, heat white wine over medium heat until bubbles form around the sides of the pan.

2. Reduce heat to medium-low; add a handful of the cheese mixture. Stir constantly, using a figure-eight motion, until the cheese is almost completely melted. Continue adding cheese, one handful at a time, allowing the cheese to almost completely melt between additions.

3. Stir the brandy mixture; gradually stir into the cheese mixture. Add the spices; cook and stir until the mixture is thickened and smooth.

4. Transfer to a fondue pot and keep warm. Serve with bread cubes, potatoes and/or pickles.

Foolproof Mushrooms

START TO FINISH: 25 MIN. **• MAKES:** 2½ DOZEN

- 1 package (6½ ounces) garlic-herb spreadable cheese
- 3 tablespoons grated Parmesan cheese, divided
- 30 small fresh mushrooms, stems removed
  Thinly sliced fresh basil, optional

1. Preheat oven to 400°. In a small bowl, combine the spreadable cheese and 2 tablespoons Parmesan cheese; spoon into the mushroom caps.

2. Transfer the mushroom caps to a foil-lined baking sheet; sprinkle with the remaining Parmesan cheese. Bake 10-12 minutes or until lightly browned. Garnish with fresh basil if desired.

❝Garlic-herb spreadable cheese, grated Parmesan and sliced fresh basil pack a surprising amount of flavor into Foolproof Mushrooms. Add some chopped artichoke hearts for extra appeal.❞

—GAIL LUCAS OLIVE BRANCH, MS

> I roll a yummy turkey filling in phyllo and bake the little cigar shapes until they're golden brown. A blend of cranberry sauce and Dijon mustard is perfect for dipping.
>
> **—DONNA MARIE RYAN** TOPSFIELD, MA

Turkey Cigars with Cranberry-Dijon Dipping Sauce

PREP: 35 MIN. • **BAKE:** 10 MIN.
MAKES: 2 DOZEN (1 CUP SAUCE)

- ½ **pound ground turkey**
- 4 **teaspoons grated Parmesan cheese**
- 2 **teaspoons minced fresh parsley**
- 2 **teaspoons jellied cranberry sauce**
- 2 **teaspoons ground walnuts, divided**
- 1 **teaspoon honey**
- 1 **teaspoon Dijon mustard**
- ½ **teaspoon salt**
- ½ **teaspoon pepper**
- 12 **sheets phyllo dough (14x9 inches)**
- 6 **tablespoons butter, melted**

DIPPING SAUCE
- ½ **cup jellied cranberry sauce**
- ¼ **cup Dijon mustard**

1. In a small skillet, cook turkey over medium heat until no longer pink; drain. Remove from the heat. Stir in the cheese, parsley, cranberry sauce, 1 teaspoon walnuts, honey, mustard, salt and pepper.

2. Place one sheet of phyllo dough on a work surface with a long side facing you; brush with butter. Repeat with three more sheets of phyllo, brushing each layer. (Keep remaining phyllo covered with plastic wrap and a damp towel to prevent it from drying out.)

3. Cut the stack widthwise into four strips. Place 2 tablespoons turkey mixture along one long side of each strip; roll up tightly. Pinch the edges to seal. Cut the roll in half; place seam side down on an ungreased baking sheet. Repeat. Brush tops with butter; sprinkle with remaining walnuts.

4. Bake at 425° for 10-12 minutes or until golden brown. For dipping sauce, in a microwave, heat cranberry sauce until softened. Stir in mustard. Serve with appetizers.

PER SERVING *76 cal., 5 g fat (2 g sat. fat), 14 mg chol., 232 mg sodium, 7 g carb., trace fiber, 2 g pro.* **Diabetic Exchanges:** *1 fat, ½ starch.*

Sesame Omelet Spinach Spirals

Tortilla spirals are always popular at a party. I give them international flair by rolling up omelets flavored with tahini, fresh ginger, sesame oil, red pepper and more.

—**ROXANNE CHAN** ALBANY, CA

PREP: 25 MIN. • **COOK:** 10 MIN.
MAKES: ABOUT 2½ DOZEN (⅓ CUP SAUCE)

- 4 **tablespoons tahini**
- 4 **spinach tortillas (8 inches), warmed**
- 6 **eggs**
- 2 **tablespoons each finely chopped green onion, sweet red pepper and canned water chestnuts**
- 2 **tablespoons shredded carrot**
- 1 **teaspoon minced fresh gingerroot**
- ¼ **teaspoon crushed red pepper flakes**
- 2 **teaspoons sesame oil, divided**

DIPPING SAUCE
- ¼ **cup reduced-sodium soy sauce**
- 1 **tablespoon minced fresh cilantro**
- 1 **garlic clove, minced**
- 1 **teaspoon sesame seeds, toasted**
- 1 **teaspoon rice vinegar**
- 1 **teaspoon sesame oil**
- ¼ **teaspoon grated orange peel**

1. Spread tahini over tortillas; set aside. In a small bowl, whisk the eggs, onion, red pepper, water chestnuts, carrot, ginger and pepper flakes.
2. Heat a large nonstick skillet over medium heat; lightly brush with some of the oil. Pour ⅓ cup egg mixture into the pan; cook for 1 minute or until set. Flip the egg mixture and cook 30 seconds to 1 minute longer or until lightly browned. Place the omelet on a tortilla; roll up. Repeat three times, brushing the skillet as needed with remaining oil. Cut the wraps into 1-in. slices.
3. Combine the sauce ingredients; serve with spirals.

Blue Cheese-Onion Steak Bites

The classic combo of blue cheese and grilled steak is so good. I've discovered it's even better with garlic and onion! Try these bites when you need a hearty appetizer or light lunch.

—**JO-ELLEN NEIL** ARROYO GRANDE, CA

PREP: 15 MIN. • **COOK:** 35 MIN. • **MAKES:** 4 DOZEN

- 3 **large onions, thinly sliced into rings**
- 3 **tablespoons butter**
- 12 **garlic cloves, minced**
- 4 **beef tenderloin steaks (6 ounces each)**
- ¼ **teaspoon salt**
- ¼ **teaspoon pepper**
- 1 **loaf (10½ ounces) French bread baguette, cut into ¼-inch slices**

SPREAD
- 4 **ounces cream cheese, softened**
- 1 **cup (4 ounces) crumbled blue cheese**
- ⅛ **teaspoon salt**
- ⅛ **teaspoon pepper**

1. In a large skillet, saute the onions in butter until onions are softened. Reduce heat to medium-low; cook, stirring occasionally, for 30 minutes or until onions are golden brown. Add garlic; cook 1 minute longer.
2. Meanwhile, sprinkle the steaks with salt and pepper. Moisten a paper towel with cooking oil; using long-handled tongs, lightly coat the grill rack.
3. Grill steaks, covered, over medium heat or broil 4 in. from the heat for 5-7 minutes on each side or until the meat reaches the desired doneness (for medium-rare, a thermometer should read 145°; medium, 160°; well-done, 170°). Cut into thin slices.
4. Place bread on ungreased baking sheets. Bake at 400° for 4-6 minutes or until lightly browned.
5. Meanwhile, place the cream cheese, blue cheese, salt and pepper in a food processor; cover and process until blended. Spread each bread slice with 1 teaspoon cheese mixture; top with steak and onions.

Lamb Pastry Bundles

I wanted to add a taste of the Mediterranean to our Thanksgiving spread, but I didn't want to turn off the less adventurous eaters in our family. Everyone liked my lamb bundles and dipping sauce.
—**TESS KONTER** NEW YORK, NY

PREP: 30 MIN. • **BAKE:** 20 MIN.
MAKES: 1½ DOZEN (2 CUPS SAUCE)

- 1 small onion, grated
- 2 teaspoons ground cumin
- 1 teaspoon paprika
- 1½ pounds ground lamb
- 1 tablespoon olive oil
- 1 package (17.3 ounces) frozen puff pastry, thawed
- 2 logs (4 ounces each) fresh goat cheese, cut into 18 slices
- 1 egg, lightly beaten

SAUCE

- ¾ cup mayonnaise
- 1 jar (24 ounces) roasted sweet red peppers, drained
- 1 garlic clove, minced
  Dash crushed red pepper flakes

1. In a large bowl, combine the onion, cumin and paprika. Crumble the lamb over mixture and mix well. Shape into eighteen ½-in.-thick mini patties. In a large skillet, cook patties in oil in batches over medium heat for 3-4 minutes on each side or until a thermometer reads 160° and juices run clear.

2. On a lightly floured surface, unfold the puff pastry. Roll each sheet into a 12x12-in. square. Cut each into nine squares. Place a burger in the center of each square; top with goat cheese. Lightly brush egg over the edges of the pastry. Bring opposite corners of pastry over burger; pinch seams to seal tightly.

3. Place seam side up on a 15x10x1-in. baking pan; brush with egg. Bake at 400° for 18-22 minutes or until the pastry is golden brown.

4. Place sauce ingredients in a food processor; cover and process until blended. Serve with bundles.

Mango Guacamole

START TO FINISH: 20 MIN. • **MAKES:** 3 CUPS

- 2 medium ripe avocados, peeled and quartered
- 1 medium mango, peeled and chopped
- ½ cup finely chopped red onion
- ¼ cup minced fresh cilantro
- 1 jalapeno pepper, seeded and finely chopped
- 2 tablespoons lime juice
- 1½ teaspoons grated lime peel
- ½ teaspoon salt
- ⅛ teaspoon coarsely ground pepper
  Tortilla or pita chips

In a small bowl, mash avocados. Stir in the mango, onion, cilantro, jalapeno, lime juice, lime peel, salt and pepper. Serve with chips.

NOTE *Wear disposable gloves when cutting hot peppers; the oils can burn skin. Avoid touching your face.*

66For a change from the usual guacamole, I mix in some mango. The sweetness complements the heat from the chili pepper. And the extra color looks great!99

—**ADAM LANDAU** ENGLEWOOD CLIFFS, NJ

Chipotle Sliders

I think these are the ultimate mini burgers—the flavor is simply fabulous! Creamy mayo and Hawaiian sweet rolls contrast perfectly with the pepper Jack cheese and chipotle peppers.

—**SHAWN SINGLETON** VIDOR, TX

START TO FINISH: 30 MIN. • **MAKES:** 10 SLIDERS

- 1 package (12 ounces) Hawaiian sweet rolls, divided
- 1 teaspoon salt
- ½ teaspoon pepper
- 8 teaspoons minced chipotle peppers in adobo sauce, divided
- 1½ pounds ground beef
- 10 slices pepper Jack cheese
- ½ cup mayonnaise

1. Place 2 sweet rolls in a food processor; process until crumbly. Transfer to a large bowl; add the salt, pepper and 6 teaspoons chipotle peppers. Crumble beef over mixture and mix well. Shape into 10 patties.

2. Grill burgers, covered, over medium heat for 3-4 minutes on each side or until a thermometer reads 160° and juices run clear. Top with cheese. Grill 1 minute longer or until cheese is melted.

3. Split the remaining rolls and grill, cut side down, over medium heat for 30-60 seconds or until toasted. Combine the mayonnaise and remaining chipotle peppers; spread over the roll bottoms. Top each with a burger. Replace the roll tops.

Smoky Cheese-Stuffed Jalapenos

Having an outdoor party? Here's a guaranteed crowd-pleaser. Wrapped around gooey stuffed jalapenos, the bacon comes off the grill cooked to an irresistible crisp. Yum!

—**LIN SINES** LITTLE ELM, TX

PREP: 40 MIN. • **GRILL:** 10 MIN. • **MAKES:** 15 APPETIZERS

- 15 large jalapeno peppers
- 2 cups (8 ounces) shredded cheddar-Monterey Jack cheese
- 4 ounces cream cheese, softened
- ½ cup minced fresh cilantro
- ¼ teaspoon garlic powder
- ¼ teaspoon paprika
- 15 bacon strips

1. Cut the stems off the jalapeno peppers; remove the seeds and membranes. In a small bowl, beat the cheeses, cilantro, garlic powder and paprika until blended. Stuff 1 tablespoon into each jalapeno; wrap a strip of bacon around each.

2. Grill the jalapenos, covered, over medium-hot heat for 4-5 minutes on each side or until the bacon is crisp and the filling is heated through. Serve warm.

NOTE *Wear disposable gloves when cutting hot peppers; the oils can burn skin. Avoid touching your face.*

Cranberry Glogg

Our chilly Wisconsin winters call for cozying up with a hot drink, and this well-spiced glogg is a family favorite. For a nonalcoholic version, just replace the wine with grape juice.

—**JUNE LINDQUIST** HAMMOND, WI

START TO FINISH: 30 MIN. • **MAKES:** 7 SERVINGS

- 4 cups cranberry juice
- 2 cups ruby port wine or grape juice
- 1 cup golden raisins
- ¼ cup sugar
- 2 cinnamon sticks (3 inches)
- 4 cardamom pods, crushed
- 6 whole cloves
  Additional cinnamon sticks, optional

1. In a large saucepan, combine the cranberry juice, wine, golden raisins and sugar. Place the cinnamon, cardamom and cloves on a double thickness of cheesecloth; bring up the corners of the cloth and tie with string to form a bag. Add to the pan.

2. Bring just to a simmer (do not boil). Reduce the heat; simmer gently, uncovered, for 15 minutes or until flavors are blended. Discard spice bag. Serve warm in mugs with additional cinnamon if desired.

Bread Pot Fondue

Our area is famous for its sourdough. My favorite way to serve it is to hollow out a loaf and fill it with a rich, decadent fondue. I cube the excess bread and pair it with fresh vegetables for dipping.

—KATIE DREIBELBIS SANTA CLARA, CA

PREP: 20 MIN. • **BAKE:** 1 HOUR 20 MIN.
MAKES: 5 CUPS

- 1 **round loaf bread (1½ pounds, 8 to 10 inches in diameter)**

FILLING
- 2 **cups (8 ounces) shredded sharp cheddar cheese**
- 2 **packages (3 ounces each) cream cheese, softened**
- 1½ **cups sour cream**
- 1 **cup (5 ounces) diced cooked ham**
- ½ **cup chopped green onions**
- 1 **can (4 ounces) chopped green chilies, drained**
- 1 **teaspoon Worcestershire sauce**
- 2 **tablespoons vegetable oil**
- 1 **tablespoon butter, melted**
  Assorted fresh vegetables

1. Slice off top of bread loaf, reserving top. Carefully hollow out inside of loaf with small sharp knife, leaving ½-in. shell. Cut the removed bread into 1-in. cubes (about 4 cups); set aside.

2. For filling, combine the cheeses and sour cream in bowl; stir in ham, onions, chilies and Worcestershire sauce. Spoon into the hollowed loaf; replace top. Wrap tightly with several layers of heavy-duty aluminum foil; place on a baking sheet.

3. Bake at 350° for 1 hour 10 minutes or until the filling is heated through. Meanwhile, combine the bread cubes, oil and melted butter. Arrange on a separate baking sheet. Bake at 350° for 10-15 minutes or until golden brown, turning occasionally. Unwrap; transfer to platter. Remove the top from bread; stir the filling and serve with toasted cubes and vegetables.

Spinach Cheese Triangles

Stuffed with three kinds of cheese—feta, Parmesan and mozzarella—and plenty of spinach, these delectable little triangles are a hit whenever I make them.

—SHERRI MELOTIK OAK CREEK, WI

PREP: 40 MIN. • **BAKE:** 10 MIN.
MAKES: 4 DOZEN

- ⅓ **cup finely chopped onion**
- 1 **tablespoon butter**
- 1 **package (10 ounces) frozen chopped spinach, thawed and squeezed dry**
- 1 **cup grated Parmesan cheese**
- ¾ **cup shredded part-skim mozzarella cheese**
- 3 **tablespoons crumbled feta cheese**
- 2 **eggs, lightly beaten**
- 2 **tablespoons soft bread crumbs**
- ¼ **teaspoon salt**
- ¼ **teaspoon pepper**
- 12 **sheets phyllo dough (14x9 inches)**
  Butter-flavored cooking spray

1. In a large skillet, saute onion in butter until tender. Stir in spinach; cook over medium-low heat just until spinach is wilted. Transfer to a large bowl; add the cheeses, eggs, bread crumbs, salt and pepper. Set aside.

2. Place one sheet of dough on a work surface with a long side facing you. (Keep remaining dough covered with plastic wrap to prevent it from drying out.) Spray sheet with cooking spray; cut into four 9x3½-in. strips.

3. Place 1 tablespoon filling on lower corner of each strip. Fold dough over filling, forming a triangle. Fold triangle up, then fold it over, forming another triangle. Continue folding, like a flag, until you come to the end of the strip.

4. Spritz the end of dough with spray and press onto triangle to seal. Turn triangle; spritz top with spray. Repeat with remaining dough and filling.

5. Place triangles on baking sheets coated with spray. Bake at 375° for 10-12 minutes or until golden brown.

Rustic Fig, Onion & Pear Tart

Here's one of the first recipes I created. The fig preserves, sweet onions and mild pears blend wonderfully in the tart crust, which is a cinch to prepare with convenient refrigerated pie pastry.

—**TINA MACKISSOCK** MANCHESTER, NH

PREP: 50 MIN. • **BAKE:** 15 MIN.
MAKES: 12 SERVINGS

- 3 **large sweet onions, halved and thinly sliced**
- 3 **medium pears, peeled and sliced**
- 4½ **teaspoons olive oil**
- 4½ **teaspoons butter**
- 1 **cup fig preserves**
- 1 **tablespoon plus 1 teaspoon cider vinegar**
- ⅛ **teaspoon salt**
- 1 **sheet refrigerated pie pastry**
- ⅛ **teaspoon pepper**
- 1 **egg, beaten**

1. In a large skillet, saute onions and pears in oil and butter until softened. Reduce the heat to medium-low; cook, stirring occasionally, for 30 minutes or until deep golden brown.
2. Add the fig preserves, vinegar and salt. Bring to a boil; cook for 5 minutes or until thickened. Cool slightly. Place half of the onion mixture in a food processor; cover and process until pureed. Set the remaining onion mixture aside.
3. Place pastry on a greased 12-in. pizza pan. Spoon the pureed onion mixture over pastry to within 2 in. of the edges; sprinkle with pepper. Top with the reserved onion mixture. Fold up the edges of pastry over the filling, leaving the center uncovered. Brush the edges of tart with egg.
4. Bake at 450° for 15-20 minutes or until the crust is golden and the filling is bubbly.

Savory Cocktail Scones

Scones as appetizers? Yes! Roasted garlic butter is the crowning touch and will have guests coming back for more.

—**DONNA MARIE RYAN** TOPSFIELD, MA

PREP: 55 MIN. • **BAKE:** 15 MIN.
MAKES: 16 SERVINGS

- 1 **whole garlic bulb**
- 2 **teaspoons olive oil**
- ½ **cup butter, softened**

SCONES
- 2 **bacon strips, chopped**
- ⅓ **cup chopped onion**
- 2 **cups all-purpose flour**
- 3 **teaspoons baking powder**
- ½ **teaspoon baking soda**
- ½ **teaspoon salt**
- ½ **cup cold butter**
- 1 **egg**
- ½ **cup sherry**
- ⅓ **cup heavy whipping cream**
- ¼ **cup 2% milk**

1. Remove the papery outer skin from the garlic (do not peel or separate the cloves). Cut the top off the garlic bulb. Brush with oil. Wrap garlic bulb in heavy-duty foil. Bake garlic at 400° for 40-45 minutes or until softened. Cool for 10-15 minutes. Squeeze softened garlic into a small bowl; mash with fork. Stir in butter; set aside.
2. In a small skillet, cook the bacon over medium heat until crisp. Remove to paper towels with a slotted spoon; drain, reserving 1 tablespoon bacon drippings. In same skillet, cook and stir onion in drippings until softened. Reduce the heat to medium-low; cook, stirring occasionally, for 30 minutes or until deep golden brown. Set aside.
3. In a large bowl, combine the flour, baking powder, baking soda and salt. Cut in the butter until the mixture resembles coarse crumbs. Whisk egg, sherry and whipping cream; stir into crumb mixture just until moistened. Fold in the onion and bacon.
4. Turn the dough onto a floured surface; knead 10 times. Pat into a 10x5-in. rectangle. Using a floured knife, cut into eight 2½-in. squares; cut each square diagonally in half.
5. Place on a parchment paper-lined baking sheet; brush with milk. Bake at 400° for 12-15 minutes or until golden brown. Serve warm with butter.

EXTRA IDEA

I combine small chunks of leftover roast beef with sweet pickles and onion in my blender or food processor. Then I add mayonnaise, onion powder, salt and pepper until the mixture is spreadable. It's great on small bread rounds or crackers as an appetizer or snack.

—**KAREN PLAMBAECK** TURLOCK, CA

Potato-Crab Cakes with Lime Butter

Adding mashed potatoes to crab cakes creates a velvety texture. Spread a little lime butter on top for a tangy accompaniment.

—EMORY DOTY JASPER, GA

PREP: 20 MIN. • **COOK:** 5 MIN./BATCH
MAKES: 1 DOZEN (½ CUP BUTTER)

- 1 cup mashed potatoes (with added milk and butter)
- 1 egg, beaten
- 1 tablespoon plus ½ cup dry bread crumbs, divided
- 1 tablespoon finely chopped onion
- 1 tablespoon minced fresh parsley
- ½ teaspoon lime juice
- ⅛ teaspoon salt
- ⅛ teaspoon pepper
- 1 pound fresh crabmeat
- ¼ cup all-purpose flour
- Oil for deep-fat frying

LIME BUTTER
- ½ cup butter, softened
- 4 teaspoons lime juice
- 1 teaspoon grated lime peel

1. In a large bowl, combine the potatoes, egg, 1 tablespoon bread crumbs, onion, parsley, lime juice, salt and pepper. Gently stir in the crab. Shape into 12 patties.
2. In a shallow bowl, combine flour and remaining bread crumbs. Coat patties with crumb mixture.
3. In an electric skillet, heat ¼ in. of oil to 375°. Fry crab cakes, a few at a time, for 2-3 minutes on each side or until golden brown. Drain on paper towels. Combine the butter, lime juice and peel. Serve with crab cakes.

Polenta Cakes with Fresh Salsa

This zippy polenta is great not only as an appetizer, but also as a meatless entree. The colorful salsa makes great use of plum tomatoes, green onions and other seasonal produce.

—JACQUE O'CONNOR CHICAGO, IL

PREP: 40 MIN. + CHILLING • **GRILL:** 10 MIN. • **MAKES:** 8 SERVINGS

- 3 cups boiling water
- ½ teaspoon salt
- 1 cup yellow cornmeal
- 1 serrano pepper, seeded and finely chopped
- 2 garlic cloves, minced
- ¼ teaspoon pepper
- ½ cup shredded Monterey Jack cheese

SALSA
- 6 plum tomatoes, seeded and chopped
- 8 fresh asparagus spears, grilled and cut into ½-inch pieces
- 4 green onions, chopped
- ½ cup minced fresh cilantro
- 1 serrano pepper, seeded and chopped
- ½ teaspoon salt
- ¼ teaspoon pepper
- Quesco fresco or Monterey Jack cheese, optional

1. In a large heavy saucepan, bring the water and salt to a boil. Reduce heat to a gentle boil; slowly whisk in cornmeal. Stir in the serrano pepper, garlic and pepper. Cook and stir with a wooden spoon for 12-17 minutes or until polenta is thickened and pulls away cleanly from the sides of the pan. Stir in cheese.
2. Spread polenta into a greased 8-in.-square baking dish. Cool slightly; cover and refrigerate for at least 4 hours.
3. For salsa, in a small bowl, combine the plum tomatoes, asparagus, green onions, cilantro, serrano pepper, salt and pepper; set aside.
4. Cut polenta into eight pieces. Moisten a paper towel with cooking oil; using long-handled tongs, lightly coat the grill rack. Grill, covered, over medium heat for 5-7 minutes on each side or until lightly browned. Serve with the salsa; garnish with cheese if desired.
NOTE *Wear disposable gloves when cutting hot peppers; the oils can burn skin. Avoid touching your face.*

Crab Pesto Cheesecake

Pesto really enhances the crabmeat in my savory seafood cheesecake. Great for spreading on crackers or baguette slices, it's often on the menu when I entertain.

—CAROLYN BUTTERFIELD

LAKE STEVENS, WA

PREP: 30 MIN. • **BAKE:** 55 MIN. + CHILLING
MAKES: 24 SERVINGS

- 1 cup crushed roasted vegetable-flavored butter crackers
- 3 tablespoons butter, melted
- 3 packages (8 ounces each) cream cheese, softened
- 1 cup sour cream
- ¾ cup shredded Asiago cheese
- 3 tablespoons prepared pesto
- 1 teaspoon grated lemon peel
- ½ teaspoon salt
- 2 eggs, lightly beaten
- 1 cup fresh crabmeat
- 1 cup canned water-packed artichoke hearts, chopped
  Additional prepared pesto
  Assorted crackers

1. Place a greased 9-in. springform pan on a double thickness of heavy-duty foil (about 18 in. square). Securely wrap foil around pan.
2. In a small bowl, combine cracker crumbs and butter. Press onto the bottom of prepared pan. Place pan on a baking sheet. Bake at 350° for 8 minutes. Cool on a wire rack.
3. In a large bowl, beat the cream cheese, sour cream, Asiago cheese, pesto, peel and salt until smooth. Add the eggs; beat on low speed just until combined. Fold in crab and artichokes. Pour over crust. Place springform pan in a large baking pan; add 1 in. of hot water to larger pan.
4. Bake at 325° for 55-65 minutes or until center is just set and top appears dull. Remove springform pan from water bath. Cool on a wire rack for 10 minutes. Carefully run a knife around edge of pan to loosen; cool 1 hour longer. Refrigerate overnight.
5. Remove sides of pan. Drizzle with additional pesto; serve with crackers.

Smoky Grilled Shrimp

Grill up a platter of these bacon-wrapped appetizers, then watch them disappear in a flash! The zesty shrimp look and taste so good, you may want to prepare extras and serve larger portions as your main course. Use the reserved Dijon sauce for dunking each delectable morsel.

—DEBBIE TAYLOR WHITE BLUFF, TN

START TO FINISH: 25 MIN.
MAKES: 2½ DOZEN (¾ CUP SAUCE)

- 1 pound bacon strips
- 1¼ cups honey Dijon salad dressing
- 4 teaspoons prepared horseradish
- 1 garlic clove, minced
- 1 pound uncooked large shrimp, peeled and deveined

1. Cut bacon strips in half widthwise. In a large skillet, cook bacon over medium heat until partially cooked but not crisp. Remove to paper towels to drain.
2. In a small bowl, combine honey Dijon salad dressing, horseradish and garlic; set aside ¾ cup for sauce. Brush the remaining salad dressing mixture over both sides of the shrimp. Wrap a piece of bacon around each shrimp; thread onto four metal or soaked wooden skewers.
3. Moisten a paper towel with cooking oil. Using long-handled tongs, lightly coat grill rack. Grill shrimp, covered, over medium heat or broil 4 in. from heat for 5-8 minutes or until shrimp turn pink, turning once. Serve with reserved sauce.

Fire-Roasted Salsa

In the mood for a fiesta? Look here! Thanks to canned tomatoes, this salsa is ready to enjoy in just 15 minutes.

—MISSY KAMPLING MOUNTAIN VIEW, CA

START TO FINISH: 15 MIN.
MAKES: 1½ CUPS (20 SERVINGS)

- 1 can (14½ ounces) fire-roasted diced tomatoes, drained
- ½ cup sliced onion
- ⅓ cup fresh cilantro leaves
- 1 tablespoon lime juice
- 1 teaspoon sugar
- ¼ teaspoon salt

In a food processor, combine the tomatoes, onion, cilantro, lime juice, sugar and salt. Cover and process until desired consistency.

PER SERVING *13 cal., trace fat (trace sat. fat), 0 chol., 141 mg sodium, 3 g carb., trace fiber, trace pro.*
Diabetic Exchange: *Free food.*

Polenta Parmigiana

Top sliced polenta with pasta sauce, cheese and basil for a warm snack or quick and easy lunch. My children like to add pepperoni or sausage to create their own little pizzas.

—**CAROLYN KUMPE** EL DORADO, CA

START TO FINISH: 30 MIN.
MAKES: 16 APPETIZERS

- **1 tube (1 pound) polenta, cut into 16 slices**
- **¼ cup olive oil**
- **1 cup tomato basil pasta sauce, warmed**
- **½ pound fresh mozzarella cheese, cut into 16 slices**
- **¼ cup grated Parmesan cheese**
- **½ teaspoon salt**
- **⅛ teaspoon pepper**
- **Fresh basil leaves, optional**

1. Preheat oven to 425°. Place polenta in a greased 15x10x1-in. baking pan; brush with oil. Bake 15-20 minutes or until edges are golden brown.

2. Spoon warmed pasta sauce over the polenta slices. Top each with a mozzarella cheese slice; sprinkle with the Parmesan cheese, salt and pepper. Bake 3-5 minutes longer or until the cheese is melted. Garnish with basil leaves if desired.

Grilled Steak Appetizers with Stilton Sauce

Chunks of juicy grilled steak paired with a creamy cheese sauce for dipping will have guests—especially meat lovers—waiting in line to fill their plates. Remind everyone to save room for dinner!

—**RADELLE KNAPPENBERGER** OVIEDO, FL

PREP: 25 MIN. • **GRILL:** 10 MIN.
MAKES: 20 APPETIZERS (¾ CUP SAUCE)

- **2 boneless beef top loin steaks (8 ounces each)**
- **¼ teaspoon salt**
- **¼ teaspoon pepper**
- **½ cup white wine or chicken broth**
- **⅓ cup heavy whipping cream**
- **3 tablespoons sour cream**
- **2 ounces Stilton cheese, cubed**

1. Sprinkle the steaks with salt and pepper. Grill the steaks, covered, over medium heat for 4-6 minutes on each side or until the meat reaches the desired doneness (for medium-rare, a thermometer should read 145°; medium, 160°; well-done, 170°). Remove the meat to a cutting board and keep warm.

2. In a small saucepan, bring white wine to a boil; cook until reduced by half. Add the heavy whipping cream. Bring to a gentle boil. Reduce the heat; simmer, uncovered, until thickened, stirring occasionally. Remove from the heat. Add sour cream and cheese; stir until cheese is melted.

3. Cut the steaks into 1-in. cubes; skewer with toothpicks. Serve with the cheese sauce.

NOTES *Top loin steak may be labeled as strip steak, Kansas City steak, New York strip steak, ambassador steak or boneless club steak in your region. You may substitute ⅓ cup crumbled blue cheese for the Stilton cheese.*

Minty-Watermelon Cucumber Salad, page 30

26

33

31

Special Salads

Toss together an exciting new creation for your family using any of the recipes in this chapter. From pasta combos to veggie medleys, they're different, delicious and **delightfully refreshing**.

Pear Salad with Sesame Vinaigrette

When I had pears, mozzarella and romaine left over from a party menu, I tossed them together and added some roasted almonds. I loved the contrasting colors, flavors and textures.
—**SHIRLEE BODFIELD** TUCSON, AZ

START TO FINISH: 15 MIN. • **MAKES:** 6 SERVINGS

- 1 package (10 ounces) hearts of romaine salad mix
- 3 medium pears, sliced
- 8 ounces fresh mozzarella cheese, sliced
- ¾ cup sesame ginger vinaigrette
- 1 package (3¾ ounces) oven-roasted sliced almonds

Divide salad mix among six plates. Top with pears and cheese; drizzle with vinaigrette. Sprinkle with almonds.

Sizzling Cheese Salad

These gooey, golden-brown cheese bites are fabulous with any mix of crisp greens, such as arugula, spinach or even cabbage. Serve pita wedges on the side for a great lunch or light dinner.
—**CLEO GONSKE** REDDING, CA

PREP: 45 MIN. • **MAKES:** 5 SERVINGS

- 4 ounces cream cheese, softened
- 1 cup (4 ounces) shredded Gjetost cheese
- 1 egg
- 1 tablespoon water
- 2 tablespoons cornmeal
- 1 tablespoon sesame seeds, toasted
- 1 tablespoon dry bread crumbs
- 2 teaspoons grated Parmesan cheese
- 2 tablespoons butter

SALAD
- 5 cups torn mixed salad greens
- 1 cup pitted ripe olives
- 5 tomato wedges

DRESSING
- ¼ cup olive oil
- 1 teaspoon sesame oil
- ¼ cup white wine vinegar
- 2 teaspoons finely chopped green onions
- 1 teaspoon Dijon mustard
- ½ teaspoon dried tarragon
- ¼ teaspoon salt
- ¼ teaspoon pepper
  Toasted pita wedges, optional

1. In a small bowl, combine the cream cheese and Gjetost cheese until blended. Shape into ten 1-in. balls; flatten into 1½-in. patties.

2. In a shallow bowl, whisk the egg and water. In another shallow bowl, combine the cornmeal, sesame seeds, bread crumbs and Parmesan cheese. Dip cheese in egg mixture, then cornmeal mixture. In a large skillet, cook the cheese patties in butter in batches for 1-2 minutes on each side or until golden brown.

3. Meanwhile, arrange the salad greens, ripe olives and tomatoes on a serving platter. Whisk the oils, white wine vinegar, onions, mustard and seasonings; drizzle over salad. Place cheese patties over the top. Serve immediately with pita wedges if desired.

NOTE *Gjetost is a soft, caramely Norwegian cheese. For a variation, substitute 1 cup shredded Parmesan cheese and 1 teaspoon sugar.*

Grilled Chicken Salad with Blueberry Vinaigrette

Here's a wonderful summer meal. Marinated chicken makes it satisfying, while the berries and oranges are refreshing. I round out the menu with a baguette and minted lemonade.
—SUSAN GAUTHIER FALMOUTH, ME

PREP: 20 MIN. + MARINATING • **GRILL:** 10 MIN.
MAKES: 4 SERVINGS

- 3 tablespoons olive oil
- 1 garlic clove, minced
- 1 teaspoon salt
- 1 teaspoon pepper
- 2 boneless skinless chicken breast halves (6 ounces each)

VINAIGRETTE
- ¼ cup olive oil
- ¼ cup blueberry preserves
- 2 tablespoons maple syrup
- 2 tablespoons balsamic vinegar
- ¼ teaspoon ground mustard
- ⅛ teaspoon salt
  Dash pepper

SALADS
- 1 package (10 ounces) ready-to-serve salad greens
- 1 cup fresh blueberries
- 1 snack-size cup (4 ounces) mandarin oranges, drained
- 1 cup crumbled goat cheese

1. In a large resealable plastic bag, combine the oil, garlic, salt and pepper; add the chicken. Seal bag and turn to coat; refrigerate for 30 minutes.

2. In a small bowl, whisk vinaigrette ingredients. Cover and refrigerate until ready to use.

3. Drain and discard marinade. Grill chicken, covered, over medium heat for 5-7 minutes on each side or until a meat thermometer reads 160°. When cool enough to handle, cut chicken into slices.

4. Divide salad greens among four serving plates. Top each with chicken, blueberries and oranges. Whisk vinaigrette and drizzle over salads; sprinkle with cheese.

Curried Chicken Salad

Curry and Dijon mustard complement the sweet-tart fruit and crunchy nuts in this standout salad. For a change of pace, spoon it on whole wheat toast or scoop it up with apple slices.
—JOANNA PERDOMO CHICAGO, IL

START TO FINISH: 15 MIN. • **MAKES:** 4 SERVINGS

- 3 cups cubed cooked chicken breast
- 1 medium apple, finely chopped
- ¼ cup slivered almonds, toasted
- 2 tablespoons golden raisins
- 2 tablespoons dried cranberries
- ½ cup fat-free plain Greek yogurt
- ¼ cup apricot preserves
- 2 tablespoons curry powder
- 1 tablespoon Dijon mustard
- ½ teaspoon salt
- ¼ to ½ teaspoon pepper
  Lettuce leaves

In a small bowl, combine the first five ingredients. In a small bowl, whisk the yogurt, preserves, curry, mustard, salt and pepper; pour over chicken mixture and toss to coat. Serve on lettuce leaves.

NOTE *If Greek yogurt is not available in your area, line a strainer with a coffee filter and place over a bowl. Place 1 cup fat-free yogurt in prepared strainer; refrigerate overnight. Discard liquid from bowl; proceed as directed.*
PER SERVING *323 cal., 7 g fat (1 g sat. fat), 81 mg chol., 477 mg sodium, 30 g carb., 3 g fiber, 36 g pro.* **Diabetic Exchanges:** *4 lean meat, 1 starch, ½ fruit, ½ fat.*

Sweet Potato Salad

A friend of mine from Maryland shared a delicious sweet potato dish with me, and I put my own spin on it.

—ELLEN MOORE SPRINGFIELD, NH

PREP: 30 MIN. + CHILLING
MAKES: 6 SERVINGS

- 2¼ **pounds sweet potatoes (about 4 medium), peeled and cut into 1-inch pieces**
- 1 **can (8 ounces) pineapple chunks, drained**
- 1 **cup pecan halves, chopped**
- ¼ **cup orange juice**
- 1 **cup mayonnaise**
- 2 **tablespoons half-and-half cream**
- 1 **teaspoon curry powder**
- 1 **teaspoon grated orange peel**
- 1 **teaspoon white vinegar**
- ¼ **to ½ teaspoon dried tarragon**
  Torn mixed salad greens and chutney, optional

1. Place the sweet potatoes in a 6-qt. stockpot; add water to cover. Bring to a boil. Reduce heat; cook, covered, 8-10 minutes or just until tender. Drain and place in a large bowl. Add pineapple, pecans and orange juice.
2. In a small bowl, mix mayonnaise, half-and-half, curry powder, orange peel, vinegar and tarragon; pour over the potato mixture and gently toss to coat. Refrigerate, covered, until cold. If desired, serve with mixed salad greens and chutney.

SWEET SECRETS

The sweet potato is a member of the morning glory family and native to Central America. Select sweet potatoes that are firm with no cracks or bruises. If stored in a cool, dark and well-ventilated place, sweet potatoes will remain fresh for approximately 2 weeks. If the temperature is above 60°, they will sprout sooner or become woody. Once cooked, sweet potatoes can be stored for up to 1 week in the refrigerator.

Fresh Broccoli and Mandarin Salad

I write a column about food for our local newspaper and consider myself a pretty good judge of recipes. But I was surprised by this one—I didn't think the ingredients would go together as well as they do!

—CONNIE BLOMMERS PELLA, IA

PREP: 30 MIN. + CHILLING
MAKES: 10-12 SERVINGS

CUSTARD DRESSING
- ½ **cup sugar**
- 1½ **teaspoons cornstarch**
- 1 **teaspoon ground mustard**
- ¼ **cup white vinegar**
- ¼ **cup water**
- 1 **egg plus 1 egg yolk, lightly beaten**
- ½ **cup mayonnaise**
- 3 **tablespoons butter, softened**

SALAD
- 4 **cups fresh broccoli florets, 1-inch cuts**
- 2 **cups sliced fresh mushrooms**
- ½ **medium red onion, sliced in ⅛-inch-thick rings**
- 1 **can (11 ounces) mandarin oranges, drained**
- 6 **slices bacon, cooked and crumbled**
- ½ **cup slivered almonds, toasted**
- ½ **cup golden raisins**

1. In a large saucepan, combine the sugar, cornstarch and ground mustard. Combine vinegar and water. Stir into sugar mixture until smooth. Cook and stir over medium-high heat until thickened and bubbly. Reduce heat; cook and stir 2 minutes longer. Remove from the heat.
2. Stir a small amount of hot filling into egg and yolk; return all to pan, stirring constantly. Bring to a gentle boil; cook and stir 2 minutes longer. Remove from the heat. Gently stir in mayonnaise and butter. Cool to room temperature without stirring. Chill.
3. In a large salad bowl, combine the broccoli, mushrooms, onion, oranges, bacon, almonds and golden raisins. Pour dressing over salad; toss to coat. Store in refrigerator.

Tropical Fusion Salad with Spicy Tortilla Ribbons

Send your taste buds on a trip to the tropics with a special medley featuring avocado, papaya and a splash of lime. Spicy tortilla strips are the perfect finishing touch.

—**JENNIFER FISHER** AUSTIN, TX

START TO FINISH: 30 MIN.
MAKES: 4 SERVINGS

- 2 cups cubed peeled papaya
- 1 can (15 ounces) black beans, rinsed and drained
- 1 medium ripe avocado, peeled and cubed
- 1 cup frozen corn, thawed
- ½ cup golden raisins
- ¼ cup minced fresh cilantro
- ¼ cup orange juice
- 2 serrano peppers, seeded and chopped
- 2 tablespoons lime juice
- 1 tablespoon cider vinegar
- 2 garlic cloves, minced
- 2 teaspoons ground ancho chili pepper, divided
- ¼ teaspoon sugar
- ¼ teaspoon salt
- 2 corn tortillas (6 inches), cut into ¼-inch strips
  Cooking spray

1. Preheat oven to 350°. In a large bowl, combine the papaya, black beans, avocado, corn, golden raisins, cilantro, orange juice, peppers, lime juice, vinegar, garlic, ½ teaspoon chili pepper, sugar and salt.

2. Place tortilla strips on a greased baking sheet; spritz with cooking spray. Sprinkle with remaining chili pepper. Bake 8-10 minutes or until crisp. Top salad with tortilla strips.

NOTE *Wear disposable gloves when cutting hot peppers; the oils can burn skin. Avoid touching your face.*

Bacon & Gorgonzola Potato Salad

A rich, creamy dressing with bacon bits and Gorgonzola cheese make this potato salad a hit. I like to prepare it ahead so the flavors have time to blend.

—**BARBARA SPITZER** LODI, CA

PREP: 25 MIN. • **COOK:** 15 MIN. + CHILLING
MAKES: 6 SERVINGS

- 1¾ pounds potatoes, peeled and cubed
- ¾ cup mayonnaise
- ¾ cup sour cream
- 4 green onions, thinly sliced
- 1 celery rib, finely chopped
- 2 tablespoons minced chives, divided
- ½ teaspoon salt
- ½ teaspoon coarsely ground pepper
- ¼ teaspoon sugar
- 1 cup (4 ounces) crumbled Gorgonzola cheese
- 1 cup bacon bits, divided
- 2 plum tomatoes, peeled, seeded and chopped

1. Place potatoes in a large saucepan and cover with water. Bring to a boil. Reduce the heat; cover and cook for 10-15 minutes or until tender. Drain and cool.

2. Meanwhile, in a large bowl, combine mayonnaise, sour cream, green onions, celery, 1 tablespoon chives, salt, pepper and sugar. Stir in the Gorgonzola cheese and ½ cup bacon bits. Fold in the plum tomatoes and potatoes. Cover and refrigerate for at least 1 hour. Just before serving, sprinkle with the remaining chives and bacon bits.

Spinach Orzo Salad

Rice-shaped orzo pasta is so versatile and fun to use. I like to toss it with spinach, feta cheese, red onion, nuts and basil. A balsamic vinaigrette brings everything together beautifully.
—**DONNA BARDOCZ** HOWELL, MI

START TO FINISH: 30 MIN. • **MAKES:** 10 SERVINGS

- 1 package (16 ounces) orzo pasta
- 1 package (6 ounces) fresh baby spinach, finely chopped
- ¾ cup crumbled feta cheese
- ¾ cup finely chopped red onion
- ¾ cup reduced-fat balsamic vinaigrette
- ½ teaspoon dried basil
- ¼ teaspoon white pepper
- ¼ cup pine nuts, toasted

1. Cook the orzo pasta according to the package directions. Drain and rinse in cold water.
2. In a large bowl, combine the spinach, feta cheese, red onion and orzo pasta. In a small bowl, combine balsamic vinaigrette, basil and white pepper. Pour over orzo pasta; toss to coat. Chill until serving. Just before serving, stir in the pine nuts.

Ham Pasta Salad

I came up with this hearty dish by combining some of my favorite recipes. I usually serve it on the side, but in summer—when my husband doesn't care for hot meals—I make it as a main course.
—**DEANNA MITCHELL** INDEPENDENCE, KS

PREP: 20 MIN. + CHILLING • **MAKES:** 4-6 SERVINGS

- 1 package (7 ounces) shell macaroni, cooked and drained
- 2 cups cubed fully cooked ham
- 1 cup chopped green pepper
- 1 cup chopped tomato
- ¼ cup chopped onion
  DRESSING
- ½ cup Miracle Whip
- ¼ cup grated Parmesan cheese
- 2 tablespoons milk
- ¼ teaspoon salt
  Additional Parmesan cheese

1. In a large bowl, toss the shell macaroni with the ham, green pepper, tomato and onion. In a small bowl, combine Miracle Whip, Parmesan cheese, milk and salt. Pour over macaroni mixture and stir to coat. Cover and refrigerate.
2. Sprinkle with additional Parmesan before serving.

[GRAND PRIZE]

Teriyaki Chicken Salad with Poppy Seed Dressing

My friend's daughter shared her deliciously different version of chicken salad. Loaded with fresh strawberries, raspberries and kiwi, it's a wonderful entree for warm evenings. The poppy seed dressing really enhances the fruit flavors.
—**C. LEONARD** WOODBRIDGE, CA

PREP: 30 MIN. + MARINATING • **GRILL:** 10 MIN.
MAKES: 6 SERVINGS

- 1 cup honey teriyaki marinade
- 1 pound boneless skinless chicken breasts
- 6 cups torn romaine
- 3 medium kiwifruit, peeled and sliced
- 1 can (20 ounces) unsweetened pineapple chunks, drained
- 1 can (11 ounces) mandarin oranges, drained
- 2 celery ribs, chopped
- 1 medium sweet red pepper, chopped
- 1 medium green pepper, chopped
- 1 cup fresh raspberries
- 1 cup sliced fresh strawberries
- 3 green onions, chopped
- ½ cup salted cashews
- ⅓ cup reduced-fat poppy seed salad dressing

1. Place marinade in a large resealable plastic bag; add the chicken. Seal bag and turn to coat; refrigerate for 8 hours or overnight. Drain and discard the marinade.
2. Grill the chicken, covered, over medium heat or broil 4 in. from the heat for 5-7 minutes on each side or until a meat thermometer reads 170°.
3. Slice the chicken. Divide the romaine, kiwi, pineapple chunks, mandarin oranges, celery, peppers, raspberries and strawberries among six plates; top with chicken. Sprinkle with the green onions and cashews. Drizzle with poppy seed salad dressing.
PER SERVING *361 cal., 11 g fat (2 g sat. fat), 42 mg chol., 761 mg sodium, 49 g carb., 7 g fiber, 20 g pro.* **Diabetic Exchanges:** *2 lean meat, 1½ starch, 1½ fat, 1 vegetable, 1 fruit.*

Minty-Watermelon Cucumber Salad

Heading to a picnic? This dish is bound to be the talk of the event. Chunks of watermelon, cucumbers, onions and fresh mint really capture the fantastic flavors of summer. Plus, the simple dressing is a breeze to prepare.

—**ROBLYNN HUNNISETT** GUELPH, ON

START TO FINISH: 20 MIN.
MAKES: 16 SERVINGS (¾ CUP EACH)

- 8 **cups cubed seedless watermelon**
- 2 **medium English cucumbers, halved lengthwise and sliced**
- 6 **green onions, chopped**
- ¼ **cup minced fresh mint**
- ¼ **cup balsamic vinegar**
- ¼ **cup olive oil**
- ½ **teaspoon salt**
- ½ **teaspoon pepper**

In a large bowl, combine watermelon, cucumbers, green onions and mint. In a small bowl, whisk the remaining ingredients. Pour over the salad and toss to coat. Serve immediately or refrigerate, covered, up to 2 hours before serving.

PER SERVING *60 cal., 3 g fat (trace sat. fat), 0 chol., 78 mg sodium, 9 g carb., 1 g fiber, 1 g pro.* **Diabetic Exchanges:** *½ fruit, ½ fat.*

WATERMELON WIZ

While watermelon belongs to the gourd family, which includes squash and cucumbers, it more closely resembles cucumbers because watermelon seeds are distributed throughout the fruit. A watermelon may have seeds or may be a seedless variety, which means it will contain some edible seeds. To test it for ripeness, slap the side with the palm of your hand. A deep thump means the watermelon is ripe.

Deli-Style Pasta Salad

Colorful spiral pasta provides the base for this tongue-tingling, make-ahead favorite. Full of satisfying ingredients, it goes over big at parties and potlucks.

—JOYCE MCLENNAN ALGONAC, MI

PREP: 20 MIN. + CHILLING
MAKES: 10-12 SERVINGS

- 1 package (7 ounces) tricolor spiral pasta
- 6 ounces thinly sliced hard salami, julienned
- 6 ounces provolone cheese, cubed
- 1 can (2¼ ounces) sliced ripe olives, drained
- 1 small red onion, thinly sliced
- 1 small zucchini, halved and thinly sliced
- ½ cup chopped green pepper
- ½ cup chopped sweet red pepper
- ¼ cup minced fresh parsley
- ¼ cup grated Parmesan cheese
- ½ cup olive oil
- ¼ cup red wine vinegar
- 1 garlic clove, minced
- 1½ teaspoons ground mustard
- 1 teaspoon dried basil
- 1 teaspoon dried oregano
- ¼ teaspoon salt
  Dash pepper
- 2 medium tomatoes, cut into wedges

1. Cook the spiral pasta according to the package directions; rinse in cold water and drain. Place in a large bowl; add the next nine ingredients.

2. In a jar with a tight-fitting lid, combine the oil, red wine vinegar, garlic, ground mustard, basil, oregano, salt and pepper; shake well.

3. Pour the dressing over the salad; toss to coat. Cover and chill for 8 hour or overnight. Toss before serving. Garnish with tomatoes.

Festive Broccoli-Cauliflower Salad

When unexpected company arrived and I didn't have enough lettuce on hand to make a traditional salad, I improvised with some fresh broccoli and cauliflower. I was thrilled when everyone liked the results! Now it's a staple on our menus.

—AVANELL HEWITT
NORTH RICHLAND HILLS, TX

PREP: 35 MIN. + CHILLING
MAKES: 14 SERVINGS (⅔ CUP EACH)

- 1 bunch broccoli, cut into florets
- 3 cups fresh cauliflowerets
- 1 medium green pepper, julienned
- 2 medium carrots, thinly sliced
- ½ cup thinly sliced red onion
- ½ cup small pitted ripe olives, halved
- ½ cup cubed sharp cheddar cheese

DRESSING

- 1 cup mayonnaise
- ½ cup ranch salad dressing
- 1 teaspoon Italian seasoning
- ½ teaspoon garlic powder
- ½ teaspoon dill weed
- ½ cup sunflower kernels

1. In a large bowl, combine the first seven ingredients.

2. In a small bowl, whisk mayonnaise, ranch salad dressing, Italian seasoning, garlic powder and dill. Pour over salad; toss to coat. Cover and refrigerate for at least 1 hour.

3. Just before serving, sprinkle salad with sunflower kernels.

Curried Egg Lettuce Cups

Need something extra-special for a ladies' luncheon, bridal shower or other event? Guests are sure to love this zippy egg salad served in crisp lettuce leaves.
—**PATRICIA NIEH** PORTOLA VALLEY, CA

PREP: 20 MIN. + CHILLING
MAKES: 6 SERVINGS

- 4 **ounces cream cheese, softened**
- ¼ **cup sour cream**
- 2 **teaspoons curry powder**
- ¼ **teaspoon salt**
- 6 **hard-cooked eggs, chopped**
- ¼ **cup finely chopped green pepper**
- ¼ **cup finely chopped green onions**
- 4 **tablespoons chopped salted peanuts, divided**
- 6 **Bibb or Boston lettuce leaves**
- ½ **cup mango chutney**

1. In a large bowl, combine the first four ingredients. Stir in the eggs, green pepper and green onions. Cover and refrigerate for at least 1 hour.

2. Just before serving, stir in 3 tablespoons chopped peanuts. Place a rounded ⅓ cupful on each lettuce leaf. Top with the mango chutney; sprinkle with remaining peanuts.

Pina Colada Fruit Salad

Just about everyone enjoys classic pina colada flavor. For even more in your fruit medley, stir in a splash of coconut rum.
—**CAROL FARNSWORTH** GREENWOOD, IN

START TO FINISH: 15 MIN.
MAKES: 9 SERVINGS

- 1½ **cups green grapes**
- 1½ **cups seedless red grapes**
- 1½ **cups fresh blueberries**
- 1½ **cups halved fresh strawberries**
- 1 **can (8 ounces) pineapple chunks, drained**
- ½ **cup fresh raspberries**
- 1 **can (10 ounces) frozen non-alcoholic pina colada mix, thawed**
- ½ **cup sugar**
- ½ **cup pineapple-orange juice**
- ⅛ **teaspoon almond extract**
- ⅛ **teaspoon coconut extract**

In a serving bowl, combine the first six ingredients. In a small bowl, whisk pina colada mix, sugar, juice and extracts until the sugar is dissolved. Pour over fruit; toss to coat. Chill until serving.

IN A CRUNCH

When I want to add a little crunch to fruit salads but don't want to add the fat content of nuts, I use broken pretzel pieces instead. I crumble a handful of pretzels on a microwave-safe plate and toast them in the microwave for 2-3 minutes (watching carefully to prevent burning). It's always a hit!
—**JOYCE L.** DAVISON, MI

Cilantro Blue Cheese Slaw

This cheesy coleslaw makes a terrific side. You could also use it to top your favorite fish tacos or sandwiches.

—**CHRISTI DALTON** HARTSVILLE, TN

START TO FINISH: 25 MIN.
MAKES: 8 SERVINGS

- 8 cups shredded cabbage
- 1 small red onion, halved and thinly sliced
- ⅓ cup minced fresh cilantro
- 1 jalapeno pepper, seeded and minced
- ¼ cup crumbled blue cheese
- ¼ cup fat-free mayonnaise
- ¼ cup reduced-fat sour cream
- 2 tablespoons rice vinegar
- 2 tablespoons lime juice
- 1 garlic clove, minced
- 1 teaspoon sugar
- 1 teaspoon grated lime peel
- ¾ teaspoon salt
- ½ teaspoon coarsely ground pepper

In a large bowl, combine the cabbage, onion, cilantro and jalapeno. In a small bowl, combine the remaining ingredients; pour over the salad and toss to coat.

NOTE *Wear disposable gloves when cutting hot peppers; the oils can burn skin. Avoid touching your face.*

PER SERVING *63 cal., 2 g fat (1 g sat. fat), 6 mg chol., 362 mg sodium, 9 g carb., 3 g fiber, 3 g pro.* **Diabetic Exchanges:** *1 vegetable, ½ fat.*

Fresh Corn Salad

PREP: 20 MIN. + CHILLING
MAKES: 10 SERVINGS

- 8 ears fresh corn, husked and cleaned
- ½ cup canola oil
- ¼ cup cider vinegar
- 1½ teaspoons lemon juice
- ¼ cup minced fresh parsley
- 2 teaspoons sugar
- 1 teaspoon salt
- ½ teaspoon dried basil
- ⅛ to ¼ teaspoon cayenne pepper
- 2 large tomatoes, seeded and coarsely chopped
- ½ cup chopped onion
- ⅓ cup chopped green pepper
- ⅓ cup chopped sweet red pepper

1. In a large saucepan, cook the corn in enough boiling water to cover for 5-7 minutes or until tender. Drain, cool and set aside.

2. In a large bowl, mix oil, vinegar, lemon juice, parsley, sugar, salt if desired, basil and cayenne. Cut cooled corn off cob (should measure 4 cups).

3. Add the corn, tomatoes, onion and peppers to the oil mixture. Mix well. Cover and chill for several hours or overnight.

❝People who prefer food that has a little tang to it are the biggest fans of my Fresh Corn Salad. If you have homegrown vegetables that are ripe for the picking, you won't need to buy much from the grocery store—just head out to the garden.❞

—**CAROL SHAFFER** CAPE GIRARDEAU, MO

Summer Chicken Salad with Raspberry Vinaigrette

Celebrate the best of the summer season with a medley of sugar snap peas, blueberries, raspberries and more. Yum!

—HEIDI FARNWORTH RIVERTON, UT

START TO FINISH: 20 MIN. • **MAKES:** 6 SERVINGS

- 1 package (10 ounces) ready-to-serve salad greens
- 3½ cups cubed cooked chicken
- 1 cup fresh sugar snap peas
- 1 cup fresh blueberries
- 1 cup fresh raspberries
- 1 celery rib, thinly sliced
- ¼ cup olive oil
- 3 tablespoons balsamic vinegar
- 1 tablespoon seedless red raspberry preserves
- ½ teaspoon salt
- ½ teaspoon onion powder
- ½ teaspoon pepper
- ¼ cup slivered almonds, toasted

Place salad greens, chicken, sugar snap peas, blueberries, raspberries and celery in a large bowl. In a small bowl, whisk the oil, balsamic vinegar, raspberry preserves, salt, onion powder and pepper. Drizzle over salad; toss gently to coat. Top with almonds.

Broccoli Mushroom Salad

START TO FINISH: 20 MIN. • **MAKES:** 8 SERVINGS

- 7 cups fresh broccoli florets
- 1 cup sliced fresh mushrooms
- ½ cup shredded cheddar cheese
- ⅓ cup prepared honey Dijon salad dressing
- 4 bacon strips, cooked and crumbled

1. In a large saucepan, bring 3 cups water to a boil. Add broccoli florets; cover and cook for 2-3 minutes or until crisp-tender. Drain and immediately place broccoli in ice water. Drain and pat dry.

2. Transfer the broccoli to a large bowl; toss with the remaining ingredients.

PER SERVING *98 cal., 7 g fat (2 g sat. fat), 11 mg chol., 203 mg sodium, 6 g carb., 2 g fiber, 5 g pro.* **Diabetic Exchanges:** *1 vegetable, 1 fat.*

❝Packed with nutrition, Broccoli Mushroom Salad gets great flavor from bacon, cheddar cheese and Dijon dressing. Plus, it all comes together in 20 minutes.❞

—DEBORAH WILLIAMS PEORIA, AZ

Black-Eyed Pea Pasta Salad

I frequently whip up this make-ahead dish for picnics and potlucks because it's a little different and always popular.

—JOAN HUGGINS WAYNESBORO, MS

PREP: 30 MIN. + CHILLING
MAKES: 8 SERVINGS

- 1 jar (7½ ounces) marinated quartered artichoke hearts
- 1 cup uncooked tricolor spiral pasta
- 1 can (15½ ounces) black-eyed peas, rinsed and drained
- 4 slices provolone cheese, cut into thin strips
- ½ cup chopped green pepper
- ½ cup chopped sweet red pepper
- ½ cup thinly sliced red onion
- ½ cup sliced pepperoni, cut into thin strips
- ½ cup mayonnaise
- ¼ cup prepared Italian salad dressing

1. Drain the artichokes, reserving ¼ cup liquid; chop artichokes and set aside. Cook the spiral pasta according to the package directions.

2. Meanwhile, in a large bowl, combine the artichokes, peas, cheese, peppers, onion and pepperoni. Drain pasta; add to artichoke mixture.

3. In a small bowl, combine the mayonnaise, Italian salad dressing and reserved artichoke liquid. Pour over pasta mixture; toss to coat. Cover and refrigerate for at least 1 hour.

CHEESE, PLEASE

Our family enjoys all kinds of pasta salads. When a recipe calls for cubed cheese, I use string cheese or cheese stick snacks. I just unwrap and slice them into chunks or cubes. Using smaller, individually wrapped pieces means I can open just the number of packages I need, and I don't end up with a partially used block of cheese that may spoil before I can use it.

—ANNETTE MARIE YOUNG
WEST LAFAYETTE, IN

GRAND PRIZE

Bulgur Greek Salad

I'm trying to eat healthier, and this is one of my staples. It doesn't skimp on flavor.

—**JENNIFER ANDRZEJEWSKI**

GRIZZLY FLATS, CA

PREP: 20 MIN. + STANDING
MAKES: 12 SERVINGS

- 1½ cups bulgur
- 3 cups boiling water
- ¼ cup plus 2 tablespoons lemon juice, divided
- 1 teaspoon salt, divided
- 1¼ cups cubed cooked chicken breast
- 1¼ cups chopped cucumber
- ½ cup cherry tomatoes, halved
- ⅓ cup Greek olives
- ¼ cup minced fresh parsley
- ¼ cup roasted sweet red peppers, drained and chopped
- ¼ cup chopped red onion
- 3 tablespoons minced fresh basil
- 3 tablespoons olive oil
- ¼ teaspoon dried oregano
- ¼ teaspoon pepper
- ⅛ teaspoon cayenne pepper
- ¼ cup crumbled feta cheese

1. Place the bulgur in a small bowl. Stir in the water, ¼ cup lemon juice and ½ teaspoon salt. Cover and let stand for 30 minutes or until most of the liquid is absorbed. Drain well.

2. In a large bowl, combine chicken, cucumber, tomatoes, Greek olives, parsley, red peppers, onion and basil. Stir in bulgur.

3. In a small bowl, whisk oil, oregano, pepper, cayenne and remaining juice and salt. Pour over bulgur mixture; toss to coat. Sprinkle with cheese.

PER SERVING *137 cal., 5 g fat (1 g sat. fat), 12 mg chol., 313 mg sodium, 16 g carb., 4 g fiber, 7 g pro.* **Diabetic Exchanges:** *1 starch, 1 lean meat, ½ fat.*

Fall Harvest Salad

PREP: 30 MIN. • **BAKE:** 25 MIN.
MAKES: 6 SERVINGS

- 2 large sweet potatoes, peeled and cubed
- 2 tablespoons olive oil
- ¼ teaspoon salt
- ¼ teaspoon pepper
- 2 cups cubed cooked turkey breast
- 2 medium apples, cubed
- 1 cup chopped walnuts, toasted
- 4 green onions, thinly sliced
- ½ cup raisins
- ½ cup minced fresh parsley

DRESSING

- ¼ cup olive oil
- 2 tablespoons rice vinegar
- 2 tablespoons orange juice
- 2 tablespoons maple syrup
- 1 tablespoon lemon juice
- 2 teaspoons minced fresh gingerroot
- ¼ teaspoon salt
- ¼ teaspoon ground cinnamon
- ⅛ teaspoon ground nutmeg
- ⅛ teaspoon pepper

1. Place the sweet potatoes in an ungreased 15x10x1-in. baking pan; drizzle with oil and sprinkle with salt and pepper. Toss to coat.

2. Bake at 400° for 25-30 minutes or until tender, stirring occasionally. Cool to room temperature.

3. In a large bowl, combine the turkey, apples, walnuts, green onions, raisins, parsley and sweet potatoes.

4. In a small bowl, whisk the dressing ingredients. Pour the dressing over the turkey mixture; toss to coat. Serve immediately.

> Just about any combination of dried fruit and nuts will work in Fall Harvest Salad. You could also substitute roasted butternut squash or pumpkin for the sweet potatoes.
> —**MARY MARLOWE LEVERETTE** COLUMBIA, SC

Cantaloupe with Chicken Salad

Blueberries are an important crop here in the fertile Willamette Valley of Oregon. They're grown for commercial use, but we usually pick about 60 pounds in summer to use in our favorite recipes, including these yummy cantaloupe bowls.
—**ELSIE TRUDE** KEIZER, OR

START TO FINISH: 20 MIN.
MAKES: 6 SERVINGS

- 2 cups cubed cooked chicken
- 1½ to 2 cups fresh blueberries
- 1 cup sliced celery
- 1 cup seedless green grapes, halved
- ½ cup sliced almonds
- 3 cantaloupe, halved and seeded

DRESSING

- ½ cup mayonnaise
- ¼ cup sour cream
- 1 tablespoon lemon juice
- 1½ teaspoons grated lemon peel
- 1½ teaspoons sugar or sugar substitute to equal 1½ teaspoons
- ½ teaspoon ground ginger
- ¼ teaspoon salt, optional

In a large bowl, combine the chicken, blueberries, celery, green grapes and sliced almonds. In a small bowl, mix the dressing ingredients. Pour the dressing over the chicken mixture; toss to coat. Spoon mixture into the cantaloupe halves.

Southwestern Bean Chowder, page 43

42

41

55

Soups & Sandwiches

Get a pot simmering on the stove and stack sliced bread high with tasty ingredients. The **comforting combo** of soup and a sandwich is perfect for busy weekdays, lazy weekends—**anytime at all**!

Red, White and Blue Pita Pockets

These steak pitas boast an all-American combo of ingredients—red peppers, white sour cream and blue cheese!

—CHARLENE CHAMBERS

ORMOND BEACH, FL

PREP: 15 MIN. + MARINATING • **COOK:** 5 MIN.
MAKES: 4 SERVINGS

- 2 tablespoons red wine vinegar
- 4 teaspoons olive oil
- 2 garlic cloves, minced
- 1 pound beef top sirloin steak, thinly sliced
- ½ cup fat-free sour cream
- ⅓ cup crumbled blue cheese
- 4 whole wheat pita pocket halves
- 2 cups torn red leaf lettuce
- ½ cup roasted sweet red peppers, drained and cut into strips
- ¼ cup sliced red onion

1. In a large resealable plastic bag, combine the red wine vinegar, oil and garlic; add the beef. Seal the bag and turn to coat; refrigerate for 8 hours or overnight.

2. In a small bowl, combine the sour cream and cheese; set aside. Drain and discard the marinade.

3. In a large nonstick skillet or wok coated with cooking spray, stir-fry the beef for 2-3 minutes or until no longer pink. Line the pita halves with lettuce, red peppers and red onion; fill each with ⅓ cup beef. Serve with the sour cream mixture.

PER SERVING *351 cal., 12 g fat (4 g sat. fat), 59 mg chol., 522 mg sodium, 26 g carb., 3 g fiber, 32 g pro.* **Diabetic Exchanges:** *4 lean meat, 1½ fat, 1 starch, 1 vegetable.*

Gnocchi Chicken Minestrone

My Italian heritage—and my mom, who was truly amazing at making a pot of soup—inspired me to experiment a little with traditional minestrone. To save some time, I take advantage of the convenient potato gnocchi available in the freezer case at the supermarket.

—BARBARA ESTABROOK RHINELANDER, WI

PREP: 30 MIN. • **COOK:** 30 MIN.
MAKES: 8 SERVINGS (2¾ QUARTS)

- 1¼ pounds chicken tenderloins, cut into ½-inch pieces
- ¾ teaspoon dried oregano
- ¼ teaspoon salt
- ¼ teaspoon pepper
- 2 tablespoons olive oil, divided
- 1 each small green, sweet red and yellow peppers, finely chopped
- 1 medium zucchini, finely chopped
- 1 cup chopped fresh baby portobello mushrooms
- ⅓ cup chopped red onion
- ⅓ cup chopped prosciutto or deli ham
- 4 garlic cloves, minced
- 2 cans (14½ ounces each) chicken broth
- 1 can (14½ ounces) Italian diced tomatoes, undrained
- ¾ cup canned white kidney or cannellini beans, rinsed and drained
- ½ cup frozen peas
- 3 tablespoons tomato paste
- 1 package (16 ounces) potato gnocchi
- ½ cup shredded Asiago cheese
- 8 fresh basil leaves, thinly sliced

1. Sprinkle the chicken with oregano, salt and pepper. In a Dutch oven, saute the chicken in 1 tablespoon oil until no longer pink. Remove from the pan and set aside.

2. In the same pan, cook the peppers, zucchini, mushrooms and red onion in remaining oil until tender. Add the prosciutto and garlic; cook 1 minute longer. Add chicken broth, tomatoes, beans, peas, tomato paste and chicken. Bring to a boil. Reduce heat; simmer, uncovered, for 20 minutes, stirring occasionally.

3. Meanwhile, cook potato gnocchi according to the package directions. Drain; stir into soup. Garnish each serving with cheese and basil.

NOTE *Look for potato gnocchi in the pasta or frozen foods section.*

Spicy Black Bean Soup

A splash of sherry really enhances this satisfying, simple-to-fix favorite.

—**TIA MUSSER** HUDSON, IN

PREP: 25 MIN. • **COOK:** 40 MIN.
MAKES: 12 SERVINGS (¾ CUP EACH)

- 1 large red onion, chopped
- 1 medium sweet red pepper, chopped
- 1 jalapeno pepper, seeded and minced
- 2 tablespoons olive oil
- 3 garlic cloves, minced
- 3 cans (15 ounces each) black beans, rinsed and drained
- 3½ cups vegetable broth
- 1 can (14½ ounces) diced tomatoes with mild green chilies, undrained
- 1 can (4 ounces) chopped green chilies
- ⅓ cup sherry or additional vegetable broth
- 2 tablespoons minced fresh cilantro
- ½ cup fat-free sour cream
- ¼ cup shredded cheddar cheese

1. In a Dutch oven, saute onion and peppers in oil until tender. Add garlic; cook 1 minute longer.

2. Stir in the black beans, vegetable broth, tomatoes and chopped green chilies. Bring to a boil. Reduce heat; simmer, uncovered, for 25 minutes. Add the sherry and cilantro; cook 5 minutes longer.

3. Remove the soup from the heat; cool slightly. Place half of the soup in a blender; cover and process until pureed. Return soup to the pan and heat through. Top each serving with 2 teaspoons sour cream and 1 teaspoon cheddar cheese.

NOTE *Wear disposable gloves when cutting hot peppers; the oils can burn skin. Avoid touching your face.*

BBQ Beef Sandwiches

After years of searching, I finally came across a recipe for shredded barbecue beef that became a big hit with my family and friends. It was worth the wait!

—**REBECCA ROHLAND** MEDFORD, WI

PREP: 15 MIN. • **COOK:** 8 HOURS
MAKES: 14 SERVINGS

- 2 cups ketchup
- 1 medium onion, chopped
- ¼ cup cider vinegar
- ¼ cup molasses
- 2 tablespoons Worcestershire sauce
- 2 garlic cloves, minced
- ½ teaspoon salt
- ½ teaspoon ground mustard
- ½ teaspoon pepper
- ¼ teaspoon garlic powder
- ¼ teaspoon crushed red pepper flakes
- 1 boneless beef chuck roast (3 pounds)
- 14 sesame seed hamburger buns, split

1. In a large bowl, combine the first 11 ingredients. Cut the roast in half; place in a 5-qt. slow cooker. Pour the ketchup mixture over roast. Cover and cook on low for 8-10 hours or until the meat is tender.

2. Remove the meat and shred with two forks. Skim fat from the cooking juices. Return meat to slow cooker; heat through. Using a slotted spoon, serve beef on buns.

GRAND PRIZE WINNER ★★★★

GRAND PRIZE

Sweet Potato & Black Bean Chili

My whole family enjoys this satisfying vegetarian chili—but my daughter is definitely its biggest fan!

—**JOY PENDLEY** ORTONVILLE, MI

PREP: 25 MIN. • **COOK:** 35 MIN.
MAKES: 8 SERVINGS (2 QUARTS)

- 3 large sweet potatoes, peeled and cut into ½-inch cubes
- 1 large onion, chopped
- 1 tablespoon olive oil
- 2 tablespoons chili powder
- 3 garlic cloves, minced
- 1 teaspoon ground cumin
- ¼ teaspoon cayenne pepper
- 2 cans (15 ounces each) black beans, rinsed and drained
- 1 can (28 ounces) diced tomatoes, undrained
- ¼ cup brewed coffee
- 2 tablespoons honey
- ½ teaspoon salt
- ¼ teaspoon pepper
- ½ cup shredded reduced-fat Monterey Jack cheese or reduced-fat Mexican cheese blend

1. In a nonstick Dutch oven coated with cooking spray, saute the sweet potatoes and onion in olive oil until crisp-tender. Add the chili powder, garlic, cumin and cayenne pepper; cook 1 minute longer. Stir in the black beans, tomatoes, coffee, honey, salt and pepper.

2. Bring to a boil. Reduce the heat; cover and simmer for 30-35 minutes or until sweet potatoes are tender. Sprinkle with cheese.

Southwestern Bean Chowder

I use white kidney beans in my chowder because I love their texture. With cumin, chilies and chili powder, every spoonful has a south-of-the-border kick.

—JULI MEYERS HINESVILLE, GA

PREP: 20 MIN. • **COOK:** 35 MIN.
MAKES: 8 SERVINGS (2 QUARTS)

- 2 cans (15 ounces each) white kidney or cannellini beans, rinsed and drained, divided
- 1 medium onion, chopped
- ¼ cup chopped celery
- ¼ cup chopped green pepper
- 1 tablespoon olive oil
- 2 garlic cloves, minced
- 3 cups vegetable broth
- 1½ cups frozen corn, thawed
- 1 medium carrot, shredded
- 1 can (4 ounces) chopped green chilies
- 1 tablespoon ground cumin
- ½ teaspoon chili powder
- 4½ teaspoons cornstarch
- 2 cups 2% milk
- 1 cup (4 ounces) shredded cheddar cheese
  Minced fresh cilantro and additional shredded cheddar cheese, optional

1. In a small bowl, mash one can of beans with a fork; set aside.
2. In a Dutch oven, saute the onion, celery and pepper in oil until tender. Add garlic; cook 1 minute longer. Stir in the mashed beans, vegetable broth, corn, carrot, green chilies, cumin, chili powder and remaining beans. Bring to a boil. Reduce the heat; simmer, uncovered, for 20 minutes.
3. Combine cornstarch and milk until smooth. Stir into bean mixture. Bring to a boil; cook and stir for 2 minutes or until thickened. Stir in cheddar cheese until melted. Serve with cilantro and additional cheese if desired.
PER SERVING *236 cal., 8 g fat (4 g sat. fat), 20 mg chol., 670 mg sodium, 31 g carb., 6 g fiber, 11 g pro.* **Diabetic Exchanges:** *2 starch, 1 lean meat, ½ fat.*

Grilled Stuffed Turkey Burgers

How do you give turkey burgers fantastic flavor? Mix the ground meat with plenty of seasonings, then stuff the patties with red pepper and mozzarella. Delicious!

—MEGAN CROW LINCOLN, NE

START TO FINISH: 25 MIN.
MAKES: 5 SERVINGS

- 2 tablespoons onion soup mix
- ½ teaspoon garlic powder
- ½ teaspoon Worcestershire sauce
- ⅛ teaspoon salt
  Dash pepper
- 1¼ pounds lean ground turkey
- ½ cup finely chopped sweet red pepper
- ½ cup shredded part-skim mozzarella cheese
- 5 whole wheat hamburger buns, split

1. In a small bowl, combine the first five ingredients. Crumble turkey over the mixture and mix well. Shape into 10 thin patties. Spoon red pepper and cheese onto center of five patties; top with the remaining patties and press edges firmly to seal.
2. Grill the burgers, covered, over medium heat or broil 4 in. from heat for 5-7 minutes on each side or until a thermometer reads 165° and juices run clear. Serve on buns.

Potato-Lentil Stew

Hash brown potatoes, lentils, tomatoes, spices...they all add up to a comforting and satisfying main course. Pair the stew with a loaf of your favorite bread, and dinner's done!

—**KRISTA GOODWIN** YPSILANTI, MI

PREP: 20 MIN. • **COOK:** 40 MIN. • **MAKES:** 6 SERVINGS (2½ QUARTS)

- 1 **large onion, chopped**
- 2 **medium carrots, chopped**
- 2 **teaspoons olive oil**
- 4 **teaspoons chili powder**
- 3 **garlic cloves, minced**
- 3 **teaspoons ground cumin**
- 1 **teaspoon dried oregano**
- 1 **carton (32 ounces) vegetable broth**
- ¾ **cup dried lentils, rinsed**
- 2 **cans (10 ounces each) diced tomatoes and green chilies**
- 3½ **cups frozen cubed hash brown potatoes**
- 1 **can (16 ounces) kidney beans, rinsed and drained**
- ½ **teaspoon salt**
- ¼ **teaspoon pepper**

1. In a Dutch oven, saute the onion and carrots in oil for 3 minutes. Add chili powder, garlic, cumin and oregano; cook 1 minute longer.

2. Stir in the broth and lentils. Bring to a boil. Reduce the heat; cover and simmer for 20-22 minutes or until lentils are tender. Stir in the tomatoes, potatoes, beans, salt and pepper. Return to a boil. Reduce heat; cover and simmer 10-15 minutes longer or until potatoes are tender.

Melt-in-Your-Mouth Sausages

My family absolutely loves this slow cooker recipe. The zesty Italian sausages are great not only in brat buns for sandwiches, but also served over a bed of hot spaghetti.

—**ILEAN SCHULTHEISS** COHOCTON, NY

PREP: 10 MIN. • **COOK:** 4 HOURS • **MAKES:** 8 SERVINGS

- 8 **Italian sausage links (2 pounds)**
- 1 **jar (26 ounces) meatless spaghetti sauce**
- ½ **cup water**
- 1 **can (6 ounces) tomato paste**
- 1 **large green pepper, thinly sliced**
- 1 **large onion, thinly sliced**
- 1 **tablespoon grated Parmesan cheese**
- 1 **teaspoon dried parsley flakes**
- 8 **brat buns, split**
  Additional Parmesan cheese, optional

1. Place sausages in a large skillet; cover with water. Bring to a boil. Reduce heat; cover and simmer for 10 minutes or until a thermometer reads 160°; drain well.

2. Meanwhile, in a 3-qt. slow cooker, combine the spaghetti sauce, water, tomato paste, green pepper, onion, cheese and parsley. Add sausages. Cover and cook on low for 4-5 hours or until vegetables are tender. Serve in buns. Sprinkle with additional cheese if desired.

Fresh garden peas combine with a hint of basil for this delightfully light spring soup. A drizzle of mushroom cream sauce on top lends even more depth and appeal.

—SALLY SIBTHORPE SHELBY TOWNSHIP, MI

Pea Soup with Mushroom Cream Sauce

PREP: 25 MIN. • **COOK:** 15 MIN.
MAKES: 6 SERVINGS

- ½ pound sliced baby portobello mushrooms, divided
- 1 tablespoon butter
- ¼ cup chopped onion
- 1 garlic clove, minced
- ½ cup half-and-half cream
- 3 tablespoons sherry or reduced-sodium chicken broth
- 1 tablespoon minced fresh thyme or 1 teaspoon dried thyme
- ¾ teaspoon salt, divided
- 5 cups fresh or frozen peas, divided
- 3 cups reduced-sodium chicken broth
- 2 tablespoons lemon juice
- 4½ teaspoons minced fresh basil or 1½ teaspoons dried basil

1. Set aside 3 tablespoons portobello mushrooms for garnish. In a large skillet, saute remaining mushrooms in butter until tender.

2. Add the onion to the skillet; saute until tender. Add the garlic; cook 1 minute longer. Stir in half-and-half cream, sherry, thyme and ¼ teaspoon salt. Bring to a boil. Reduce the heat; simmer, uncovered, for 2 minutes. Cool slightly. Transfer to a blender; process until smooth. Set aside.

3. In a Dutch oven, combine 4½ cups peas, chicken broth and remaining salt. Bring to a boil. Reduce the heat; simmer, uncovered, for 4 minutes or until the peas are tender. Stir in the lemon juice and basil; heat through. Transfer to a blender; process in batches until blended.

4. Ladle the soup into serving bowls; top with the mushroom cream sauce. Garnish with reserved mushrooms and remaining peas.

PER SERVING *169 cal., 5 g fat (3 g sat. fat), 15 mg chol., 612 mg sodium, 22 g carb., 7 g fiber, 10 g pro.* **Diabetic Exchanges:** *1½ starch, 1 fat.*

French Dip

PREP: 15 MIN. • **COOK:** 5 HOURS • **MAKES:** 8 SERVINGS

- 1 beef chuck roast (3 pounds), trimmed
- 2 cups water
- ½ cup reduced-sodium soy sauce
- 1 teaspoon dried rosemary, crushed
- 1 teaspoon dried thyme
- 1 teaspoon garlic powder
- 1 bay leaf
- 3 to 4 whole peppercorns
- 8 French rolls, split

1. Place the roast in a 5-qt. slow cooker. Add the water, soy sauce and seasonings. Cover and cook on high for 5-6 hours or until beef is tender.

2. Remove meat from broth; shred with two forks and keep warm. Strain broth; skim fat. Pour broth into small cups for dipping. Serve beef on rolls.

> ❝For a French dip that offers a little more pizzazz than the traditional version, try this one. The rosemary, garlic and other seasonings add great flavor to the broth, served on the side for dipping the shredded beef sandwich. Using a slow cooker makes preparation easy, too.❞

—MARGARET MCNEIL GERMANTOWN, TN

Day After Easter Soup

My recipe gets its name from an Easter years ago, when I tossed some extra asparagus into the pan. Now, I wait impatiently each spring for the next crop of fresh-picked spears.

—SUSAN WILSON MILWAUKEE, WI

PREP: 25 MIN. • **COOK:** 45 MIN. • **MAKES:** 9 SERVINGS (2¼ QUARTS)

- 2 medium leeks (white portion only), chopped
- 2 tablespoons butter
- 2 tablespoons all-purpose flour
- 1 carton (32 ounces) vegetable broth
- 1 cup water
- 1 tablespoon minced fresh parsley
- 1 teaspoon herbes de Provence
- 1 teaspoon minced chives
- ½ teaspoon celery seed
- ¼ teaspoon ground nutmeg
- 1 pound fresh asparagus, trimmed
- 5 medium red potatoes, peeled and cut into ½-inch cubes
- 1½ cups cubed fully cooked lean ham
- 1¼ cups half-and-half cream
- 3 tablespoons shredded Gruyere or Swiss cheese

1. In a large saucepan, saute leeks in butter until tender. Stir in flour until blended. Gradually add vegetable broth, water, parsley, herbes de Provence, chives, celery seed and nutmeg. Bring to a boil; cook and stir for 2 minutes or until thickened.

2. Cut the tips off asparagus and set aside. Cut stalks into ½-in. pieces; add to pan. Reduce heat; cover and simmer for 10-15 minutes or until asparagus is tender. Cool slightly.

3. In a blender, process the soup in batches until smooth. Return all to the pan. Stir in the potatoes. Bring to a boil. Reduce heat; cover and simmer for 10 minutes. Stir in the asparagus tips; cover and simmer 5-8 minutes longer or until the vegetables are tender. Stir in the ham and cream; heat through. Sprinkle with cheese.

NOTE *Look for herbes de Provence in the spice aisle.*

Bean Beef Burgers

If you're looking for a healthier burger that's lower in fat and higher in fiber, this variation is for you. Black beans and bulgur combine with ground beef for the delicious patties, which are stacked with spinach, onion and tomato on whole wheat buns.
—**JENNIFER KUNZ** AUSTIN, TX

START TO FINISH: 30 MIN. • **MAKES:** 6 SERVINGS

- 1 cup water
- ½ cup bulgur
- 1 can (15 ounces) black beans, rinsed and drained
- 3 green onions, sliced
- 1 tablespoon stone-ground mustard
- 1 garlic clove, halved
- ¼ teaspoon salt
- ¼ teaspoon pepper
- 1 egg, lightly beaten
- ½ pound lean ground beef (90% lean)
- 1 tablespoon canola oil
- 6 whole wheat hamburger buns, split
  Spinach leaves, sliced red onion and tomato

1. In a small saucepan, bring the water to a boil. Stir in bulgur. Reduce heat; cover and simmer for 15-20 minutes or until tender. In a food processor, combine the black beans, green onions, mustard and garlic. Cover and pulse until blended. Stir in salt and pepper.
2. In a large bowl, combine egg, bulgur and bean mixture. Crumble the beef over the mixture and mix well. Shape into six patties.
3. In a large nonstick skillet, cook patties in oil in batches for 4-5 minutes on each side or until a thermometer reads 160° and juices run clear. Serve on buns with spinach, onion and tomato.
PER SERVING *307 cal., 8 g fat (2 g sat. fat), 54 mg chol., 517 mg sodium, 42 g carb., 9 g fiber, 17 g pro.* **Diabetic Exchanges:** *2 starch, 2 lean meat, 1 fat.*

Asian Chicken Noodle Soup

One night when I discovered I didn't have the usual noodles on hand for my chicken soup, I improvised and gave it an Asian twist with wonton wrappers. It was a success!
—**NOELLE MYERS** GRAND FORKS, ND

PREP: 15 MIN. • **COOK:** 40 MIN. • **MAKES:** 10 SERVINGS (2½ QUARTS)

- 1½ pounds boneless skinless chicken breasts, cut into 1-inch cubes
- 1 tablespoon sesame oil
- 3 medium carrots, sliced
- 2 celery ribs, chopped
- 1 medium onion, chopped
- 6 cups chicken broth
- ⅓ cup teriyaki sauce
- ¼ cup chili garlic sauce
- 1 package (12 ounces) wonton wrappers, cut into ¼-inch strips
- 2 cups sliced fresh shiitake mushrooms
- ⅓ cup chopped celery leaves
- ¼ cup minced fresh basil
- 2 tablespoons minced fresh cilantro
- 2 green onions, sliced

1. In a Dutch oven, cook chicken in oil over medium heat until no longer pink. Remove and keep warm. In the same pan, saute the carrots, celery and onion until tender. Stir in the broth, teriyaki sauce, garlic sauce and chicken. Bring to a boil. Reduce heat; simmer, uncovered, for 20 minutes.
2. Add wonton wrapper strips, shiitake mushrooms, celery leaves, basil and cilantro. Cook and stir for 4-5 minutes or until wonton wrapper strips and mushrooms are tender. Sprinkle with green onions.

Baked Lasagna in a Bun

Love classic lasagna but not the fuss? My family really goes for Italian meat sauce and cheese tucked into hollowed-out buns.

—**CINDY MORELOCK** AFTON, TN

PREP: 20 MIN. • **BAKE:** 25 MIN. • **MAKES:** 8 SERVINGS

- 8 submarine or hoagie buns (8 inches)
- 1 pound ground beef
- 1 cup spaghetti sauce
- 1 tablespoon garlic powder
- 1 tablespoon Italian seasoning
- 1 cup ricotta cheese
- ¼ cup grated Parmesan cheese
- 1 cup (4 ounces) shredded cheddar cheese, divided
- 1 cup (4 ounces) shredded part-skim mozzarella cheese, divided

1. Preheat oven to 350°. Make a 2-in.-wide V-shaped cut in the center of each bun to within 1 inch of bottom. Remove the cut portion and save for another use. Place buns on an ungreased baking sheet.

2. In a large skillet, cook the ground beef over medium heat 6-8 minutes or until no longer pink, breaking the meat into crumbles; drain. Stir in the spaghetti sauce, garlic powder and Italian seasoning; heat through.

3. Meanwhile, in a small bowl, mix the ricotta cheese, Parmesan cheese and half of the cheddar and mozzarella cheese. Spoon the meat sauce into buns; top with ricotta mixture. Cover loosely with foil.

4. Bake 20 minutes. Sprinkle tops with remaining cheddar and mozzarella cheese; bake, uncovered, 3-5 minutes or until the cheese is melted.

Crouton-Topped Garlic Soup

Pan-roasted garlic lends robust flavor to this rich cream soup. Shredded cheese and croutons make the perfect toppings.

—**CAROLYN KUMPE** EL DORADO, CA

PREP: 20 MIN. • **COOK:** 1 HOUR • **MAKES:** 4 SERVINGS

- 20 garlic cloves, peeled
- 1 tablespoon olive oil
- 2 large onions, halved and sliced
- 2 tablespoons butter
- 2½ cups reduced-sodium chicken broth
- 1 tablespoon minced fresh thyme or 1 teaspoon dried thyme
- 1 bay leaf
- 1 cup heavy whipping cream

CROUTONS
- 2 cups cubed sourdough bread, crusts removed
- 2 tablespoons olive oil
- 1 teaspoon minced fresh rosemary or ¼ teaspoon dried rosemary, crushed
- ¼ teaspoon salt
- ⅛ teaspoon pepper

TOPPINGS
- ½ cup shredded Gruyere or Swiss cheese
- 2 tablespoons minced fresh parsley

1. In a small skillet, cook the garlic in oil over low heat for 3-5 minutes or until golden brown. Remove from the heat; set aside.

2. In a Dutch oven over medium-high heat, cook onions in butter until softened. Reduce the heat to medium-low; cook, stirring occasionally, for 30 minutes or until deep golden brown.

3. Add the chicken broth, thyme, bay leaf and reserved garlic. Bring to a boil. Reduce the heat; cover and simmer for 20 minutes to allow the flavors to blend. Stir in cream; heat through. Discard bay leaf.

4. For croutons, place sourdough bread in a small bowl. Combine the oil, rosemary, salt and pepper; drizzle over bread and toss to coat. Place in an ungreased 15x10x1-in. baking pan. Bake at 400° for 15-20 minutes or until golden brown, stirring occasionally.

5. Divide the soup among four bowls. Top with croutons, cheese and parsley.

SUPER SOUP

Adding a garnish such as shredded cheese, minced parsley or croutons to soup before serving gives it extra color, flavor and texture. Other garnish ideas include finely chopped green onions or chives, bacon bits, grated cheese and sour cream. Kids are sure to love fun toppings like goldfish crackers and sliced cheese cut with a cookie cutter.

Gazpacho

Served as an appetizer, first course or light lunch, this chilled classic is a wonderfully refreshing choice for warm summer days. The recipe is versatile, too—you can add or omit various ingredients to suit your taste. Have fun experimenting!

—AGNES GATES LUBBOCK, TX

PREP: 20 MIN. + CHILLING • **MAKES:** 5 CUPS

SOUP BASE

- 2½ cups tomato juice
- 3 tablespoons red wine vinegar
- ½ teaspoon Worcestershire sauce
- 2 tablespoons olive oil
- 1 teaspoon minced garlic
- 2 teaspoons minced fresh parsley
- ⅛ teaspoon hot pepper sauce or to taste
- ½ teaspoon salt
- ⅛ teaspoon pepper
- 1 tablespoon lemon juice

VEGETABLES

- 1 cup finely chopped tomatoes
- ½ cup finely chopped celery
- ½ cup finely chopped green pepper
- ½ cup finely chopped onion
- 1 small cucumber, peeled, seeded, finely chopped

GARNISHES

- Chopped avocado
- Croutons

1. In a bowl, combine the soup base ingredients. Stir in the vegetables. Cover and refrigerate for 4 hours or overnight.

2. Garnish soup with avocado and croutons; serve cold.

AVOCADO EASE

The easiest avocados to peel and cut are those that are ripe yet firm. To seed and peel an avocado, start by cutting it in half lengthwise. Twist the halves in opposite directions to separate. Carefully tap the seed with the blade of a sharp knife. Rotate the knife to loosen the seed and lift it out. To remove the peel, use a large metal spoon to scoop out the flesh from each avocado half, staying close to the peel.

Hearty Chipotle Chicken Soup

Sweet corn and cool sour cream tame the heat of chipotles in my soup. I love sitting down to a hot bowlful on a cold night.

—SONALI RUDER NEW YORK, NY

PREP: 15 MIN. • **COOK:** 30 MIN.
MAKES: 8 SERVINGS (3¼ QUARTS)

- 1 large onion, chopped
- 1 tablespoon canola oil
- 4 garlic cloves, minced
- 4 cups reduced-sodium chicken broth
- 2 cans (15 ounces each) pinto beans, rinsed and drained
- 2 cans (14½ ounces each) fire-roasted diced tomatoes, undrained
- 3 cups frozen corn
- 2 chipotle peppers in adobo sauce, seeded and minced
- 2 teaspoons adobo sauce
- 1 teaspoon ground cumin
- ¼ teaspoon pepper
- 2 cups cubed cooked chicken breast
- ½ cup fat-free sour cream
- ¼ cup minced fresh cilantro

1. In a Dutch oven, saute the onion in oil until tender. Add the garlic; cook 1 minute longer. Add chicken broth, pinto beans, tomatoes, corn, chipotle peppers, adobo sauce, cumin and pepper. Bring to a boil. Reduce heat; simmer, uncovered, for 20 minutes.

2. Stir in the chicken; heat through. Garnish with sour cream; sprinkle with cilantro.

PER SERVING *287 cal., 4 g fat (1 g sat. fat), 29 mg chol., 790 mg sodium, 42 g carb., 7 g fiber, 21 g pro.* **Diabetic Exchanges:** *2 starch, 2 lean meat, 2 vegetable.*

Caribbean Potato Soup

An unusual vegetable combination goes into this bright, exotic blend. If you don't have kale, use spinach instead.

—CRYSTAL BRUNS ILIFF, CO

START TO FINISH: 30 MIN.
MAKES: 6 SERVINGS

- 2 **medium onions, chopped**
- 2 **teaspoons canola oil**
- 3 **garlic cloves, minced**
- 2 **teaspoons minced fresh gingerroot**
- 2 **teaspoons ground coriander**
- 1 **teaspoon ground turmeric**
- ½ **teaspoon dried thyme**
- ¼ **teaspoon ground allspice**
- 5 **cups vegetable broth**
- 2 **cups cubed peeled sweet potato**
- 3 **cups chopped fresh kale**
- 1 **cup frozen sliced okra**
- 1 **cup coconut milk**
- 1 **cup canned diced tomatoes, drained**
- 1 **cup canned black-eyed peas, rinsed and drained**
- 2 **tablespoons lime juice**

1. In a Dutch oven, saute onions in oil until tender. Add the garlic, ginger and spices; cook 1 minute longer.
2. Stir in broth and potato. Bring to a boil. Reduce heat; cover and simmer for 5 minutes. Stir in kale and okra. Return to a boil; cover and simmer 10 minutes longer or until potato is tender. Add the milk, tomatoes, peas and lime juice; heat through.

Tomato-Basil Turkey Burgers

I always prepare my burgers with regular, not lean, ground turkey so they're extra-moist and juicy. If the weather isn't right for grilling, I just cook them under the broiler.

—JAMIE MILLER MAPLE GROVE, MN

START TO FINISH: 30 MIN.
MAKES: 4 SERVINGS

- 1 **large sweet onion**
- 1 **package (6½ ounces) sun-dried tomato and basil cheese spread, divided**
- 1¼ **pounds ground turkey**
- 1 **large sweet red pepper, quartered**
- 4 **ciabatta rolls, split**

1. Cut the sweet onion into three ½-in. slices; chop remaining onion and place in a large bowl. Stir in ⅓ cup cheese spread. Crumble turkey over the mixture and mix well. Shape into four patties.
2. Moisten a paper towel with cooking oil. Using long-handled tongs, lightly coat the grill rack. Grill the burgers, onion slices and pepper, covered, over medium-high heat for 5-7 minutes on each side or until a thermometer reads 165° and juices run clear. Chop grilled onion and pepper.
3. Spread rolls with remaining cheese spread; top each with a burger and grilled vegetables. Replace tops.

Spicy Fajita Chili

I like to serve my zesty chili with rolls or corn bread for soaking up every last drop. If your family prefers more heat, just use spicier versions of V8 juice and chili beans.
—**CATHY BELL** JOPLIN, MO

PREP: 15 MIN. • **COOK:** 30 MIN.
MAKES: 8 SERVINGS (2 QUARTS)

- 1½ pounds ground pork
- 1 medium onion, chopped
- 1 medium green pepper, chopped
- 1 medium sweet red pepper, chopped
- 1 garlic clove, minced
- 2 cans (11½ ounces each) V8 juice
- 1 can (16 ounces) chili beans, undrained
- 1 can (10 ounces) diced tomatoes and green chilies
- 2 tablespoons chili powder
- 1 teaspoon seasoned salt
- ½ teaspoon seasoned pepper
  Shredded cheddar cheese

1. In a Dutch oven, cook pork, onion and peppers over medium heat until the meat is no longer pink. Add garlic; cook 1 minute longer. Drain.
2. Stir in the V8 juice, chili beans, tomatoes, chili powder, seasoned salt and seasoned pepper. Bring to a boil. Reduce heat; simmer, uncovered, for 20 minutes or until slightly thickened. Serve with cheese.
FREEZER OPTION *Serve desired amount. Cool the remaining chili; transfer to freezer containers. Chili may be frozen for up to 3 months. To use frozen chili, thaw in refrigerator. Place in a saucepan; heat through. Sprinkle with additional cheese.*

Grilled Turkey Pitas

These creamy pita pockets featuring marinated turkey, feta cheese and lots of fresh vegetables are a complete meal from the grill—and a great way to shake up your cookout routine.
—**PENELOPE MALCOLM** AMERICUS, GA

PREP: 20 MIN. + MARINATING
GRILL: 20 MIN. • **MAKES:** 4 SERVINGS

- 1 cup fat-free plain Greek yogurt
- 2 tablespoons olive oil
- 1 tablespoon lemon juice
- 1 tablespoon honey
- 2 garlic cloves, minced
- 1 teaspoon minced fresh oregano or ¼ teaspoon dried oregano
- ¼ teaspoon salt
- ⅛ teaspoon pepper
- 1 package (20 ounces) turkey breast tenderloins
- 3 medium tomatoes, seeded and chopped
- 1 small cucumber, chopped
- 1 small red onion, chopped
- 1 small green pepper, chopped
- ½ cup crumbled feta cheese
- ⅓ cup Greek olives, chopped
- 8 pita pocket halves

1. In a small bowl, combine the first eight ingredients. Pour ¼ cup yogurt mixture into a large resealable plastic bag; add turkey. Seal the bag and turn to coat; refrigerate turkey for 8 hours or overnight. Cover and refrigerate remaining yogurt mixture.
2. Drain and discard the marinade. Moisten a paper towel with cooking oil. Using long-handled tongs, lightly coat the grill rack.
3. Grill turkey, covered, over medium heat or broil 4 in. from the heat for 15-20 minutes or until a thermometer reads 170°, turning occasionally. Let stand for 5 minutes before slicing.
4. To the remaining yogurt mixture, add the tomatoes, cucumber, red onion, green pepper, feta cheese and Greek olives.
5. Grill the pita halves, uncovered, over medium heat for 1-2 minutes on each side or until warm. Fill each with turkey and ⅓ cup yogurt mixture.

Pizza Burgers

Children tend to go for anything with the word "pizza" in it, so I came up with a recipe for top-your-own Pizza Burgers. The hearty open-face sandwiches bring some fun to our weeknight dinners.
—ROBIN KORNEGAY SEFFNER, FL

PREP: 20 MIN. • **GRILL:** 15 MIN.
MAKES: 6 SERVINGS

- 6 pieces frozen garlic Texas toast
- 1¾ pounds ground beef
- 1 cup pizza sauce, divided
- 18 slices pepperoni
- 12 slices part-skim mozzarella cheese, divided
- 1 cup sliced fresh mushrooms
- 2 teaspoons butter
- 6 teaspoons grated Parmesan cheese
  Sliced green pepper and ripe olives, optional

1. Prepare Texas toast according to package directions. Meanwhile, shape beef into 12 thin patties.
2. Top six patties with 1 tablespoon pizza sauce, three slices of pepperoni and one slice of mozzarella cheese. Top with remaining patties; press edges firmly to seal.
3. Grill, covered, over medium heat for 6-8 minutes on each side or until a thermometer reads 160° and the juices run clear. Meanwhile, in a small skillet, saute mushrooms in butter.
4. Top burgers with remaining sauce and mozzarella cheese. Cover and cook 3 minutes longer or until cheese is melted. Serve burgers on toast with mushrooms, Parmesan cheese and peppers and olives if desired.

BURGER BOOST

When I want to give my burgers a little extra pizzazz, I combine 2 pounds of ground beef with an envelope of ranch salad dressing mix. Then I form the seasoned meat into patties and pop them on the grill. Everyone who tries them gives them a thumbs-up.
—CAROLYN ZIMMERMAN
FAIRBURY, IL

Champion Lamb Burgers

I give our cookouts a Mediterranean twist with these Greek-style burgers. The ground lamb patties get great flavor from rosemary, garlic, mustard, red onions and more.

—**CHARLENE CHAMBERS** ORMOND BEACH, FL

START TO FINISH: 25 MIN. • **MAKES:** 6 SERVINGS

- 2 large red onions, thinly sliced
- 2 teaspoons olive oil
- 1 tablespoon red wine vinegar
- 2 teaspoons minced fresh rosemary
- 1½ teaspoons sugar
- 1 teaspoon stone-ground mustard
- ¼ teaspoon salt
- ¼ teaspoon pepper
- **BURGERS**
- 2 pounds ground lamb
- 2 garlic cloves, minced
- 1 teaspoon salt
- ¼ teaspoon pepper
- 6 pita pocket halves
- 2 tablespoons olive oil
- 1½ cups spring mix salad greens

1. In a large skillet, saute onions in oil until tender. Add the red wine vinegar, rosemary, sugar, stone-ground mustard, salt and pepper; cook 5 minutes longer. Keep warm.

2. Crumble the lamb into a large bowl; sprinkle with garlic, salt and pepper and mix well. Shape the mixture into six patties. Grill burgers, covered, over medium heat or broil 4 in. from the heat for 4-6 minutes on each side or until a thermometer reads 160° and juices run clear.

3. Brush pita pockets with oil; lightly grill on both sides. Serve burgers in pockets with lettuce and onions.

CHANGE-UP

Pitas are a great alternative to the usual buns or sliced bread for sandwiches and burgers. Also try biscuits, tortillas, bagels, English muffins or pastry shells.

Cheesy Cauliflower Soup

Here's one of my cold-weather favorites. Like your soup chunky? Skip the blender step in the recipe and just stir the cheddar and cream into the slow cooker. Then heat on high until the cheese is melted.

—SHERYL PUNTER WOODSTOCK, ON

PREP: 25 MIN. • **COOK:** 5½ HOURS
MAKES: 9 SERVINGS (2¼ QUARTS)

- 1 large head cauliflower, broken into florets
- 2 celery ribs
- 2 large carrots
- 1 large green pepper
- 1 small sweet red pepper
- 1 medium red onion
- 4 cups chicken broth
- ½ teaspoon Worcestershire sauce
- ¼ teaspoon salt
- ⅛ teaspoon pepper
- 2 cups (8 ounces) shredded cheddar cheese
- 2 cups half-and-half cream

1. Place the cauliflower in a 4-qt. slow cooker. Chop celery, carrots, peppers and red onion; add to the slow cooker. Stir in chicken broth, Worcestershire sauce, salt and pepper. Cover; cook on low for 5-6 hours or until vegetables are tender.

2. In a blender, process the soup in batches until smooth. Return all to the slow cooker; stir in the cheddar cheese and half-and-half cream. Cover and cook on high for 30 minutes or until the cheese is melted.

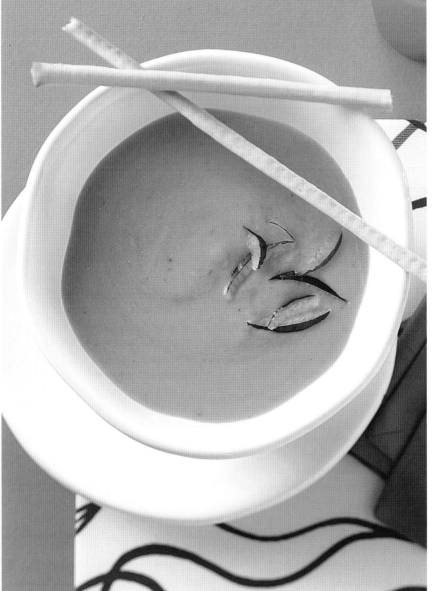

Chipotle Cheeseburgers

These are guaranteed to get your taste buds fired up! Feel free to use turkey in place of beef—the chipotle pepper and spices add plenty of zip to either meat.

—CRYSTAL BRUNS ILIFF, CO

START TO FINISH: 25 MIN.
MAKES: 4 SERVINGS

- 1 small onion, finely chopped
- 2 tablespoons minced fresh cilantro
- 1 chipotle pepper in adobo sauce, finely chopped
- 1 teaspoon onion powder
- 1 teaspoon garlic powder
- 1 teaspoon seasoned salt
- ¼ teaspoon pepper
- 1 pound ground beef
- 4 slices part-skim mozzarella cheese
- 4 hamburger buns, split and toasted
  Lettuce leaves and tomato slices, optional

1. In a small bowl, combine the first seven ingredients. Crumble the beef over the mixture and mix well. Shape into four patties.

2. Grill, covered, over medium heat or broil 4 in. from heat for 5-7 minutes on each side or until a thermometer reads 160° and the juices run clear. Top with mozzarella cheese. Cook 1-2 minutes longer or until the cheese is melted. Serve on buns with lettuce and tomato if desired.

Chicken Caesar Wraps

Think outside the bowl! With tortillas full of tender chicken, Parmesan, croutons and a creamy dressing, the classic Caesar salad becomes a grab-and-go wrap.

—**NANCY PRATT** LONGVIEW, TX

START TO FINISH: 15 MIN.
MAKES: 6 SERVINGS

- ¾ **cup fat-free creamy Caesar salad dressing**
- ¼ **cup grated Parmesan cheese**
- ½ **teaspoon garlic powder**
- ¼ **teaspoon pepper**
- 3 **cups cubed cooked chicken breast**
- 2 **cups torn romaine**
- ¾ **cup Caesar salad croutons, coarsely chopped**
- 6 **whole wheat tortillas (8 inches), room temperature**

In a large bowl, combine the salad dressing, Parmesan cheese, garlic powder and pepper. Add the chicken, romaine and croutons. Spoon ⅔ cup chicken mixture down the center of each tortilla; roll up.

PER SERVING *332 cal., 7 g fat (1 g sat. fat), 57 mg chol., 689 mg sodium, 37 g carb., 4 g fiber, 27 g pro.* **Diabetic Exchanges:** *3 lean meat, 2½ starch, ½ fat.*

Picadillo in Pita Bread

When my children were young, I relied on these Cuban-style pockets because they were easy to fix after work. Now my kids are grown, but I still serve these tasty pitas.

—**SHIRLEY SMITH** ORANGE, CA

START TO FINISH: 30 MIN.
MAKES: 6 SERVINGS

- 1 **pound ground beef**
- 1 **garlic clove, minced**
- ½ **medium onion, chopped**
- 1 **small apple, peeled and chopped**
- ¼ **cup beef broth**
- 1 **tablespoon vinegar**
- 1 **can (8 ounces) tomato sauce or 1 can (7¾ ounces) Mexican-style hot tomato sauce**
- 1 **teaspoon salt**
- ½ **teaspoon ground cinnamon**
- ½ **teaspoon ground cumin**
- ¼ **cup raisins**
- ⅓ **cup sliced almonds**
- 6 **pita pocket halves**
- 1 **avocado, sliced**
- ½ **cup sour cream**

1. In a large skillet over medium heat, cook the beef, garlic and onion until the meat is no longer pink, breaking meat into crumbles; drain. Stir in the apple, broth, vinegar, tomato sauce, salt, cinnamon and cumin; simmer, stirring occasionally, until liquid is absorbed, about 15 minutes. Stir in raisins and almonds. Adjust seasoning if necessary.

2. To serve, fill each pita half with beef mixture and top with an avocado slice and a dollop of sour cream.

Herb & Cheese-Stuffed Burgers

Bored with burgers that have the same old ground beef patties? Stuff them with a gooey, mouthwatering filling.

—SHERRI COX LUCASVILLE, OH

START TO FINISH: 30 MIN.
MAKES: 4 SERVINGS

- ¼ cup shredded cheddar cheese
- 2 tablespoons cream cheese, softened
- 2 tablespoons minced fresh parsley
- 3 teaspoons Dijon mustard, divided
- 2 green onions, thinly sliced
- 3 tablespoons dry bread crumbs
- 2 tablespoons ketchup
- ½ teaspoon salt
- ½ teaspoon dried rosemary, crushed
- ¼ teaspoon dried sage leaves
- 1 pound lean ground beef (90% lean)
- 4 hard rolls, split
  Lettuce leaves and tomato slices, optional

1. In a small bowl, combine cheddar cheese, cream cheese, parsley and 1 teaspoon mustard; set aside.

2. In another bowl, combine green onions, dry bread crumbs, ketchup, salt, rosemary, sage and remaining mustard. Crumble beef over mixture and mix well.

3. Shape into eight thin patties. Spoon cheese mixture onto the center of four patties; top with the remaining patties and press edges firmly to seal.

4. Grill the burgers, covered, over medium heat or broil 4 in. from heat for 5-7 minutes on each side or until a thermometer reads 160° and juices run clear. Serve on rolls with lettuce and tomato if desired.

Ham and Brie Melts

These golden melts take ham-and-cheese sandwiches to a whole new level. Apricot preserves and Brie are the key ingredients in this simple but special recipe.

—BONNIE BAHLER ELLINGTON, CT

START TO FINISH: 20 MIN.
MAKES: 4 SERVINGS

- 8 slices multigrain bread
- ¼ cup apricot preserves, divided
- ½ pound sliced deli ham
- 1 round (8 ounces) Brie cheese, rind removed, sliced
- 3 tablespoons butter, softened

1. Spread four bread slices with half of the apricot preserves. Layer with ham and cheese. Spread the remaining bread with the remaining preserves; place over the cheese, preserves side down. Spread outsides of sandwiches with butter.

2. In a large skillet, toast sandwiches over medium heat 2-3 minutes on each side or until golden brown and cheese is melted.

Potato Crust Quiche, page 60

62

70

66

Breakfast & Brunch

Make mornings the tastiest time of day with the top-rated treats in this chapter. From drizzled cinnamon rolls and golden pancakes to hearty casseroles, these sunny sensations are **impossible to resist!**

Basil Marmalade Scones

Orange marmalade and basil give scones a slightly sweet, fresh flavor—the perfect accompaniment for a cup of tea.

—HANNAH WALLACE WENATCHEE, WA

PREP: 20 MIN. • **BAKE:** 15 MIN.
MAKES: 8 SCONES

- 2 cups all-purpose flour
- 3 tablespoons sugar
- 2 teaspoons baking powder
- ½ teaspoon salt
- 3 tablespoons cold butter
- 3 tablespoons minced fresh basil or 1 tablespoon dried basil
- 2 eggs
- ⅓ cup fat-free milk
- ⅓ cup orange marmalade

1. In a small bowl, combine the flour, sugar, baking powder and salt. Cut in the butter until the mixture resembles coarse crumbs. Stir in the basil. Whisk the eggs and milk; stir into the crumb mixture just until moistened. Turn the dough onto a floured surface; knead 5 times.

2. Divide the dough in half. Transfer one portion to a baking sheet coated with cooking spray. Pat into a 7-in. circle. Spread the orange marmalade to within ½ in. of the edge. Pat the remaining dough into a 7-in. circle. Place over the orange marmalade; seal the edges. Cut into eight wedges, but do not separate.

3. Bake at 400° for 15-20 minutes or until golden brown. Serve warm.

Potato Crust Quiche

We've lived in four different states and have grown our own potatoes in every one of them. I like to shred our spuds and use them to form the crust for this satisfying quiche. It goes over well with both my family and company. To round out the menu, I serve a salad on the side.

—NANCY SMITH SCOTTSDALE, AZ

PREP: 20 MIN. • **BAKE:** 35 MIN.
MAKES: 8 SERVINGS

CRUST
- 4 cups coarsely shredded uncooked potatoes (about 4 large)
- ½ cup chopped onion
- 1 egg, lightly beaten
- 1 cup all-purpose flour
- ½ teaspoon salt

FILLING
- 1½ cups (6 ounces) shredded Colby cheese, divided
- ½ cup chopped onion
- 1½ cups cubed fully cooked ham
- 1½ cups fresh broccoli florets
- 3 eggs, lightly beaten
- 1 cup half-and-half cream
- ½ teaspoon salt
  Dash ground nutmeg
  Paprika

1. In a large bowl, combine the crust ingredients; press into a well-greased 10-in. deep-dish pie plate. Bake at 400° for 20 minutes.

2. Remove from the oven; reduce the heat to 350°. Add 1 cup Colby cheese, onion, ham and broccoli to the crust. Whisk eggs, cream, salt and nutmeg; pour over the broccoli. Sprinkle with the paprika.

3. Bake for 35-40 minutes or until a knife inserted near the center comes out clean. Sprinkle with the remaining Colby cheese. Let stand for 5 minutes before serving.

Apple Crisp Muffins

With a wonderful aroma and even better taste, these dessert-inspired goodies are guaranteed to start any morning off right. The oats and pecans in the topping add crunch, and the cream cheese filling in the center is a luscious bonus. For a variation, substitute pears for the apples.

—CONNIE BOLL CHILTON, WI

PREP: 30 MIN. • **BAKE:** 20 MIN.
MAKES: 1 DOZEN

- 2 cups all-purpose flour
- ⅓ cup packed brown sugar
- 2 teaspoons baking powder
- ½ teaspoon salt
- ½ teaspoon ground cinnamon
- 1 egg, beaten
- 1 cup 2% milk
- ½ cup canola oil
- 2 cups finely chopped peeled apples

FILLING
- 1 package (8 ounces) cream cheese, softened
- 2 tablespoons maple syrup
- 4 teaspoons grated orange peel
- ¼ teaspoon ground nutmeg

TOPPING
- ¼ cup all-purpose flour
- ¼ cup old-fashioned oats
- ¼ cup packed brown sugar
- ¼ teaspoon ground cinnamon
- 3 tablespoons cold butter
- ¼ cup chopped pecans

1. Preheat oven to 400°. In a large bowl, combine the flour, sugar, baking powder, salt and cinnamon. In another bowl, combine the egg, milk and oil. Stir into the dry ingredients just until moistened. Fold in the apples. Fill greased or paper-lined muffin cups three-fourths full.
2. In a small bowl, beat the filling ingredients until smooth. Drop by tablespoonfuls into centers of muffins.
3. For the topping, in a small bowl, combine the flour, oats, brown sugar and cinnamon. Cut in butter until crumbly. Stir in pecans. Sprinkle over filling. Bake 16-20 minutes or until a toothpick inserted in muffin comes out clean. Cool 5 minutes before removing from pan to wire rack.

Enchilada Hash Brown Casserole

Olé! Make breakfast a fiesta with a colorful, spicy Mexican bake.

—GERALDINE SAUCIER
ALBUQUERQUE, NM

PREP: 15 MIN. • **BAKE:** 40 MIN. + STANDING
MAKES: 6 SERVINGS

- 1½ cups enchilada sauce
- 1 garlic clove, minced
- 1 teaspoon onion powder
- ½ teaspoon pepper
- ¼ teaspoon ground coriander
- ⅛ teaspoon ground cumin
- 3 cups frozen cubed hash brown potatoes, thawed
- 1¼ cups (5 ounces) shredded Mexican cheese blend, divided
- 1 cup cubed fully cooked ham
- 1 cup canned black beans, rinsed and drained
- 1 can (4 ounces) chopped green chilies
- 6 eggs
- 2 tablespoons butter

1. In a large bowl, combine the first six ingredients; stir in the hash brown potatoes, 1 cup Mexican cheese blend, ham, black beans and green chilies. Transfer the mixture to a greased 8-in.-square baking dish; sprinkle with remaining cheese.
2. Cover; bake at 350° for 30 minutes. Uncover; bake 10-15 minutes longer or until heated through and the cheese is melted. Let stand for 10 minutes.
3. Meanwhile, in a large skillet, fry the eggs in butter as desired. Serve with the casserole.

Fines Herbes & Mushroom Omelets Deluxe

Fines herbes is a traditional French herb blend of chives, chervil, tarragon and parsley. The combination really complements the baby portobello mushrooms, Asiago cheese and other ingredients in these extra-special omelets.

—**LEE LOCKWOOD** MAYBROOK, NY

PREP: 30 MIN. • **COOK:** 15 MIN. • **MAKES:** 4 SERVINGS

- 1 **pound sliced baby portobello mushrooms**
- 2 **tablespoons butter**
- ¼ **cup white wine**
- 1 **teaspoon each minced fresh parsley, tarragon and chives**
- ½ **teaspoon dried chervil**
- ⅛ **teaspoon salt**
- ⅛ **teaspoon pepper**

ASIAGO SAUCE
- 2 **tablespoons butter**
- 2 **tablespoons all-purpose flour**
- 1 **cup 2% milk**
- ¼ **cup shredded Asiago cheese**
- ¼ **teaspoon salt**

OMELETS
- 4 **teaspoons butter, divided**
- 8 **eggs**
- ½ **cup water**
  Additional minced fresh herbs, optional

1. In a large skillet, saute the mushrooms in butter until tender. Add wine, stirring to loosen browned bits from pan. Stir in herbs, salt and pepper. Remove from heat; set aside.
2. In a small saucepan, melt the butter; stir in flour until smooth. Gradually add the milk. Bring to a boil; cook and stir for 1-2 minutes or until thickened. Stir in the Asiago cheese and salt. Keep warm.

3. In a small nonstick skillet, melt 1 teaspoon butter over medium-high heat. Whisk eggs and water until blended. Add ⅔ cup egg mixture to skillet (the mixture should set immediately at the edges).
4. As the eggs set, push the cooked edges toward the center, letting the uncooked portion flow underneath. When the eggs are set, spoon ½ cup mushroom mixture on one side; fold the other side over the filling. Slide the omelet onto a plate; top with ¼ cup sauce. Sprinkle with additional herbs if desired. Repeat.

Oven French Toast with Nut Topping

My family loves French toast, and I love the make-ahead ease of assembling it the night before. All I have to do in the morning is add the sweet, buttery pecan topping and bake.

—**DONNA JUSTIN** SPARTA, WI

PREP: 15 MIN. + CHILLING • **BAKE:** 50 MIN. • **MAKES:** 8-10 SERVINGS

- 1 **loaf (12 ounces) French bread, cut in 1-inch slices**
- 8 **eggs**
- 2 **cups milk**
- 2 **cups half-and-half cream**
- 2 **teaspoons vanilla extract**
- ½ **teaspoon ground nutmeg**
- ½ **teaspoon ground cinnamon**
- ½ **teaspoon ground mace**

TOPPING
- 1⅓ **cups packed brown sugar**
- ¾ **cup butter, softened**
- 3 **tablespoons dark corn syrup**
- 1⅓ **cups chopped pecans, walnuts or hickory nuts**

1. Fill a well-greased 13x9x2-in. baking dish with French bread slices to within ½ in. of top; set aside.
2. In blender, combine the eggs, milk, half-and-half cream, vanilla, nutmeg, cinnamon and mace; cover and process until blended. Pour over French bread slices. Cover and refrigerate overnight.
3. Remove from the refrigerator 30 minutes before baking. Meanwhile, combine topping ingredients. Spread over top.
4. Bake, uncovered, at 350° for 50-55 minutes or until puffed and golden. (Cover with foil if top browns too quickly.)

EGGS AND EGG SUBSTITUTE

People who are watching their cholesterol often prefer to use egg substitute instead of whole eggs. Egg substitute can be used to replace whole eggs in many recipes with good results, especially in omelets, frittatas and quiches, or for coating purposes (such as breading chicken). In most baked goods, however, the *Taste of Home* Test Kitchen has found that totally replacing the eggs may not produce the best results. That's because yolks, which are high in fat, give baked goods a more tender crumb and add flavor.

Light Sour Cream Coffee Cake

Pair your morning coffee or tea with a guilt-free treat—a piece of reduced-fat sour cream coffee cake. It's so moist, tender and scrumptious, no one ever guesses it's light!

—AMY MCBRIDE COLUMBIA, MO

PREP: 25 MIN. • **BAKE:** 30 MIN. + COOLING • **MAKES:** 20 SERVINGS

- 2 cups all-purpose flour
- 1½ cups sugar
- 1 teaspoon baking powder
- ½ teaspoon salt
- ½ teaspoon ground cinnamon
- 2 eggs, beaten
- 1 cup (8 ounces) reduced-fat sour cream
- ½ cup vanilla yogurt
- ½ cup butter, melted
- 1 teaspoon vanilla extract

STREUSEL

- ½ cup packed brown sugar
- ⅓ cup all-purpose flour
- 2 tablespoons butter, melted
- 1 teaspoon ground cinnamon

1. In a large bowl, combine the first five ingredients. In another bowl, combine the eggs, sour cream, yogurt, butter and vanilla. Stir into dry ingredients just until moistened.
2. In a small bowl, combine streusel ingredients. Spoon half of batter into a 13x9x2-in. baking pan coated with cooking spray; sprinkle with half of the streusel. Top with remaining batter and streusel. Bake at 350° for 30-35 minutes or until a toothpick inserted near the center comes out clean. Place the pan on a wire rack to cool.
PER SERVING *210 cal., 7 g fat (4 g sat. fat), 40 mg chol., 140 mg sodium, 33 g carb., trace fiber, 3 g pro.* **Diabetic Exchanges:** *2 starch, 1 fat.*

Spinach & Bacon Hash Brown Quiche

With a crust of crispy hash browns and a rich egg filling studded with spinach and bacon, this cheesy quiche is comfort food at its best. Serve a side of fresh fruit for a complete meal.

—SONYA LABBE WEST HOLLYWOOD, CA

PREP: 25 MIN. • **BAKE:** 25 MIN. + STANDING • **MAKES:** 6 SERVINGS

- 3 cups frozen shredded hash brown potatoes, thawed
- ¼ cup butter, melted
- 6 bacon strips, diced
- 1 small onion, chopped
- 3 eggs
- 1 cup half-and-half cream
- ¼ teaspoon salt
- ⅛ teaspoon pepper
- 2 cups chopped fresh spinach
- ⅔ cup shredded part-skim mozzarella cheese
- ⅓ cup shredded Swiss cheese

1. Preheat oven to 425°. Press the hash browns between paper towels to remove excess moisture; toss with butter. Press onto the bottom and up the sides of a 9-in. pie plate. Bake 20-25 minutes or until edges are browned. Reduce oven temperature to 350°.
2. Meanwhile, in a large skillet, cook bacon and onion over medium heat until bacon is crisp. Remove to paper towels to drain. In a large bowl, combine the eggs, cream, salt and pepper. Stir in spinach, cheeses and bacon mixture; pour into crust.
3. Bake 25-30 minutes or until a knife inserted near center comes out clean. Let stand 10 minutes before cutting.

Vegetarian Egg Strata

I used to make my strata with turkey or chicken sausage, but then I adapted it for a vegetarian friend. The meatless version was a hit! I've also served it for lunch with bowls of tomato bisque.

—DANNA ROGERS WESTPORT, CT

PREP: 25 MIN. + CHILLING • **BAKE:** 45 MIN. + STANDING
MAKES: 12 SERVINGS

- 1 medium zucchini, finely chopped
- 1 medium sweet red pepper, finely chopped
- 1 cup sliced baby portobello mushrooms
- 1 medium red onion, finely chopped
- 2 teaspoons olive oil
- 3 garlic cloves, minced
- 2 teaspoons minced fresh thyme or ½ teaspoon dried thyme
- ½ teaspoon salt
- ¼ teaspoon pepper
- 1 loaf (1 pound) day-old French bread, cubed
- 2 packages (5.3 ounces each) fresh goat cheese, crumbled
- 1¾ cups grated Parmesan cheese
- 6 eggs, lightly beaten
- 2 cups fat-free milk
- ¼ teaspoon ground nutmeg

1. In a large skillet, saute zucchini, red pepper, mushrooms and onion in oil until tender. Add the garlic, thyme, salt and pepper; saute 1 minute longer.

2. In a 13x9x2-in. baking dish coated with cooking spray, layer half the bread cubes, zucchini mixture, goat cheese and Parmesan cheese. Repeat layers.

3. In a small bowl, whisk eggs, milk and nutmeg. Pour over top. Cover and refrigerate overnight.

4. Remove from the refrigerator 30 minutes before baking. Preheat oven to 350°. Bake, uncovered, 45-50 minutes or until a knife inserted near the center comes out clean. Let stand 10 minutes before cutting.

Apple Cider Cinnamon Rolls

Feeling creative, I gave my usual cinnamon rolls a twist with chopped apples and cider. A warm-from-the-oven panful is such a treat on a cool fall or winter morning.

—**KIM FORNI** LACONIA, NH

PREP: 1 HOUR + RISING • **BAKE:** 30 MIN. • **MAKES:** 1 DOZEN

- 3¾ cups all-purpose flour
- ¼ cup sugar
- 1 package (¼ ounce) quick-rise yeast
- ½ teaspoon salt
- ¾ cup 2% milk
- ¼ cup apple cider or juice
- ¼ cup plus ⅓ cup butter, softened, divided
- 1 egg
- 2 cups finely chopped peeled tart apples
- 1¼ cups packed brown sugar
- ¾ cup finely chopped walnuts
- 3 teaspoons ground cinnamon

APPLE CIDER CREAM CHEESE FROSTING

- 2 cups apple cider or juice
- 1 cinnamon stick (3 inches)
- 1 package (8 ounces) cream cheese, softened
- ¼ cup butter, softened
- 1 cup confectioners' sugar

1. In a large bowl, combine 2¼ cups flour, sugar, yeast and salt. In a small saucepan, heat milk, apple cider and ¼ cup butter to 120°-130°. Add to dry ingredients; beat just until moistened. Add the egg; beat until smooth. Stir in enough remaining flour to form a soft dough (dough will be sticky).

2. Turn the dough onto a floured surface; knead until smooth and elastic, about 6-8 minutes. Cover and let rest for 10 minutes. Roll into a 15x10x1-in. rectangle. Spread the remaining butter to within ½ in. of the edges of rectangle. Combine the apples, brown sugar, walnuts and cinnamon; sprinkle over butter.

3. Roll up jelly-roll style, starting with a long side; pinch the seam to seal. Cut into 12 slices. Place slices, cut side down, in a greased 13x9x2-in. baking dish. Cover and let rise in a warm place for 30 minutes.

4. Bake at 325° for 30-35 minutes or until golden brown. For the frosting, place cider and cinnamon stick in a small saucepan. Bring to a boil; cook until the liquid is reduced to ¼ cup, about 20 minutes. Discard stick; cool cider.

5. In a large bowl, beat the cream cheese and butter until fluffy. Add the confectioners' sugar and reduced cider; beat until smooth. Spread over warm rolls.

Cranberry-White Chocolate Cinnamon Rolls

What's better than fresh-baked cinnamon rolls? Add some white chocolate and dried cranberries, and you'll have sheer bliss!

—**MEG MARRIOTT** TACOMA, WA

PREP: 45 MIN. + CHILLING • **BAKE:** 30 MIN. + COOLING
MAKES: 16 SERVINGS

- 2 packages (¼ ounce each) active dry yeast
- 2 cups warm water (110° to 115°)
- 1 cup butter, melted
- ½ cup sugar
- 2 teaspoons salt
- 5 to 6 cups all-purpose flour

FILLING
- 1 cup butter, softened
- ½ cup packed brown sugar
- 2 teaspoons ground cinnamon
- 1 package (10 to 12 ounces) white baking chips
- 1 cup dried cranberries
- ½ cup chopped pecans

GLAZE
- 2 cups confectioners' sugar
- 2 teaspoons vanilla extract
- 5 to 6 tablespoons heavy whipping cream

1. In a large bowl, dissolve the yeast in the warm water. Add butter, sugar, salt and 4 cups flour; beat until smooth. Stir in enough remaining flour to form a soft dough.

2. Turn onto a floured surface; knead until smooth and elastic, about 6-8 minutes. Place in a greased bowl, turning once to grease the top. Cover and refrigerate overnight.

3. Punch dough down. On a lightly floured surface, roll into a 24x12-in. rectangle. For the filling, combine butter, brown sugar and cinnamon; spread over the dough to within ½ in. of the edges. Sprinkle with white chips, dried cranberries and pecans. Roll up jelly-roll style, starting with a long side; pinch seam to seal.

4. Cut into 16 slices. Place cut side down in two greased 13x9x2-in. baking pans. Cover and let rise in a warm place until doubled, about 45 minutes.

5. Bake at 350° for 30-35 minutes or until golden brown. Meanwhile, in a small bowl, combine confectioners' sugar, vanilla and enough cream to achieve desired consistency; drizzle over warm rolls. Cool on wire racks.

Fresh Corn Cakes

This is one of the first recipes I made for my husband. The savory cakes are nice not only for breakfast, but also for dinner with ham.

—**GAYNELLE FRITSCH** WELCHES, OR

START TO FINISH: 30 MIN. • **MAKES:** 20 PANCAKES

- 1 cup all-purpose flour
- ½ cup yellow or blue cornmeal
- 1 tablespoon sugar
- 1 tablespoon baking powder
- ½ teaspoon salt
- 2 eggs, separated
- 1 cup milk
- ½ cup butter, melted
- 1 cup cooked whole kernel corn
- 4 green onions, thinly sliced
- ½ medium sweet red pepper, finely chopped
- 1 can (4 ounces) chopped green chilies
  Oil for frying
  Maple syrup, optional

1. In a medium bowl, combine the flour, cornmeal, sugar, baking powder and salt. In a small bowl, beat the egg yolks; blend in milk and butter. Add to dry ingredients; stir until just mixed. (Batter may be slightly lumpy.) Stir in the corn, green onions, red pepper and green chilies; set aside.

2. In a small bowl, beat egg whites until stiff peaks form. Gently fold into the batter.

3. For each pancake, pour about ¼ cup batter onto a lightly greased hot griddle; turn when bubbles form on the tops of the pancakes. Cook the second side until golden brown. Serve immediately with syrup if desired.

Eggs Benedict Casserole

If you're a fan of classic eggs Benedict, you'll love this variation. It tastes just as special as the traditional dish but is easier to serve a crowd. Plus, the casserole goes together the night before. In the morning, I just sprinkle on paprika, then whip up the rich sauce during baking.

—**SANDIE HEINDEL** LIBERTY, MO

PREP: 25 MIN. + CHILLING • **BAKE:** 45 MIN.
MAKES: 12 SERVINGS (1⅔ CUPS SAUCE)

- 12 ounces Canadian bacon, chopped
- 6 English muffins, split and cut into 1-inch pieces
- 8 eggs
- 2 cups 2% milk
- 1 teaspoon onion powder
- ¼ teaspoon paprika

HOLLANDAISE SAUCE

- 4 egg yolks
- ½ cup heavy whipping cream
- 2 tablespoons lemon juice
- 1 teaspoon Dijon mustard
- ½ cup butter, melted

1. Place half of the Canadian bacon in a greased 3-qt. or 13x9x2-in. baking dish; top with the English muffins and remaining Canadian bacon. In a large bowl, whisk the eggs, milk and onion powder; pour over the top. Refrigerate, covered, overnight.

2. Preheat oven to 375°. Remove the casserole from the refrigerator while the oven heats. Sprinkle the top with paprika. Bake, covered, for 35 minutes. Uncover; bake 10-15 minutes longer or until a knife inserted near the center comes out clean.

3. In the top of a double boiler or a metal bowl over simmering water, whisk the egg yolks, heavy whipping cream, lemon juice and mustard until blended; cook until the mixture is just thick enough to coat a metal spoon and the temperature reaches 160°, whisking constantly. Reduce heat to very low. Very slowly drizzle in the warm butter, whisking constantly. Serve immediately with casserole.

Crab Quiche with Hollandaise

A diner I went to served a quiche that was so amazing, I duplicated it at home.

—AMY KNIGHT LAKE LINDEN, MI

PREP: 25 MIN. • **BAKE:** 35 MIN.
MAKES: 6 SERVINGS (⅔ CUP SAUCE)

Pastry for single-crust pie
  (9 inches)
1 can (6 ounces) crabmeat, drained,
  flaked and cartilage removed
1 cup (4 ounces) shredded
  cheddar-Monterey Jack cheese
¾ cup frozen asparagus stir-fry
  vegetable blend, thawed
¼ cup finely chopped onion
3 eggs
1 cup evaporated milk
½ teaspoon salt
¼ teaspoon pepper
¼ teaspoon seafood seasoning
⅛ teaspoon hot pepper sauce

SAUCE
3 egg yolks
1 tablespoon water
1 tablespoon lemon juice
½ cup butter, melted
  Dash pepper

1. Roll out the pastry to fit a 9-in. pie plate. Transfer the pastry to the pie plate. Trim pastry to ½ in. beyond the edge of the plate; flute the edges. Line the unpricked pastry with a double thickness of heavy-duty foil. Bake at 450° for 8 minutes. Remove foil; bake 5 minutes longer. Place on a wire rack.

2. In a small bowl, combine crab, cheese, vegetable blend and onion; transfer to crust. In another bowl, whisk eggs, milk, salt, pepper, seasoning and pepper sauce. Pour over crab mixture.

3. Bake at 375° for 35-40 minutes or until a knife inserted near the center comes out clean. Cover edges with foil during the last 15 minutes to prevent overbrowning if necessary. Let stand for 5 minutes before cutting.

4. In a double boiler or metal bowl over simmering water, constantly whisk the egg yolks, water and lemon juice until the mixture reaches 160° or is thick enough to coat the back of a metal spoon. Reduce the heat to low. Slowly drizzle in warm melted butter, whisking constantly. Whisk in pepper. Serve immediately with quiche.

Hash Brown Supreme

I like to cut my hash browns into wedges and garnish them with sour cream.

—JENNIFER BISTLINE CONFLUENCE, PA

PREP: 20 MIN. • **COOK:** 15 MIN.
MAKES: 4 SERVINGS

- 1 **small onion, finely chopped**
- ½ **cup sliced fresh mushrooms**
- ½ **cup chopped green pepper**
- 1 **tablespoon canola oil**
- 3 **cups frozen shredded hash brown potatoes**
- 1 **medium tomato, finely chopped**
- ½ **cup shredded reduced-fat cheddar cheese**
- 2 **tablespoons sliced ripe olives**
- 1 **jalapeno pepper, seeded and sliced**
- ¼ **teaspoon seasoned salt**
- ⅛ **teaspoon pepper**
- 1 **tablespoon minced chives**

1. In a large nonstick skillet, saute the onion, mushrooms and green pepper in the oil until tender. Add the hash brown potatoes; cook over medium heat for 8-10 minutes or until the hash brown potatoes are browned, stirring occasionally.

2. Stir in the tomato, cheddar cheese, ripe olives, jalapeno pepper, seasoned salt and pepper. Cover and cook for 2 minutes or until the cheddar cheese is melted. Sprinkle with chives; cut into wedges.

NOTE *Wear disposable gloves when cutting hot peppers; the oils can burn skin. Avoid touching your face.*

PER SERVING *142 cal., 7 g fat (2 g sat. fat), 10 mg chol., 233 mg sodium, 15 g carb., 2 g fiber, 6 g pro.* **Diabetic Exchanges:** *1 medium-fat meat, 1 vegetable, ½ starch.*

Sweet Potato Waffles with Nut Topping

These homemade waffles have a sweet, crunchy topping featuring walnuts and pecans. What a yummy way to wake up!

—CHRISTINE KEATING NORWALK, CA

PREP: 20 MIN. • **COOK:** 5 MIN./BATCH
MAKES: 12 WAFFLES

- 2 **cups biscuit/baking mix**
- 2 **tablespoons brown sugar**
- ½ **teaspoon ground cinnamon**
- ¼ **teaspoon ground ginger**
- ¼ **teaspoon ground nutmeg**
- 1 **egg**
- 1⅓ **cups 2% milk**
- 1 **cup canned sweet potatoes, mashed**
- 2 **tablespoons canola oil**
- 1 **teaspoon vanilla extract**

TOPPING
- 1 **tablespoon butter**
- ½ **cup chopped pecans**
- ½ **cup chopped walnuts**
- 2 **tablespoons brown sugar**
- 1 **tablespoon water**
- ⅛ **teaspoon ground cinnamon**
  Dash salt
  Dash ground nutmeg
  Maple syrup

1. In a large bowl, combine the biscuit mix, brown sugar and spices. In another bowl, whisk egg, milk, sweet potatoes, oil and vanilla. Stir into dry ingredients just until combined.

2. Bake in a preheated waffle iron according to the manufacturer's directions until golden brown.

3. Meanwhile, in a small skillet, melt the butter over medium heat. Add the pecans and walnuts. Cook and stir for 2 minutes. Add the brown sugar, water, cinnamon, salt and nutmeg. Cook and stir until the sugar is dissolved. Serve waffles with topping and syrup.

Brunch Pizza

Pizza for brunch? Absolutely! I top a crescent dough crust with popular breakfast foods such as eggs, sausage, bacon and cheese. Picante sauce and sour cream are great on the side.

—MARTY SCHWARTZ SARASOTA, FL

PREP: 35 MIN. • **BAKE:** 15 MIN. • **MAKES:** 12 PIECES

- 1 tube (8 ounces) refrigerated crescent rolls
- ½ pound bacon strips, chopped
- ½ pound bulk pork sausage
- ½ pound sliced fresh mushrooms
- 1 small onion, finely chopped
- 1 small green pepper, finely chopped
- 1 tablespoon butter
- 8 eggs, lightly beaten
- 1 package (3 ounces) cream cheese, softened
- ⅓ cup sour cream
- 1 garlic clove, minced
- ¼ teaspoon Italian seasoning
- 2 plum tomatoes, chopped
- 1½ cups (6 ounces) shredded part-skim mozzarella cheese
  Picante sauce and additional sour cream, optional

1. Unroll the crescent dough into a greased 13x9x2-in. baking dish; seal seams and perforations. Bake at 375° for 6-8 minutes or until golden brown.
2. Meanwhile, in a small skillet, cook bacon and sausage over medium heat until bacon is crisp and sausage is no longer pink. Using a slotted spoon, remove meat to paper towels; drain, reserving 2 tablespoons drippings. In the drippings, saute the mushrooms, onion and green pepper. Remove and set aside.
3. Heat butter in a large skillet over medium heat. Add the eggs; cook and stir until almost set.
4. In a small bowl, beat cream cheese, sour cream, garlic and Italian seasoning; spread over the crust. Layer with the eggs, sausage and bacon, sauteed vegetables, tomatoes and mozzarella cheese.
5. Bake at 375° for 15-18 minutes or until the mozzarella cheese is melted. Serve with picante sauce and additional sour cream if desired.

Berry Smoothies

Smooth out the workday rush with a burst of berries. Tangy and sweet, this refreshing five-minute blend requires just a handful of ingredients—fruit, juice, yogurt and ice.

—ELISABETH LARSEN PLEASANT GROVE, UT

START TO FINISH: 5 MIN. • **MAKES:** 5 SERVINGS

- 2 cups cranberry juice
- 2 containers (6 ounces each) raspberry yogurt
- 1 cup frozen unsweetened raspberries
- 1 cup frozen unsweetened blueberries
- 8 ice cubes

1. In a blender, combine all ingredients; cover and process for 30-45 seconds or until blended. Pour into chilled glasses; serve immediately.

Lemon-Blueberry Muffins

Fresh-baked muffins are always a treat, and this lemon-blueberry recipe is one of my favorites. Bake a batch to enjoy with your morning coffee or to snack on during an afternoon break.

—KATHY HARDING RICHMOND, MO

PREP: 30 MIN. • **BAKE:** 25 MIN. • **MAKES:** 11 MUFFINS

- ½ cup butter, softened
- 1 cup sugar
- 2 eggs
- ½ cup 2% milk
- 2 tablespoons lemon juice
- 2 teaspoons grated lemon peel
- 2 cups all-purpose flour
- 2 teaspoons baking powder
  Dash salt
- 2 cups fresh or frozen blueberries

GLAZE

- 1½ cups confectioners' sugar
- 2 tablespoons lemon juice
- 1 teaspoon butter, melted
- ¼ teaspoon vanilla extract

1. Preheat oven to 400°. In a large bowl, cream the butter and sugar until light and fluffy. Add the eggs, one at a time, beating well after each addition. Beat in the milk, lemon juice and lemon peel. Combine the flour, baking powder and salt; add to the creamed mixture just until moistened. Fold in blueberries.

2. Fill paper-lined regular-size muffin cups three-fourths full. Bake 25-30 minutes or until a toothpick inserted in muffin comes out clean. Cool 5 minutes before removing from pan to a wire rack.

3. In a small bowl, combine confectioners' sugar, lemon juice, butter and vanilla; drizzle over warm muffins.

FREEZE OPTION *Freeze cooled muffins in resealable plastic freezer bags. To use, thaw at room temperature or, if desired, microwave each muffin on high for 20-30 seconds or until heated through.*

NOTE *If using frozen blueberries, use without thawing to avoid discoloring the batter.*

GRAND PRIZE

Sunny-Side-Up Herbed Tart

Feel free to be creative and give your tart a personal touch. Replace the pancetta with Canadian bacon or ham, or add different toppings such as thyme, chopped spinach or goat cheese to suit your taste.

—DIANA NEVES LAFAYETTE, CA

PREP: 30 MIN. • **BAKE:** 20 MIN.
MAKES: 4 SERVINGS

- 4 **slices pancetta or 4 bacon strips**
- 1 **cup sliced fresh mushrooms**
- 2 **tablespoons chopped shallot**
- 1 **tablespoon olive oil**
- 1 **tablespoon minced fresh tarragon or 1 teaspoon dried tarragon**
- 1 **teaspoon sherry, optional**
- ¼ **cup shredded Gruyere or Swiss cheese**
- ¼ **cup shredded cheddar cheese**
- 3 **tablespoons sour cream**
- ⅛ **teaspoon salt**
  Dash pepper

TART

- 1 **sheet frozen puff pastry, thawed**
- 5 **eggs**
- 1 **teaspoon water**
- 1 **tablespoon minced chives**
  Dash each salt and pepper

1. Preheat oven to 425°. In a large skillet, cook pancetta over medium heat until partially cooked but not crisp. Remove to paper towels to drain. In a small skillet, saute the mushrooms and shallot in oil until tender. Add tarragon and, if desired, sherry; cook 1 minute longer.

2. Remove from the heat; stir in the cheeses, sour cream, salt and pepper. Set aside.

3. On a lightly floured surface, unfold the puff pastry. Roll into a 10x9-in. rectangle. Transfer to a 15x10x1-in. parchment paper-lined baking sheet. Prick with a fork.

4. Spread the mushroom mixture over the puff pastry to within 1 in. of the edges. Top with sliced pancetta

(place pancetta near the edges of the mushroom mixture). Score the edges of the pastry with a fork. Beat 1 egg and the water; brush over the pastry edges. Bake 10-12 minutes or until pastry is golden brown.

5. Carefully crack the remaining eggs off-center into each corner. Bake 8-10 minutes longer or until eggs are set. Sprinkle with chives, salt and pepper. Cut into four pieces. Serve warm.

DOUGH DETAILS

Rich and delicate, frozen puff pastry dough has dozens of paper-thin layers of dough separated by butter. Thaw frozen puff pastry dough at room temperature for about 20 minutes before handling. Handle it as little as possible to avoid stretching and tearing.

Spring Frittata

Here's a great way to savor springtime flavor. The baked egg dish boasts roasted asparagus and leek, as well as mushrooms and Asiago cheese. It's an impressive main course that's surprisingly easy to make.

—DIANE HIGGINS TAMPA, FL

PREP: 35 MIN. • **BAKE:** 30 MIN.
MAKES: 6 SERVINGS

- ½ cup chopped leek (white portion only)
- ½ cup cut fresh asparagus (1-inch pieces)
- 2 teaspoons olive oil
- ¼ teaspoon salt
- ¼ teaspoon pepper
- 1 cup sliced fresh mushrooms
- 1 cup shredded Asiago cheese
- 4 eggs
- 1 cup egg substitute
- ¼ cup fat-free milk
- 1 tablespoon snipped fresh dill or 1 teaspoon dill weed
- 1 tablespoon minced fresh parsley or 1 teaspoon dried parsley flakes

1. In small bowl, combine leek and asparagus. Drizzle with oil and sprinkle with salt and pepper; toss to coat.
2. Transfer to a baking sheet coated with cooking spray. Bake at 400° for 20-25 minutes or until tender, stirring occasionally. Reduce heat to 350°.
3. Place mushrooms on the bottom of a 9-in. deep-dish pie plate coated with cooking spray. Top with roasted vegetables and cheese. In a large bowl, whisk the remaining ingredients; pour over the cheese.
4. Bake for 30-35 minutes or until a knife inserted near the center comes out clean. Let stand for 5 minutes. Cut into wedges.

Ultimate Fruity Granola

Enjoy this crunchy treat on its own, with milk or in a yogurt parfait.

—SARAH VASQUES
MILFORD, NH

PREP: 15 MIN. • **BAKE:** 20 MIN. + COOLING
MAKES: 9 CUPS

- 5 cups old-fashioned oats
- 1 cup sliced almonds
- ½ cup sunflower kernels
- ½ cup ground flaxseed
- ½ cup packed brown sugar
- ¼ cup maple syrup
- ¼ cup honey
- 2 tablespoons canola oil
- ½ teaspoon salt
- ½ teaspoon ground cinnamon
- 1 teaspoon vanilla extract
- ½ cup dried cranberries
- ½ cup dried banana chips
- ½ cup dried apricots, halved

1. In a large bowl, combine the oats, almonds, sunflower kernels and flax. In a small saucepan, combine brown sugar, maple syrup, honey, oil, salt and cinnamon. Cook and stir over medium heat for 2-3 minutes or until brown sugar is dissolved and the mixture is heated through. Remove from heat; stir in vanilla. Pour over oat mixture and toss to coat.
2. Transfer to a 15x10x1-in. baking pan coated with cooking spray. Bake at 350° for 20-25 minutes or until golden brown, stirring every 8 minutes. Cool completely on a wire rack. Stir in dried cranberries, banana chips and apricots. Store in an airtight container.

PER SERVING *253 cal., 10 g fat (2 g sat. fat), 0 chol., 86 mg sodium, 38 g carb., 5 g fiber, 6 g pro.* **Diabetic Exchanges:** *2½ starch, 1 fat.*

Steak au Poivre for 2, page 85

90

78

85

Beef Entrees

Meat lovers, get ready! Rave-review steaks, cheesy burritos, comforting roasts, grilled kabobs, loaded pizzas...these hearty helpings will **satisfy even the biggest appetites.**

Spiced Cran-Apple Brisket

Everyone who tastes this tender, flavorful brisket becomes a fan. Pop it into the slow cooker before you head out the door in the morning, then just whip up the savory gravy when you get home.
—**AYSHA SCHURMAN** AMMON, ID

PREP: 20 MIN. • **COOK:** 8 HOURS • **MAKES:** 9 SERVINGS

- 1 **fresh beef brisket (4 pounds)**
- ½ **cup apple butter**
- ¼ **cup ruby port wine**
- 2 **tablespoons cider vinegar**
- 1 **teaspoon coarsely ground pepper**
- ½ **teaspoon salt**
- 1 **medium tart apple, peeled and cubed**
- 1 **celery rib, chopped**
- 1 **small red onion, chopped**
- ⅓ **cup dried apples, diced**
- ⅓ **cup dried cranberries**
- 2 **garlic cloves, minced**
- 1 **tablespoon cornstarch**
- 3 **tablespoons cold water**

1. Cut the brisket in half; place in a 5-qt. slow cooker.
2. In a large bowl, combine the apple butter, wine, vinegar, pepper and salt. Stir in the tart apple, celery, onion, dried apples, cranberries and garlic. Pour over brisket. Cover and cook on low for 8-10 hours or until meat is tender.
3. Remove meat to a serving platter; keep warm. Skim fat from cooking juices; transfer to a small saucepan. Bring liquid to a boil.
4. Combine the cornstarch and cold water until smooth. Gradually stir into the pan. Bring to a boil; cook and stir for 2 minutes or until thickened. Serve with meat.
NOTES *This is a fresh beef brisket, not corned beef. The recipe was tested with commercially prepared apple butter.*
PER SERVING *334 cal., 9 g fat (3 g sat. fat), 86 mg chol., 208 mg sodium, 18 g carb., 1 g fiber, 42 g pro.* **Diabetic** *Exchanges: 6 lean meat, 1 starch.*

Roadside Diner Cheeseburger Quiche

Love the kind of hearty, all-American food that's served up at roadside diners? Here's a recipe for you! Every bite of quiche will remind you of a big, juicy bacon cheeseburger.

—BARB MILLER OAKDALE, MN

PREP: 20 MIN. • **BAKE:** 50 MIN. + STANDING
MAKES: 8 SERVINGS

- 1 sheet refrigerated pie pastry
- ¾ pound ground beef
- 2 plum tomatoes, seeded and chopped
- 1 medium onion, chopped
- ½ cup dill pickle relish
- ½ cup crumbled cooked bacon
- 5 eggs
- 1 cup heavy whipping cream
- ½ cup 2% milk
- 2 teaspoons prepared mustard
- 1 teaspoon hot pepper sauce
- ½ teaspoon salt
- ¼ teaspoon pepper
- 1½ cups (6 ounces) shredded cheddar cheese
- ½ cup shredded Parmesan cheese
  Optional garnishes: mayonnaise, additional pickle relish, crumbled cooked bacon, and chopped onion and tomato

1. Unroll pastry into a 9-in. deep-dish pie plate; flute edges and set aside. In a large skillet, cook beef over medium heat until no longer pink, breaking the meat into crumbles; drain. Stir in the tomatoes, onion, relish and bacon. Transfer to prepared pastry.

2. In a large bowl, whisk the eggs, heavy whipping cream, milk, mustard, pepper sauce, salt and pepper. Pour over the beef mixture. Sprinkle with the cheeses.

3. Bake at 375° for 50-60 minutes or until a knife inserted near the center comes out clean. Cover edges with foil during the last 15 minutes to prevent overbrowning if necessary. Let stand for 10 minutes before cutting. Garnish with optional ingredients if desired.

Southwest Beef & Rice Skillet

My family likes this skillet dinner because it's so tasty. I like the fact that I can get a satisfying meal on the table in less than half an hour. It's win-win!

—JANE PORRAS PLANO, TX

START TO FINISH: 25 MIN.
MAKES: 5 SERVINGS

- 1½ cups uncooked instant rice
- 1 pound ground beef
- 1 medium onion, chopped
- 1 garlic clove, minced
- 1 can (15 ounces) Ranch Style beans (pinto beans in seasoned tomato sauce)
- 1 cup beef broth
- 1 cup tomato sauce
- 2 teaspoons chili powder
- ½ teaspoon salt
- ½ teaspoon ground cumin
- ¼ teaspoon pepper
- ½ cup shredded pepper jack cheese

1. Cook the rice according to the package directions.

2. Meanwhile, in a large skillet, cook the beef, onion and garlic over medium heat until meat is no longer pink, breaking meat into crumbles; drain. Stir in rice, beans, broth, tomato sauce, chili powder, salt, cumin and pepper; heat through. Sprinkle with cheese. Cover and cook for 1-2 minutes or until cheese is melted.

Chili Tortilla Bake

Here's a casserole that will get them running to the dinner table. Thanks to the Southwestern flavors and bubbly cheese topping, you won't have to worry about leftovers!

—**CELINE WELDY** CAVE CREEK, AZ

PREP: 20 MIN. • **BAKE:** 25 MIN. • **MAKES:** 6 SERVINGS

- 1 pound extra-lean ground beef (95% lean)
- 2 cans (8 ounces each) no-salt-added tomato sauce
- 1 can (15 ounces) black beans, rinsed and drained
- 1 cup frozen corn
- 1 can (4 ounces) chopped green chilies
- 2 tablespoons dried minced onion
- 2 tablespoons chili powder
- 1 teaspoon ground cumin
- ½ teaspoon garlic powder
- ½ teaspoon dried oregano
- 6 whole wheat tortillas (8 inches)
- 1 cup (4 ounces) shredded reduced-fat cheddar cheese

1. In a large skillet, cook the beef over medium heat until no longer pink, breaking meat into crumbles. Stir in tomato sauce, black beans, corn, green chilies, onion, chili powder, cumin, garlic powder and oregano; heat through.

2. In an 11x7-in. baking dish coated with cooking spray, layer half of the whole wheat tortillas, beef mixture and cheddar cheese. Repeat the layers. Bake, uncovered, at 350° for 25-30 minutes or until bubbly.

Hearty Shepherd's Pie

Fresh rosemary helps dress up the convenience products in this comforting but easy pie. Try slices of corn bread on the side.

—**MELISSA BIRDSONG** WALESKA, GA

PREP: 35 MIN. • **BAKE:** 20 MIN. • **MAKES:** 6 SERVINGS

- 1 pound lean ground beef (90% lean)
- 1 medium onion, chopped
- 1 can (10¾ ounces) condensed cream of celery soup, undiluted
- 1 can (8½ ounces) peas and carrots, drained
- 1 jar (4½ ounces) sliced mushrooms, drained
- ¼ cup water
- 1 tablespoon minced fresh rosemary or 1 teaspoon dried rosemary, crushed
- 1 teaspoon garlic powder, divided
- ½ teaspoon salt
- ¼ teaspoon pepper
- 2 cups prepared instant mashed potatoes
- 1 package (3 ounces) cream cheese, softened and cubed
- ¼ cup sour cream
- ¼ cup grated Parmesan cheese

1. In a large skillet, cook the beef and onion over medium heat until the meat is no longer pink, breaking the meat into crumbles; drain. Stir in the soup, peas and carrots, mushrooms, water, rosemary, ½ teaspoon garlic powder, salt and pepper; heat through. Transfer to a greased 9-in. deep-dish pie plate.

2. In a large bowl, beat the mashed potatoes, cream cheese, sour cream and remaining garlic powder until blended. Spread over top. Sprinkle with Parmesan cheese.

3. Bake, uncovered, at 350° for 20-25 minutes or until heated through and potatoes are lightly browned.

Slow-Cooked Caribbean Pot Roast goes over well whenever I serve it, but I think it's especially good in fall and winter. The spicy meat and veggies warm you right up!

—JENNIFER TIDWELL FAIR OAKS, CA

GRAND PRIZE

Slow-Cooked Caribbean Pot Roast

PREP: 30 MIN. • COOK: 6 HOURS • MAKES: 10 SERVINGS

- 2 medium sweet potatoes, cubed
- 2 large carrots, sliced
- ¼ cup chopped celery
- 1 boneless beef chuck roast (2½ pounds)
- 1 tablespoon canola oil
- 1 large onion, chopped
- 2 garlic cloves, minced
- 1 tablespoon all-purpose flour
- 1 tablespoon sugar
- 1 tablespoon brown sugar
- 1 teaspoon ground cumin
- ¾ teaspoon salt
- ¾ teaspoon ground coriander
- ¾ teaspoon chili powder
- ½ teaspoon dried oregano
- ⅛ teaspoon ground cinnamon
- ¾ teaspoon grated orange peel
- ¾ teaspoon baking cocoa
- 1 can (15 ounces) tomato sauce

1. Place sweet potatoes, carrots and celery in a 5-qt. slow cooker. In a large skillet, brown the meat in oil on all sides. Transfer meat to slow cooker.

2. In the same skillet, saute the onion in the drippings until tender. Add the garlic; cook 1 minute longer. Combine flour, sugar, brown sugar, seasonings, orange peel and baking cocoa. Stir in the tomato sauce; add to the skillet and heat through. Pour over beef.

3. Cover and cook on low for 6-8 hours or until beef and vegetables are tender.

PER SERVING *278 cal., 12 g fat (4 g sat. fat), 74 mg chol., 453 mg sodium, 16 g carb., 3 g fiber, 25 g pro.* **Diabetic Exchanges:** *3 lean meat, 1 starch, 1 vegetable, ½ fat.*

Peppered Filets with Cherry Port Sauce for 2

Need dinner for just the two of you? Make it extra-special but easy with this standout steak, ready to enjoy in just 30 minutes. I like to serve the peppery beef with a light side dish of vegetables to round out the meal. If you prefer, substitute dried cranberries for the cherries or use feta instead of blue cheese.

—**BARBARA LENTO** HOUSTON, PA

START TO FINISH: 30 MIN. • **MAKES:** 2 SERVINGS

- 2 beef tenderloin steaks (8 ounces each)
- 2 teaspoons coarsely ground pepper
- 1 cup dry red wine
- ½ cup chopped red onion
- ⅓ cup golden raisins
- ⅓ cup dried cherries
- 2 tablespoons sugar
- 1½ teaspoons cornstarch
- ¼ teaspoon ground mustard
  Dash salt
- 2 teaspoons cold water
- ¼ cup crumbled blue cheese

1. Sprinkle the steaks with pepper. Grill, covered, over medium heat or broil 4 in. from the heat for 6-8 minutes on each side or until meat reaches desired doneness (for medium-rare, a thermometer should read 145°; medium, 160°; well-done, 170°).

2. Meanwhile, in a small saucepan, combine wine, onion, raisins, cherries and sugar. Bring to a boil; cook until liquid is reduced by half.

3. Combine the cornstarch, mustard, salt and cold water until smooth. Gradually stir into the pan. Bring to a boil; cook and stir for 2 minutes or until thickened. Serve sauce with steaks; sprinkle with cheese.

Cream Cheese and Swiss Lasagna

PREP: 40 MIN. + SIMMERING • **BAKE:** 55 MIN. + STANDING
MAKES: 12 SERVINGS

- 1½ pounds lean ground beef (90% lean)
- 1 pound bulk Italian sausage
- 1 medium onion, finely chopped
- 3 garlic cloves, minced
- 2 cans (15 ounces each) tomato sauce
- 1 can (14½ ounces) Italian diced tomatoes, undrained
- 1 can (6 ounces) tomato paste
- 2 teaspoons dried oregano
- 1 teaspoon dried basil
- 1 teaspoon Italian seasoning
- ½ teaspoon sugar
- ½ teaspoon salt
- ¼ teaspoon pepper
- 9 no-cook lasagna noodles
- 12 ounces cream cheese, softened
- 2 cups shredded part-skim mozzarella cheese, divided
- 2 cups shredded Parmesan cheese
- 2 cups shredded Swiss cheese

1. In a Dutch oven over medium heat, cook beef, sausage and onion until meat is no longer pink, breaking beef into crumbles. Add garlic; cook 1 minute longer. Drain. Stir in the tomato sauce, tomatoes, tomato paste, oregano, basil, Italian seasoning, sugar, salt and pepper. Bring to a boil. Reduce heat; simmer, uncovered, for 30 minutes.

2. Spread 1 cup sauce in a greased 13x9x2-in. baking dish. Top with three lasagna noodles. Drop a third of the cream cheese by teaspoonfuls over the top. Sprinkle with ½ cup mozzarella and ⅔ cup each of Parmesan cheese and Swiss cheese; spoon a third of the remaining sauce over the top. Repeat with layers of noodles, cheeses and sauce twice (dish will be full). Place dish on a baking sheet.

3. Cover and bake at 350° for 45 minutes. Sprinkle with the remaining mozzarella cheese. Bake, uncovered, 10-15 minutes longer or until bubbly and the cheese is melted. Let stand for 15 minutes before cutting.

> ❝I fix the sauce for Cream Cheese and Swiss Lasagna the day before so the flavors can blend. The recipe makes 12 servings, but be ready to dish out second helpings!❞

—**BETTY PEARSON** EDGEWATER, MD

Italian Shepherd's Pies

Served in individual baking cups, my little shepherd's pies have biscuit-like tops and a meaty marinara filling. If you like, prepare the recipe using a 1½-quart casserole dish instead.
—**SONYA LABBE** WEST HOLLYWOOD, CA

PREP: 20 MIN. • **BAKE:** 15 MIN. • **MAKES:** 4 SERVINGS

- 1 **pound ground beef**
- 1 **medium onion, finely chopped**
- 2 **cups marinara sauce**
- ⅛ **teaspoon salt**
- ⅛ **teaspoon pepper**

TOPPING
- 1 **cup all-purpose flour**
- ¼ **cup grated Parmesan cheese**
- 1½ **teaspoons baking powder**
- ½ **teaspoon salt**
- ¼ **teaspoon Italian seasoning**
- ½ **cup 2% milk**
- ¼ **cup butter, melted**

1. In a large skillet, cook beef and onion over medium heat until meat is no longer pink, breaking meat into crumbles; drain. Add the marinara sauce, salt and pepper; cook and stir for 8-10 minutes or until thickened. Spoon into four 8-oz. ramekins or custard cups; set aside.

2. In a small bowl, combine flour, cheese, baking powder, salt and Italian seasoning. Stir in milk and butter just until moistened. Spoon the dough over the meat mixture; place ramekins on a baking sheet.

3. Bake at 450° for 12-15 minutes or until golden brown.

FREEZE OPTION *Cover and freeze unbaked pies. To use, remove from freezer 30 minutes before baking (do not thaw). Preheat oven to 400°. Place pies on a baking sheet; cover edges loosely with foil. Bake as directed, increasing time as necessary to heat through and for a thermometer inserted in center to read 165°.*

Beef & Bacon Stroganoff

When I'm in the mood for comfort food, I get the stove going and start cooking a Stroganoff using bacon and garlic, plus some horseradish for a little kick. It really hits the spot!
—**MELISSA MILLWOOD** LYMAN, SC

PREP: 20 MIN. • **COOK:** 20 MIN. • **MAKES:** 6 SERVINGS

- 1 **pound lean ground beef (90% lean)**
- 5 **thick-sliced bacon strips, chopped**
- 1 **cup sliced fresh mushrooms**
- 1 **medium onion, chopped**
- 2 **garlic cloves, minced**
- 2 **tablespoons all-purpose flour**
- 1 **can (14½ ounces) beef broth**
- 1 **can (10¾ ounces) condensed cream of mushroom with roasted garlic soup, undiluted**
- 2 **tablespoons Worcestershire sauce**
- 1 **teaspoon pepper**
- ¼ **teaspoon salt**
- ¼ **teaspoon paprika**
- 6 **cups uncooked egg noodles**
- 1 **cup (8 ounces) sour cream**
- 2 **teaspoons prepared horseradish**
- ½ **cup shredded white cheddar cheese**
  Minced fresh parsley, optional

1. In a large skillet over medium heat, cook the beef, bacon, mushrooms and onion until beef is no longer pink, breaking beef into crumbles. Add the garlic; cook 1 minute longer. Drain. Stir in the flour until blended. Add beef broth, cream soup, Worcestershire sauce, pepper, salt and paprika. Bring to a boil. Reduce heat; simmer, uncovered, for 10-15 minutes, stirring occasionally.

2. Meanwhile, cook the noodles according to the package directions; drain.

3. Stir the sour cream and horseradish into beef mixture; heat through (do not boil). Serve with noodles. Sprinkle with cheese. Garnish with parsley if desired.

Bacon Cheeseburger Pizza

PREP: 30 MIN. + STANDING • **BAKE:** 15 MIN. • **MAKES:** 6 SLICES

- 3 **cups bread flour**
- 2 **tablespoons sugar**
- 1 **package (¼ ounce) quick-rise yeast**
- 1½ **teaspoons salt**
- ¾ **cup warm water (120° to 130°)**
- 2 **tablespoons olive oil**
- 1 **pound lean ground beef (90% lean)**
- 3 **garlic cloves, minced**
- ⅛ **teaspoon pepper**
- 1 **cup grated Parmesan cheese**
- 1 **jar (10 ounces) sun-dried tomato pesto**
- 1 **large red onion, chopped**
- ¼ **cup bacon bits**
- 1 **cup (4 ounces) shredded part-skim mozzarella cheese**
- 1 **cup (4 ounces) sharp shredded cheddar cheese**

1. In a large bowl, combine 2 cups flour, sugar, yeast and salt. Add water and oil; mix until smooth. Stir in enough remaining flour to form a firm dough.

2. Turn the dough onto a lightly floured surface; knead until smooth and elastic, about 6-8 minutes. Cover and let rest for 10 minutes.

3. Meanwhile, in a large skillet over medium heat, cook the beef, garlic and pepper until meat is no longer pink, breaking meat into crumbles; drain.

4. On a floured surface, roll prepared pizza crust dough into a 15-in. circle. Transfer to a greased 14-in. pizza pan. Build up the edges of the dough slightly. Prick the dough thoroughly with a fork. Bake at 450° for 5-8 minutes or until lightly browned.

5. Sprinkle the pizza crust with Parmesan cheese. Top with the pesto, meat mixture, red onion, bacon bits, mozzarella cheese and cheddar cheese. Bake for 15-20 minutes or until the cheese is melted.

❝ You can have this terrific from-scratch pizza ready in less time than it takes for the delivery guy to show up. Turn it into a fun family event and let your children help. ❞

—**VIVIAN TAYLOR** MIDDLEBURG, FL

Tacoritos

These mild Southwestern roll-ups loaded with sausage, ground beef and refried beans combine the popular flavor of tacos with the heartiness of burritos. Your family will love 'em!
—**MONICA FLATFORD** KNOXVILLE, TN

PREP: 40 MIN. • **BAKE:** 20 MIN. • **MAKES:** 8 SERVINGS

- ¼ **cup butter, cubed**
- ¼ **cup all-purpose flour**
- 4 **cups water**
- 3 **tablespoons chili powder**
- 1 **teaspoon garlic salt**
- 1 **pound ground beef**
- 1 **pound bulk pork sausage**
- ¼ **cup chopped onion**
- 1 **cup refried beans**
- 8 **flour tortillas (8 inches), warmed**
- 3 **cups (12 ounces) shredded Monterey Jack cheese**
  Optional toppings: shredded lettuce, chopped tomatoes, sliced ripe olives and sour cream

1. In a large saucepan, melt the butter. Stir in the flour until smooth; gradually add the water. Bring to a boil; cook and stir for 1 minute or until thickened. Stir in chili powder and garlic salt. Bring to a boil. Reduce heat; simmer, uncovered, for 10 minutes.

2. In a large skillet over medium heat, cook beef, sausage and onion until meat is no longer pink, breaking beef into crumbles; drain. Stir in refried beans; heat through.

3. Spread ¼ cup sauce in a greased 13x9x2-in. baking dish. Spread 1 tablespoon sauce over each tortilla; place ⅔ cup meat mixture down the center of each. Top each with ¼ cup cheese. Roll up and place seam side down in the prepared dish. Pour the remaining sauce over the top; sprinkle with remaining cheese.

4. Bake, uncovered, at 350° for 18-22 minutes or until bubbly and the cheese is melted. Serve with optional toppings if desired.

Steak au Poivre for 2

With the punch of peppercorns and a smooth sauce, this is everything you could want in a steak dinner. A little chocolate adds an unexpected hint of sweetness.

—**CRYSTAL BRUNS** ILIFF, CO

START TO FINISH: 30 MIN.
MAKES: 2 SERVINGS

- 2 **beef tenderloin steaks (1 inch thick and 5 ounces each)**
- 2 **tablespoons olive oil, divided**
- 1 **tablespoon whole white or black peppercorns, crushed**
- ¼ **teaspoon salt**
- 1 **tablespoon finely chopped shallot**
- ¼ **cup port wine**
- 1 **tablespoon balsamic vinegar**
- ¼ **cup condensed beef consomme, undiluted**
- 1 **teaspoon minced fresh rosemary or ¼ teaspoon dried rosemary, crushed**
- ½ **ounce bittersweet chocolate, chopped**

1. Rub the steaks with 1 tablespoon oil; sprinkle with the peppercorns and salt. In a skillet, heat 2 teaspoons oil over medium heat. Add the steaks; cook 5-7 minutes on each side or until the meat reaches the desired doneness (for medium-rare, a thermometer should read 145°; medium, 160°; well-done, 170°). Remove the steaks and keep warm.

2. In the same pan, heat the remaining oil over medium-high heat. Add the shallot; cook and stir about 1 minute or until tender. Add the port wine and balsamic vinegar, stirring to loosen browned bits from the pan. Bring to a boil; cook and stir 2-3 minutes or until slightly thickened.

3. Stir in the beef consomme and rosemary; bring to a boil. Add the bittersweet chocolate; cook and stir until melted and sauce is slightly thickened. Serve with steaks.

Grilled Beef Kabobs

When I needed to fix a quick dinner using on-hand ingredients, I improvised and put together some meat-and-veggie skewers. Now my husband requests them regularly.

—**DOLORES LUEKEN** FERDINAND, IN

PREP: 15 MIN. + MARINATING
GRILL: 10 MIN. • **MAKES:** 4 SERVINGS

- 1 **bottle (8 ounces) French or Russian salad dressing**
- 2 **tablespoons lemon juice**
- 2 **tablespoons Worcestershire sauce**
- ⅛ **teaspoon garlic powder**
- ⅛ **teaspoon pepper**
- 1 **pound beef top sirloin steak, cut into 1½-inch cubes**
- 8 **to 10 bacon strips, cut in half**
- 1 **sweet red pepper, cut into chunks**
- 1 **green pepper, cut into chunks**
- 2 **small zucchini squash, cut into chunks**
- 8 **medium fresh mushrooms**
- 1 **large onion, quartered, optional**

1. In a small bowl, whisk the first five ingredients. Place half of the marinade in a large resealable plastic bag. Add the beef; seal the bag and turn to coat. Refrigerate for 8 hours or overnight. Cover and refrigerate the remaining marinade.

2. Drain beef, discarding marinade in bag. Wrap bacon around beef cubes. On metal or soaked wooden skewers, alternately thread beef and vegetables.

3. Grill, covered, over medium heat 10-15 minutes or until meat reaches desired doneness and vegetables are tender, basting frequently with the reserved marinade.

Mexican Stuffed Peppers

I especially like to prepare this main dish in summer because I can use my homegrown peppers. Sour cream is a great garnish, and tortilla chips with salsa are perfect on the side.

—**KIM COLEMAN** COLUMBIA, SC

PREP: 25 MIN. • **BAKE:** 30 MIN. • **MAKES:** 8 SERVINGS

- 8 medium green peppers
- 1 pound lean ground beef (90% lean)
- 1 can (14½ ounces) diced tomatoes and green chilies, undrained
- 1½ cups water
- 1 envelope (5.4 ounces) Mexican-style rice and pasta mix
- 2 cups (8 ounces) shredded Mexican cheese blend

1. Preheat oven to 375°. Cut off the tops of peppers and remove the seeds. In a Dutch oven, cook peppers in boiling water 3-5 minutes. Drain and rinse in cold water; set aside.
2. In a large skillet, cook beef over medium heat until no longer pink, breaking into crumbles; drain. Add tomatoes, water and pasta mix. Bring to a boil. Reduce heat; cover and simmer 6-8 minutes or until liquid is absorbed.
3. Place ⅓ cup rice mixture in each pepper; sprinkle each with 2 tablespoons cheese. Top with remaining rice mixture. Place in a greased 13x9x2-in. baking dish. Cover and bake 25 minutes. Sprinkle with the remaining cheese; bake 5-10 minutes longer or until the cheese is melted and the peppers are tender.

Rootin'-Tootin' Cincinnati Chili

What's the secret ingredient in my Cincinnati chili? Root beer! I think it adds just the right touch of sweetness.

—**HOLLY GOMEZ** SEABROOK, NH

PREP: 25 MIN. • **COOK:** 30 MIN. • **MAKES:** 4 SERVINGS

- 1 pound ground beef
- 1 small onion, chopped
- 1 small green pepper, chopped
- 1 garlic clove, minced
- 1 can (14½ ounces) fire-roasted diced tomatoes, undrained
- 1 cup root beer
- 2 tablespoons chili powder
- 2 tablespoons tomato paste
- 2 tablespoons minced chipotle peppers in adobo sauce
- 1 tablespoon ground cumin
- 1 beef bouillon cube
  Hot cooked spaghetti
  Optional toppings: crushed tortilla chips, chopped green onions, and shredded cheddar and Parmesan cheeses

1. In a large saucepan, cook the beef, onion and green pepper over medium heat until the meat is no longer pink, breaking the meat into crumbles. Add garlic; cook 1 minute longer. Drain. Add the tomatoes, root beer, chili powder, tomato paste, chipotle peppers, cumin and beef bouillon. Bring to a boil.
2. Reduce heat; cover and simmer for 20-30 minutes to allow flavors to blend. Serve with spaghetti. Garnish with chips, green onions and cheeses if desired.

Tex-Mex Pizza

Loaded with toppings that include black beans and corn, this knife-and-fork pizza is packed with popular Tex-Mex flavors. Get ready to make mouths water!

—CHARLENE CHAMBERS
ORMOND BEACH, FL

PREP: 25 MIN. • **BAKE:** 15 MIN.
MAKES: 8 SLICES

- ½ pound lean ground beef (90% lean)
- ⅔ cup chopped red onion
- 2 garlic cloves, minced
- 1 cup salsa
- 1 can (4 ounces) chopped green chilies, drained
- 1 prebaked 12-inch pizza crust
- 1½ cups (6 ounces) shredded cheddar cheese
- 1 cup canned black beans, rinsed and drained
- ½ cup frozen corn, thawed
- 1 can (2¼ ounces) sliced ripe olives, drained
- 1 medium ripe avocado, peeled and cubed
- 2 teaspoons lemon juice
- ½ cup sour cream

1. In a large skillet, cook the beef, red onion and garlic over medium heat until meat is no longer pink, breaking meat into crumbles; drain. Stir in the salsa and green chilies.

2. Place the crust on an ungreased pizza pan. Top with the beef mixture, cheese, beans, corn and olives.

3. Bake at 425° for 15-20 minutes or until edges are lightly browned and cheese is melted. Toss avocado with lemon juice. Serve pizza with avocado and sour cream.

TACO TWIST

When I have leftovers from taco night, I use them for a fuss-free pizza. After spreading the crust with a mixture of refried beans and sour cream, I sprinkle on the taco meat and bake until heated through. Leftover shredded cheese, ripe olives, tomatoes and lettuce are tasty toppings.

—MICHELLE KOORN OAK HARBOR, WA

Steak Lo Mein

Years ago, I picked up a wok at a rummage sale. That handy appliance has proven to be a great purchase—especially when it comes to fixing family-pleasing recipes like this one.

—JO GROTH PLAINFIELD, IA

START TO FINISH: 30 MIN.
MAKES: 6 SERVINGS

- 1 **pound beef top round steak, trimmed**
- 2 **tablespoons cornstarch**
- 1 **teaspoon beef bouillon granules**
- ¾ **cup water**
- ¼ **cup soy sauce**
- 2 **tablespoons vegetable oil**
- 1 **garlic clove, minced**
- 2 **cups shredded cabbage**
- 1 **cup diagonally sliced carrots, partially cooked**
- 1 **medium onion, sliced into rings**
- ½ **cup sliced fresh mushrooms**
- ½ **cup diagonally sliced celery**
- ⅓ **cup sliced green onions**
- 15 **fresh snow pea pods, trimmed**
- 1 **can (8 ounces) sliced water chestnuts, drained**
- 4 **ounces thin spaghetti, cooked and drained**

1. Freeze the steak just until firm; slice diagonally across the grain into ¼-in. strips.

2. Combine the cornstarch, beef bouillon, water and soy sauce until smooth; set aside.

3. In a wok or large skillet, heat oil on medium-high. Add the meat and garlic; stir-fry until meat is no longer pink, about 5 minutes. Remove meat to a platter.

4. Add the cabbage, carrots, onion, mushrooms, celery and green onions; stir-fry for about 3 minutes. Add the pea pods and water chestnuts; stir-fry 2 minutes. Add meat.

5. Stir bouillon mixture and pour into skillet; cook and stir until thickened. Gently toss in the spaghetti and heat through for 1 minute.

PER SERVING *329 cal., 8 g fat (0 sat. fat), 52 mg chol., 834 mg sodium, 34 g carb., 0 fiber, 29 g pro.* **Diabetic Exchanges:** *2 lean meat, 1¾ starch, 1 vegetable.*

GRAND PRIZE WINNER ★★★★

GRAND PRIZE

Slow Cooker Tamale Pie

Why go out for Mexican? Stay in and sit down to a delicious south-of-the-border dinner straight from your slow cooker. Canned beans and a corn bread/muffin mix speed up the preparation.

—JILL POKRIVKA YORK, PA

PREP: 25 MIN. • **COOK:** 7 HOURS
MAKES: 8 SERVINGS

- 1 **pound ground beef**
- 1 **teaspoon ground cumin**
- ½ **teaspoon salt**
- ½ **teaspoon chili powder**
- ¼ **teaspoon pepper**
- 1 **can (15 ounces) black beans, rinsed and drained**
- 1 **can (14½ ounces) diced tomatoes with mild green chilies, undrained**
- 1 **can (11 ounces) whole kernel corn, drained**
- 1 **can (10 ounces) enchilada sauce**
- 2 **green onions, chopped**
- ¼ **cup minced fresh cilantro**
- 1 **package (8½ ounces) corn bread/muffin mix**
- 2 **eggs**
- 1 **cup (4 ounces) shredded Mexican cheese blend**
  Sour cream and additional minced fresh cilantro, optional

1. In a large skillet, cook beef over medium heat until no longer pink, breaking into crumbles; drain. Stir in cumin, salt, chili powder and pepper.

2. Transfer to a 4-qt. slow cooker; stir in black beans, tomatoes, corn, enchilada sauce, onions and cilantro. Cover and cook on low for 6-8 hours or until heated through.

3. In a small bowl, combine muffin mix and eggs; spoon over the meat mixture. Cover and cook 1 hour longer or until a toothpick inserted near the center comes out clean.

4. Sprinkle with the cheese; cover and let stand for 5 minutes. Serve with sour cream and additional cilantro if desired.

Beef with Red Sauce

I use a homemade rub and gingersnap crumbs to spice up my saucy roast. If you don't have the cookies on hand—or they don't suit your taste—simply substitute crushed plain graham crackers.

—LAURIE TIETZE LONGVIEW, TX

PREP: 25 MIN. • **COOK:** 8 HOURS
MAKES: 8 SERVINGS

- 2 tablespoons canola oil
- 2 tablespoons baking cocoa
- 1 tablespoon chili powder
- 2 teaspoons dried oregano
- 1 teaspoon salt
- 1 teaspoon pepper
- 1 teaspoon ground cumin
- ½ teaspoon ground cloves
- ½ teaspoon ground cinnamon
- 1 beef rump roast or bottom round roast (3 pounds), cut into 1½-in. cubes
- 1 large onion, chopped
- 1 can (28 ounces) whole tomatoes, undrained
- 3 tablespoons cider vinegar
- 1½ cups crushed gingersnap cookies (about 30 cookies)
- 9 garlic cloves, peeled
- 1 tablespoon sugar
  Hot cooked noodles, rice or mashed potatoes

1. In a small bowl, combine the first nine ingredients; set aside.

2. Place the beef cubes and onion in a 4-qt. slow cooker; rub the beef with the spice mixture. Pour the tomatoes over the top; sprinkle with the cider vinegar, crushed gingersnap cookies and garlic.

3. Cover; cook on low for 8-10 hours or until the meat is tender. Stir in the sugar. Serve with noodles.

Beef Stroganoff

Say goodbye to standing and stirring at the stove. This creamy Stroganoff starts off in a skillet, then cooks all day while you're away. You'll love it!

—SARAH VASQUES MILFORD, NH

PREP: 20 MIN. • **COOK:** 6 HOURS
MAKES: 7 SERVINGS

- 2 pounds beef top sirloin steak, cut into thin strips
- 3 tablespoons olive oil
- 1 cup water
- 1 envelope (1½ ounces) beef Stroganoff seasoning for the slow cooker
- 1 pound sliced baby portobello mushrooms
- 1 small onion, chopped
- 3 tablespoons butter
- ¼ cup port wine or beef broth
- 2 teaspoons ground mustard
- 1 teaspoon sugar
- 1½ cups (12 ounces) sour cream
  Hot cooked egg noodles
  Minced fresh parsley, optional

1. In a large skillet, brown meat in oil. Add water and seasoning mix, stirring to loosen browned bits from the pan. Transfer the meat and drippings to a 3-qt. slow cooker.

2. In the same skillet, saute portobello mushrooms and onion in butter until tender. Combine the wine, mustard and sugar; stir into the mushroom mixture. Add to the slow cooker; stir to combine.

3. Cover; cook on low for 6-8 hours or until the meat is tender. Stir in sour cream. Serve with noodles. Sprinkle with parsley if desired.

French Onion Pizza au Gratin

I love a hot bowl of French onion soup and also am a big fan of pizza. I decided to combine those two favorites so I can enjoy both at the same time! The unusual but yummy pie is great when you're in the mood for a change of pace.

—BONNIE LONG LAKEWOOD, OH

PREP: 30 MIN. • **BAKE:** 10 MIN.
MAKES: 8 SLICES

- 1 large onion, sliced
- 2 tablespoons brown sugar
- 2 tablespoons olive oil, divided
- 3 tablespoons balsamic vinegar
- 3 garlic cloves, minced
- 1 tablespoon bourbon, optional
- 1 cup sliced fresh mushrooms
- ¼ pound thickly sliced deli roast beef, coarsely chopped
- 1 prebaked 12-inch pizza crust
- ¾ cup French onion dip
- ¾ cup shredded part-skim mozzarella cheese
- 1 medium sweet red pepper, chopped
- ¾ cup shredded Gruyere or Swiss cheese
- 1 teaspoon minced fresh rosemary

1. In a large skillet, saute the onion with the brown sugar in 1 tablespoon olive oil until softened. Reduce the heat to medium-low; cook, stirring occasionally, for 30 minutes or until deep golden brown. Stir in balsamic vinegar and garlic. Remove from the heat; add the bourbon if desired. Continue cooking until the liquid is nearly evaporated.

2. In another skillet, saute mushrooms in the remaining oil until tender; add the roast beef and heat through.

3. Place prebaked pizza crust on a pizza pan; spread with French onion dip. Layer with the mozzarella cheese, onion mixture, red pepper, mushroom mixture and Gruyere cheese.

4. Bake at 425° for 10-15 minutes or until the cheese is melted. Sprinkle with rosemary.

Beef Tips & Caramelized Onion Casserole

Sweet caramelized onions contrast so deliciously with the savory meat in this recipe. The toast and mozzarella on top make it look and taste even more special.
—**LINDA STEMEN** MONROEVILLE, IN

PREP: 40 MIN. • **BAKE:** 1½ HOURS
MAKES: 8 SERVINGS

- 4 **pounds beef sirloin tip roast, cut into 1-inch cubes**
- ½ **teaspoon salt**
- ½ **teaspoon pepper**
- 2 **tablespoons olive oil**
- 4 **large sweet onions, halved and thinly sliced**
- 3 **tablespoons butter**
- 4 **garlic cloves, minced**
- ⅔ **cup all-purpose flour**
- 2 **cans (10½ ounces each) condensed beef consomme, undiluted**
- 1 **can (14½ ounces) reduced-sodium beef broth**
- 2 **tablespoons Worcestershire sauce**
- 2 **bay leaves**
- ½ **cup heavy whipping cream**
- 8 **slices French bread (½ inch thick), toasted**
- 1 **cup (4 ounces) shredded part-skim mozzarella cheese**

1. Sprinkle beef with salt and pepper. In a large skillet, brown meat in oil in batches; drain. Transfer to a greased 13x9x2-in. baking dish.

2. In the same skillet, cook the onions in butter over medium-low heat for 25-30 minutes or until golden brown, stirring occasionally. Add garlic; cook 1 minute longer.

3. Preheat oven to 325°. Stir the flour into the onion mixture until blended; gradually add the beef consomme and broth. Stir in the Worcestershire sauce and bay leaves. Bring to a boil; cook and stir for 1 minute or until thickened. Pour over beef.

4. Cover and bake 1 hour. Carefully stir in cream; discard bay leaves. Bake, uncovered, 25-35 minutes or until meat is tender. Place toast over beef mixture; sprinkle with cheese. Bake 5 minutes or until cheese is melted.

Southwest Beef Burritos

Have just 20 minutes to come up with dinner? No problem! Grab some refrigerated beef tips, frozen mixed veggies and other convenience products to roll out quick burritos.
—**PATRICIA HARMON** BADEN, PA

START TO FINISH: 20 MIN.
MAKES: 4 SERVINGS

- 1 **package (17 ounces) refrigerated beef tips with gravy**
- 1 **medium onion, chopped**
- 1 **tablespoon canola oil**
- 2 **cups frozen mixed vegetables, thawed**
- 1 **can (4 ounces) chopped green chilies, drained**
- ¾ **teaspoon ground cumin**
- 4 **flour tortillas (10 inches), warmed**
- ¾ **cup shredded Mexican cheese blend**

1. Cut beef tips into ½-inch pieces. In a large skillet, saute the onion in oil until tender. Add beef tips with gravy, mixed vegetables, green chilies and cumin; heat through.

2. Spoon ¾ cup filling off center on each tortilla. Sprinkle with the cheese. Fold the sides and ends over the filling and roll up.

Curried Beef-Stuffed Squash

Acorn squash stuffed with ground beef is so filling, my husband and I often make a meal out of it during fall and winter.

—EDNA LEE GREELEY, CO

PREP: 35 MIN. • **BAKE:** 20 MIN. • **MAKES:** 6 SERVINGS

- 3 medium acorn squash (about 1 pound each), halved and seeded
- 1 pound ground beef
- ½ cup chopped onion
- 2 garlic cloves, minced
- 1 teaspoon beef bouillon granules
- ½ cup hot water
- ½ cup cooked rice
- 2 tablespoons chopped fresh parsley
- 1 tablespoon orange juice concentrate
- 1 teaspoon brown sugar
- 1 teaspoon curry powder
- ½ teaspoon ground ginger
- ¼ teaspoon salt

1. Invert the acorn squash halves in a greased 15x10x1-in. baking pan. Bake, uncovered, at 350° for 35-45 minutes or until almost tender.

2. Meanwhile, in a skillet, cook the beef, onion and garlic over medium heat until meat is no longer pink and onion is tender, breaking meat into crumbles; drain.

3. Dissolve the beef bouillon in the hot water; add to the skillet. Stir in the remaining ingredients; mix well. Turn the acorn squash halves cut side up in the pan and fill with the meat mixture.

4. Fill the pan with hot water to a depth of ¼ in.; cover loosely with foil. Bake at 350° for 20-30 minutes or until heated through.

Hot Tamale Casserole

If you like tamales, you'll love this casserole spinoff. It has all the Southwestern flavor you crave and just the right amount of heat.

—SHARON DELANEY-CHRONIS SOUTH MILWAUKEE, WI

PREP: 35 MIN. • **BAKE:** 30 MIN. • **MAKES:** 6 SERVINGS

- 2 cups water
- ¼ teaspoon salt
- ⅛ teaspoon cayenne pepper
- ½ cup cornmeal
- 1½ pounds lean ground beef (90% lean)
- 1 large onion, chopped
- 1 medium green pepper, chopped
- 2 garlic cloves, minced
- 1 can (16 ounces) kidney beans, rinsed and drained
- 1 can (10 ounces) enchilada sauce
- 1 can (4 ounces) chopped green chilies
- 1 can (2¼ ounces) sliced ripe olives, drained
- 2 teaspoons chili powder
- 2 teaspoons minced fresh cilantro
- ¾ cup shredded cheddar cheese

1. In a small heavy saucepan, bring the water, salt and cayenne to a boil. Reduce the heat to a gentle boil; slowly whisk in cornmeal. Cook and stir with a wooden spoon for 15-20 minutes or until polenta is thickened and pulls away cleanly from the sides of the pan.

2. Meanwhile, in a large skillet, cook the beef, onion, green pepper and garlic over medium heat until meat is no longer pink, breaking meat into crumbles. Stir in beans, enchilada sauce, chilies, olives, chili powder and cilantro; heat through.

3. Spread the polenta into a greased 8-in.-square baking dish. Top with the meat mixture. Cover and bake at 350° for 25 minutes. Sprinkle with the cheese. Bake, uncovered, for 2-5 minutes or until filling is bubbly and cheese is melted.

Greek Meat Loaves

Sun-dried tomatoes, olives and feta cheese give traditional meat loaf a Mediterranean twist. This recipe makes two, so I can freeze one for a fuss-free dinner another time. Add a simple Greek salad and loaf of crusty bread on the side.

—RADELLE KNAPPENBERGER OVIEDO, FL

PREP: 20 MIN. • **BAKE:** 50 MIN.
MAKES: 2 LOAVES (6 SERVINGS EACH)

- 2 **eggs, lightly beaten**
- ½ **cup ketchup**
- ¼ **cup 2% milk**
- 1 **large red onion, finely chopped**
- ¾ **cup quick-cooking oats**
- ⅓ **cup oil-packed sun-dried tomatoes, patted dry and finely chopped**
- ⅓ **cup pitted Greek olives, chopped**
- 2 **garlic cloves, minced**
- 1 **teaspoon salt**
- 1 **teaspoon pepper**
- 2 **pounds lean ground beef (90% lean)**
- ½ **cup crumbled feta cheese**

1. In a large bowl, combine the first 10 ingredients. Crumble beef over mixture and mix well. Pat into two greased 8x4-in. loaf pans. Cover and freeze one meat loaf for up to 3 months.
2. Bake the remaining meat loaf, uncovered, at 350° for 50-60 minutes or until no pink remains and a thermometer reads 160°. Let stand for 5 minutes. Transfer to a serving plate; sprinkle with feta cheese.
TO USE FROZEN MEAT LOAF *Thaw frozen meat loaf in the refrigerator overnight. Bake as directed; sprinkle with feta cheese.*

Grilled Teriyaki Pork Tenderloin, page 97

101

106

111

Pork Entrees

Ham, sausage, tenderloin, bacon...they're all here in this chapter of **pork prizewinners**. So choose your favorites, then get ready to serve a meaty main dish you'll be asked for **again and again.**

Ham and Vegetable Linguine

When I'm having dinner guests, I like to serve my rich ham linguine. The delicate cream sauce blends well with the meat and colorful vegetables. I chop them in advance to save time later.

—KERRY KERR MCAVOY ROCKFORD, MI

START TO FINISH: 20 MIN.
MAKES: 4 SERVINGS

- 1 **package (8 ounces) linguine**
- ½ **pound fresh asparagus, trimmed and cut into 1-inch pieces**
- ½ **pound fresh mushrooms, sliced**
- 1 **medium carrot, thinly sliced**
- 1 **medium zucchini, diced**
- 2 **cups julienned fully cooked ham**
- ¼ **cup butter**
- 1 **cup heavy whipping cream**
- ½ **cup frozen peas**
- 3 **green onions, sliced**
- ¼ **cup grated Parmesan cheese**
- 1 **teaspoon dried basil**
- ¾ **teaspoon salt**
  Dash ground nutmeg
  Dash pepper
  Additional Parmesan cheese, optional

1. Cook the linguine according to the package directions. Meanwhile, in a large skillet, saute the asparagus, mushrooms, carrot, zucchini and ham in butter until vegetables are tender.

2. Add the heavy whipping cream, peas, onions, Parmesan cheese, basil, salt, nutmeg and pepper; bring to a boil. Reduce the heat; simmer for 3 minutes or until heated through, stirring frequently.

3. Rinse and drain the linguine; add to the vegetable mixture and toss to coat. Sprinkle with Parmesan if desired.

HAM IT UP

Make the most of your leftover holiday ham with Ham and Vegetable Linguine (recipe above). To julienne the cooked ham, simply cut it into long, thin matchstick shapes about 2 inches long and ½ inch thick.

Glazed Pork Chops with Corn Bread Dressing

Baking the glazed pork chops and corn bread stuffing together allows part of the stuffing to get some crispness, bringing a nice texture to this home-style dinner. Every bite is sweet, savory and delicious.

—DAWN KLOMAN WATERTOWN, WI

PREP: 10 MIN. • **BAKE:** 25 MIN.
MAKES: 6 SERVINGS

- 1¼ **cups reduced-sodium chicken broth**
- ¾ **cup chopped onion**
- ¾ **cup frozen corn**
- 1 **celery rib, chopped**
  Dash cayenne pepper
- 3 **cups crushed corn bread stuffing**
- 6 **boneless pork loin chops (6 ounces each)**
- 2 **tablespoons brown sugar**
- 2 **teaspoons spicy brown mustard**

1. Preheat oven to 400°. In a large saucepan, bring broth, onion, corn, celery and cayenne to a boil. Remove from the heat; stir in stuffing.

2. Transfer to a 13x9x2-in. baking dish coated with cooking spray. Top with the pork chops. Combine brown sugar and mustard; spread over chops. Bake, uncovered, 25-30 minutes or until meat reaches desired doneness (for medium-rare, a thermometer should read 145°; medium, 160°). Let stand 5 minutes before serving.

GLAZED PORK CHOPS WITH APPLE DRESSING *Omit the corn and cayenne. Saute 2 chopped, peeled medium tart apples, the onion and the celery in 2 tablespoons butter until tender. Stir in the chicken broth, ¼ cup dried cranberries, ¼ teaspoon rubbed sage, ¼ teaspoon salt and the stuffing. Proceed as recipe directs.*

Grilled Teriyaki Pork Tenderloin

I let my tenderloin marinate overnight in a simple blend of honey mustard, teriyaki marinade and garlic, then grill. It's so easy!
—**TAHNIA FOX** TRENTON, MI

PREP: 10 MIN. + MARINATING • **GRILL:** 20 MIN.
MAKES: 4 SERVINGS

- ¾ cup honey mustard
- ¾ cup teriyaki marinade
- 1 pork tenderloin (1 pound)
- 2 garlic cloves, minced
- 1 green onion, chopped

1. In a small bowl, combine mustard and teriyaki marinade; pour 1 cup into a large resealable plastic bag. Add the pork and garlic; seal bag and turn to coat. Refrigerate 6 hours or overnight. Cover and refrigerate the remaining marinade.

2. Prepare grill for indirect heat using a drip pan. Moisten a paper towel with cooking oil; using long-handled tongs, rub on grill rack to coat lightly. Drain and discard marinade from pork.

3. Place pork over drip pan and grill, covered, over indirect medium-hot heat for 25-40 minutes or until the meat reaches desired doneness (for medium-rare, a thermometer should read 145°; medium, 160°), basting with the reserved marinade and turning occasionally. Let stand 5 minutes before slicing. Sprinkle with onion.

Italian Stuffed Portobellos

PREP: 1 HOUR • **BAKE:** 10 MIN.
MAKES: 4 SERVINGS

- 4 ounces sliced pancetta or bacon strips, finely chopped
- 1 tablespoon plus 1 teaspoon olive oil, divided
- 4 cups sliced onions
- 2 tablespoons finely chopped oil-packed sun-dried tomatoes
- ¼ teaspoon salt
- ⅛ teaspoon pepper
- 1 whole garlic bulb
- 3 tablespoons crumbled goat cheese

PIZZAS

- 4 large portobello mushrooms
- 2 tablespoons olive oil
- ⅓ cup shredded part-skim mozzarella cheese
- 3 tablespoons shredded Parmesan cheese
- 1 tablespoon minced fresh basil or 1 teaspoon dried basil

Take your taste buds to Italy without leaving the comfort of home! Pizza-like Italian Stuffed Portobellos will make you feel like you're in a Roman ristorante. To add some heat, stir in red pepper flakes while sauteeing the onions.
—**JEANNE HOLT** MENDOTA HEIGHTS, MN

1. In a large skillet over medium heat, cook pancetta in 1 tablespoon oil until crisp. Remove to paper towels with a slotted spoon; set aside.

2. In the same skillet, cook and stir the onions until softened. Reduce the heat to medium-low; cook, stirring occasionally, for 30 minutes or until deep golden brown. Stir in sun-dried tomatoes, salt, pepper and pancetta. Remove from the heat; keep warm.

3. Remove the papery outer skin from the garlic (do not peel or separate the cloves). Cut the top off of the garlic bulb. Brush with the remaining oil. Wrap the garlic bulb in heavy-duty foil. Bake at 425° for 30-35 minutes or until softened. Cool for 10-15 minutes. Squeeze the softened garlic into a small bowl; stir in crumbled goat cheese and onions.

4. Brush the portobello mushrooms with oil. Grill, covered, over medium heat or broil 4 in. from the heat for 6-8 minutes on each side or until tender. Fill mushrooms with the onion mixture. Sprinkle with the mozzarella and Parmesan cheeses.

5. Place on a greased baking sheet. Bake at 375° for 8-10 minutes or until cheese is melted. Sprinkle with basil.

Sweet & Sour Sausage

I always keep Polish sausage in the freezer so I can whip up this 20-minute meal on busy nights. Everyone likes the sweet-sour taste, and rice is an easy way to complete the meal.

—CAROL MATTHEWS LIMA, NY

START TO FINISH: 20 MIN. • **MAKES:** 4 SERVINGS

- 1 can (20 ounces) pineapple chunks
- ½ cup apricot preserves
- 2 teaspoons cornstarch
- 1 tablespoon cider vinegar
- 1 tablespoon soy sauce
- ½ teaspoon ground ginger
- 1 pound smoked Polish sausage, cut into ½-inch slices
- 1 large onion, cut into 1-inch pieces
- 1 medium green pepper, cut into 1-inch pieces
- 1 tablespoon canola oil
  Hot cooked rice

1. Drain pineapple, reserving ¼ cup juice; set pineapple aside. In a small bowl, combine the preserves, cornstarch, vinegar, soy sauce, ginger and reserved juice.
2. In a large skillet, saute the sausage, onion and pepper in oil until vegetables are tender. Add sauce mixture and pineapple. Bring to a boil; cook and stir for 2 minutes or until thickened. Serve with rice.

Apricot-Glazed Pork Tenderloin

Pork tenderloin doesn't get much easier! Apricot preserves and a few other basic ingredients create a wonderful glaze, and the Dijon flavor comes through nicely.

—CRYSTAL HOLSINGER SURPRISE, AZ

PREP: 15 MIN. • **BAKE:** 20 MIN. • **MAKES:** 6 SERVINGS

- 2 pork tenderloins (1 pound each)
- 2 tablespoons olive oil
- ½ teaspoon salt
- ¼ teaspoon pepper
- 1 cup apricot preserves
- 3 tablespoons sherry or reduced-sodium chicken broth
- 1 tablespoon Dijon mustard
- 2 garlic cloves, minced
- 1 teaspoon minced fresh thyme or ¼ teaspoon dried thyme

1. Place pork tenderloins on a rack in a shallow roasting pan. Combine oil, salt and pepper; rub over tenderloins.
2. Bake at 425° for 10 minutes. In a small bowl, combine the remaining ingredients; spoon over the tenderloins. Bake 10-17 minutes longer or until a thermometer reads 145°, basting occasionally with the pan juices. Let stand for 5 minutes before slicing.

Classic Spinach Pizza

In the mood for something different? Top a prebaked crust with a combination of pancetta, spinach, mushrooms and more.

—GILDA LESTER MILLSBORO, DE

PREP: 35 MIN. • **BAKE:** 10 MIN. • **MAKES:** 6 SLICES

- 2 ounces pancetta or sliced bacon, finely chopped
- 4 garlic cloves, minced
- 1 package (6 ounces) fresh baby spinach
- 1 cup sliced fresh mushrooms
- 1 tablespoon olive oil
- ¼ teaspoon crushed red pepper flakes
- ⅛ teaspoon salt
- ⅛ teaspoon pepper
- ⅓ cup Mascarpone cheese
- ¼ cup chopped ripe olives
- 1 prebaked 12-inch pizza crust
- 1 cup (4 ounces) shredded provolone cheese
- ⅓ cup grated Romano cheese

1. In a large skillet, cook pancetta over medium heat until crisp. Using a slotted spoon, remove to paper towels to drain. Saute garlic in drippings for 1 minute. Add spinach; cook just until wilted. Drain mixture on paper towels.
2. In the same skillet, saute mushrooms in oil until tender; add the pepper flakes, salt and pepper. Remove from the heat; transfer to a small bowl and let stand for 5 minutes. Stir in the Mascarpone cheese, olives and pancetta.
3. Place the crust on an ungreased pizza pan. Spread the mushroom mixture over the crust; layer with the spinach mixture, provolone cheese and Romano cheese. Bake at 450° for 10-12 minutes or until cheese is melted.

Broccoli-Ham Macaroni

Creamy and hearty, this dressed-up version of mac and cheese
has all the goodness of comfort food without the extra fat.
—NANCY LATULIPPE SIMCOE, ON

PREP: 30 MIN. • **BAKE:** 25 MIN. • **MAKES:** 6 SERVINGS

- 1½ **cups uncooked elbow macaroni**
- 4 **cups fresh broccoli florets**
- 1 **large onion, finely chopped**
- 1 **cup cubed fully cooked ham**
- 1 **medium sweet red pepper, chopped**
- 1 **tablespoon butter**
- ⅓ **cup all-purpose flour**
- 4 **cups fat-free milk**
- 2½ **cups (10 ounces) shredded reduced-fat cheddar cheese**
- ¼ **cup minced fresh parsley**
- 2 **teaspoons Dijon mustard**
- ½ **teaspoon garlic powder**
- ½ **teaspoon Italian seasoning**
- ¼ **teaspoon pepper**

TOPPING
- ¼ **cup dry bread crumbs**
- 1 **tablespoon butter, melted**

1. Cook the macaroni according to package directions.
Meanwhile, place 1 in. of water in a large saucepan; add
broccoli. Bring to a boil. Reduce heat; cover and simmer
for 4-5 minutes or until crisp-tender.

2. In another saucepan, saute the onion, ham and red
pepper in 1 tablespoon butter until the vegetables are
crisp-tender. Sprinkle with the flour; stir until blended.
Gradually stir in the milk. Bring to a boil; cook and stir for
2 minutes or until thickened.

3. Stir in cheese, parsley, Dijon mustard and seasonings
until blended. Drain the broccoli and macaroni; stir into
the cheese sauce. Transfer to a greased 2-qt. baking dish
(the dish will be full).

4. Combine the dry bread crumbs and butter. Sprinkle
over the top. Bake, uncovered, at 350° for 25-30 minutes
or until heated through.

Saucy Stuffed Zucchini

When I grew too much zucchini, I used it to create an Italian entree. My husband isn't a fan of veggies, but he gobbled it up.

—**BARBARA EDGINGTON** FRANKFORT, OH

PREP: 30 MIN. • **BAKE:** 25 MIN.
MAKES: 3-4 SERVINGS

- 3 to 4 medium zucchini (1¾ to 2 pounds)
- 12 ounces Italian sausage, cooked and drained
- ½ cup chopped sweet red pepper
- ½ cup chopped green pepper
- 2 tablespoons chopped onion
- 1½ teaspoons Italian seasoning
- 1 can (8 ounces) tomato sauce
- 2 tablespoons butter
- 2 tablespoons all-purpose flour
- ¼ teaspoon salt
- 1¼ cups milk
- ½ cup grated Parmesan cheese, divided
- 1 teaspoon Dijon mustard

1. Cut zucchini in half lengthwise. Scoop out pulp, leaving a ¼-in. shell. Reserve pulp. Cook shells in salted water for 2 minutes. Remove and drain. Set aside.

2. Chop the zucchini pulp. Place the pulp in a saucepan; add the sausage, peppers, onion, Italian seasoning and tomato sauce. Bring to a boil. Reduce heat; cover and simmer for 5 minutes. Place the zucchini shells in a greased 13x9x2-in. baking dish. Spoon filling into shells.

3. In a saucepan, melt the butter; whisk in flour and salt until smooth. Gradually add the milk. Bring to a boil. Cook and stir for 2 minutes or until thickened and bubbly. Remove from the heat. Add ¼ cup Parmesan cheese and mustard.

4. Pour over the zucchini. Sprinkle with the remaining Parmesan. Bake, uncovered, at 350° for 25-30 minutes or until heated through.

Kickin' Hawaiian Pizza

Tangy pineapple is great with the peppers and pepperoni on this standout pie.

—**JOHN WEAKLAND** LACEY, WA

PREP: 30 MIN. • **BAKE:** 15 MIN.
MAKES: 12 PIECES

- 4 plum tomatoes, coarsely chopped
- 1 can (6 ounces) tomato paste
- ¼ cup water
- ¼ cup roasted sweet red peppers
- 1 tablespoon dried oregano
- 1 tablespoon honey
- 2 teaspoons dried minced garlic
- 2 teaspoons paprika
- 1 teaspoon salt
- ¼ teaspoon crushed red pepper flakes
- 2 tubes (13.8 ounces each) refrigerated pizza crust
- 2 cups (8 ounces) shredded part-skim mozzarella cheese, divided
- 1 cup (4 ounces) shredded Romano cheese, divided
- 1 package (3½ ounces) sliced pepperoni
- 1 cup pineapple tidbits, drained

1. For pizza sauce, place the first 10 ingredients in a food processor; cover and process until blended. Transfer sauce to a small saucepan; heat through.

2. Meanwhile, press the pizza dough into a greased 15x10x1-in. baking pan; build up edges slightly and seal seam. Bake at 425° for 6-8 minutes or until lightly browned.

3. Spread 1¾ cups sauce over the crust (refrigerate the remaining sauce for another use). Sprinkle with 1 cup mozzarella cheese and ½ cup Romano cheese; top with pepperoni, pineapple and remaining cheeses.

4. Bake for 14-18 minutes or until the cheese is melted and the crust is golden brown.

HONEY OF A HINT

Store honey in a cool, dry place for up to 1 year. Do not keep it in the refrigerator—that speeds up the crystallization process.

Marsala Pork Chops

Knowing that my husband and I love onions and garlic, a dear friend served us her amazing Marsala pork. She gave me the recipe, and I've prepared it countless times since.

—JAN HUNTINGTON PAINESVILLE, OH

PREP: 15 MIN. • **COOK:** 20 MIN. • **MAKES:** 4 SERVINGS

- ½ cup seasoned bread crumbs
- 4 bone-in center-cut pork loin chops (6 ounces each)
- 3 tablespoons olive oil, divided
- 3 medium onions, thinly sliced
- 6 garlic cloves, minced
- ½ cup white wine or chicken broth
- 1 tablespoon Marsala wine or chicken broth
- ¼ teaspoon pepper
- ⅛ teaspoon salt
- ¼ cup cold butter, cubed
  Hot cooked egg noodles

1. Place the bread crumbs in a large resealable plastic bag. Add pork chops, one at a time, and shake to coat. In a large skillet, cook chops in 2 tablespoons oil over medium heat for 4-6 minutes on each side or until a thermometer reads 160°. Remove and keep warm.

2. In the same skillet, saute onions in remaining oil until tender. Add garlic; cook 2 minutes longer. Add the white wine, Marsala, pepper and salt, stirring to loosen browned bits from pan. Cook, stirring occasionally, until liquid is nearly evaporated. Stir in butter until melted. Serve with pork chops and noodles.

Campfire Bundles

I created these bundles during a family camping trip. I'd brought along a hodgepodge of ingredients and decided to throw them all together into foil packets. Now I grill them at home, too.

—LAURI KRAUSE JACKSON, NE

PREP: 15 MIN. • **GRILL:** 1 HOUR • **MAKES:** 6 SERVINGS

- 1 large sweet onion, sliced
- 1 each large green, sweet red and yellow pepper
- 4 medium potatoes, cut into ¼-inch slices
- 6 medium carrots, cut into ¼-inch slices
- 1 small head cabbage, sliced
- 2 medium tomatoes, chopped
- 1 to 1½ pounds smoked Polish sausage, cut into ½-inch slices
- ½ cup butter, cubed
- 1 teaspoon salt
- ½ teaspoon pepper

1. Place the onion, peppers, potatoes, carrots, cabbage and tomatoes on three pieces of double-layered heavy-duty foil (about 18 in. square). Top with the sausage; dot with butter. Sprinkle with salt and pepper. Fold foil around the mixture and seal tightly.

2. Grill, covered, over medium heat for 30 minutes. Turn and grill 30 minutes longer or until vegetables are tender. Open foil carefully to allow steam to escape.

Jerk Pork & Pineapple Kabobs

Bring on the heat! Before assembling my kabobs, I put the meat in a homemade jerk marinade that includes a habanero pepper. For a refreshing counterpoint, pair each colorful skewer with a bowl of pina colada yogurt for dipping.
—**AVA BRYAN** EAST HARTFORD, CT

PREP: 30 MIN. + MARINATING
GRILL: 10 MIN. • **MAKES:** 4 KABOBS

- 2 **bunches green onions, coarsely chopped**
- 1 **medium onion, coarsely chopped**
- 1 **habanero pepper, halved and seeded**
- 2 **tablespoons white vinegar**
- 2 **tablespoons orange juice**
- 1 **tablespoon olive oil**
- 1 **tablespoon reduced-sodium soy sauce**
- 2 **teaspoons salt**
- 2 **teaspoons brown sugar**
- 2 **teaspoons ground allspice**
- 2 **garlic cloves, peeled**
- 2 **teaspoons minced fresh gingerroot**
- 2 **teaspoons minced fresh thyme**
- ½ **teaspoon pepper**
- ¼ **teaspoon ground cinnamon**
- ¼ **teaspoon ground nutmeg**
- ¼ **teaspoon lime juice**
- 1 **pound pork tenderloin, cut into 1-inch pieces**
- 1 **can (8 ounces) unsweetened pineapple chunks, drained**
- 1 **large green pepper, cut into 1-inch pieces**
- 1 **large sweet red pepper, cut into 1-inch pieces**

1. In a food processor, combine the first 17 ingredients; cover and process until blended. Transfer marinade to a large resealable plastic bag; add pork. Seal bag and turn to coat; refrigerate for at least 3 hours.

2. Drain and discard marinade. On four metal or soaked wooden skewers, alternately thread pork, pineapple and peppers. Grill, covered, over medium heat or broil 4 in. from the heat for 10-15 minutes or until the meat is tender, turning occasionally.

NOTE *Wear disposable gloves when cutting hot peppers; the oils can burn skin. Avoid touching your face.*

Ham and Asparagus Casserole

This family favorite is popular at get-togethers. With asparagus and eggs, it's especially nice for spring brunches.

—**DONETTA BRUNNER** SAVANNA, IL

PREP: 15 MIN. • **BAKE:** 25 MIN. • **MAKES:** 4 SERVINGS

- 1 package (10 ounces) frozen cut asparagus or 1 pound fresh asparagus, ½-inch cuts
- 4 hard-cooked eggs, peeled and chopped
- 1 cup cubed fully cooked ham
- 2 tablespoons quick-cooking tapioca
- ¼ cup shredded process cheese (Velveeta)
- 2 tablespoons chopped green pepper
- 2 tablespoons chopped onion
- 1 tablespoon minced fresh parsley
- 1 tablespoon lemon juice
- ½ cup half-and-half cream or evaporated milk
- 1 cup condensed cream of mushroom soup, undiluted

TOPPING
- 1 cup soft bread crumbs
- 2 tablespoons butter, melted

1. In a large saucepan, bring ½ in. of water to a boil. Add the asparagus; cover and boil for 3 minutes. Drain; immediately place asparagus in ice water. Drain and pat dry.
2. In a 2½-qt. baking dish, combine the asparagus, eggs and ham; sprinkle tapioca evenly over all. Stir in the cheese, green pepper, onion and parsley.
3. In a small bowl, combine the lemon juice, half-and-half cream and cream of mushroom soup; add to the casserole and mix thoroughly. Combine the topping ingredients; sprinkle over the top.
4. Bake, uncovered, at 375° for 25-30 minutes or until heated through. Let stand a few minutes before serving.

Texas Pork Burritos

When I was doing some experimenting with green enchilada sauce, I created a recipe for pork burritos. The meat always comes out of the slow cooker nice and tender.

—**SALLY SIBTHORPE** SHELBY TOWNSHIP, MI

PREP: 40 MIN. • **COOK:** 6½ HOURS • **MAKES:** 10 SERVINGS

- 1 boneless pork shoulder butt roast (3 to 4 pounds), cubed
- 1 teaspoon salt
- ½ teaspoon pepper
- 2 tablespoons canola oil
- 2 cans (10 ounces each) green enchilada sauce
- 1 large onion, thinly sliced
- 2 medium carrots, thinly sliced
- 2 cans (2¼ ounces each) sliced ripe olives, drained
- ½ cup chicken broth
- 2 tablespoons ground cumin
- 3 garlic cloves, minced
- 2 teaspoons dried oregano
- 2 tablespoons all-purpose flour
- 1 cup (8 ounces) sour cream
- ½ cup minced fresh cilantro
- 10 flour tortillas (8 inches), warmed
- 2 cups (8 ounces) shredded Mexican cheese blend

1. Sprinkle the pork with salt and pepper. In a large skillet, brown the meat in oil in batches. Transfer to a 3-qt. slow cooker. Combine the green enchilada sauce, onion, carrots, ripe olives, chicken broth, cumin, garlic and oregano; pour over the meat. Cover and cook on low for 6-8 hours or until meat is tender.
2. Combine flour and sour cream; stir into meat mixture. Cover and cook on high for 30 minutes or until thickened. Stir in cilantro.
3. Spoon ⅔ cup pork mixture onto each tortilla; top with about 3 tablespoons cheese. Roll up tightly.

TORTILLA TIME

If I have leftover flour tortillas, I use them to make sweet snacks. I just cut the tortillas into wedges or strips and fry them on both sides in a lightly oiled skillet until golden. Then I sprinkle them with sugar and sometimes a bit of cinnamon. Yum!

—**JUDITH L.** LITTLETON, MA

Cranberry-Maple Pork Chops

A tangy cranberry sauce with a hint of maple syrup makes pork chops special enough for company. Try seasoned roasted potato wedges on the side.

—**HEATHER BATES** ATHENS, ME

START TO FINISH: 30 MIN.
MAKES: 6 SERVINGS

- 6 boneless pork loin chops (5 ounces each)
- ½ teaspoon salt
- ½ teaspoon pepper
- 2 tablespoons butter
- 1 can (14 ounces) whole-berry cranberry sauce
- ⅓ cup grape jelly
- 2 tablespoons ketchup
- 1 tablespoon soy sauce
- ⅓ cup maple syrup

1. Sprinkle the pork chops with salt and pepper. In a large skillet, brown the pork chops in butter. Remove and keep warm.

2. In the same skillet, combine the cranberry sauce, grape jelly, ketchup and soy sauce; cook and stir until blended. Return chops to the pan; drizzle with syrup. Bring to a boil. Reduce heat; cover and simmer for 15-20 minutes or until meat is tender.

Sweet and Spicy Jerk Ribs

Here's a a no-fuss recipe that gives baby back ribs a Caribbean twist. The spicy jerk seasoning combines with sweet preserves and honey for lip-smacking flavor.

—**GERI LESCH** NEW PORT RICHEY, FL

PREP: 10 MIN. • **COOK:** 6 HOURS
MAKES: 5 SERVINGS

- 4½ pounds pork baby back ribs
- 3 tablespoons olive oil
- ⅓ cup Caribbean jerk seasoning
- 3 cups honey barbecue sauce
- 3 tablespoons apricot preserves
- 2 tablespoons honey

1. Cut the pork baby back ribs into serving-size pieces; brush with the olive oil and rub with the Caribbean jerk seasoning. Place in a 5- or 6-qt. slow cooker. Combine the remaining ingredients; pour over ribs.

2. Cover; cook on low for 6-8 hours or until the meat is tender. Skim fat from sauce before serving.

Big Kahuna Pizza

Want something different for pizza night? Go big! Top a convenient prebaked crust with refrigerated barbecued pork, onion, pineapple chunks and mozzarella cheese. The hefty slices are sure to win raves.

—**JONI HILTON** ROCKLIN, CA

START TO FINISH: 30 MIN.
MAKES: 6 SERVINGS

- 1 prebaked 12-inch pizza crust
- 1 carton (16 ounces) refrigerated fully cooked barbecued shredded pork
- 1 can (20 ounces) pineapple chunks, drained
- ⅓ cup chopped red onion
- 2 cups (8 ounces) shredded part-skim mozzarella cheese

1. Place pizza crust on an ungreased 12-in. pizza pan. Spread shredded pork over the crust; top with pineapple and onion. Sprinkle with cheese.

2. Bake at 350° for 20-25 minutes or until cheese is melted.

Pecan Pork Medallions with Cambozola Cream

With these elegant medallions and cream, you can treat your family to fine dining straight from your kitchen.

—**MARIE RIZZIO** INTERLOCHEN, MI

PREP: 25 MIN. • **COOK:** 20 MIN.
MAKES: 6 SERVINGS

- ½ cup white wine
- 1 tablespoon chopped shallot
- 1½ cups heavy whipping cream
- 3 ounces Cambozola cheese, chopped
- ½ teaspoon Worcestershire sauce
- ¼ teaspoon hot pepper sauce
- ⅛ teaspoon salt
- ⅛ teaspoon white pepper

PORK

- ⅓ cup dried tart cherries
- 3 tablespoons port wine
- 1½ pounds pork tenderloin
- ½ cup chopped pecans
- ⅓ cup dry bread crumbs
- ¼ teaspoon salt
- ⅛ teaspoon pepper
- 2 tablespoons butter

1. In a small saucepan, combine the white wine and shallot. Bring to a boil; cook until the liquid is reduced to about 2 tablespoons. Add cream, Cambozola cheese, Worcestershire sauce, pepper sauce, salt and white pepper. Return to a boil; cook until slightly thickened, about 15 minutes. In small bowl, combine cherries and port wine; set aside.

2. Meanwhile, cut pork into 12 slices; flatten slices to ½-in. thickness. Place the pecans in a food processor; cover and process until finely chopped. In a large resealable plastic bag, combine the pecans, dry bread crumbs, salt and pepper. Add the pork, a few pieces at a time; shake to coat.

3. In a large skillet over medium-high heat, cook pork in butter in batches for 3-4 minutes on each side or until tender. Drain the cherries; serve with pork and sauce.

NOTE *You may substitute 2 ounces Brie and 1 ounce blue cheese for the Cambozola cheese.*

Antipasto Pizza

This distinctive pie piles on salami, ham, artichokes and other ingredients that are traditionally used for an Italian antipasto platter. For an appetizer instead of an entree, cut smaller wedges or squares.

—**MINDEE CURTIS** OMAHA, NE

START TO FINISH: 25 MIN.
MAKES: 8 SLICES

- 1 prebaked 12-inch pizza crust
- ¾ cup pizza sauce
- 2 cups (8 ounces) shredded part-skim mozzarella cheese, divided
- ½ cup julienned roasted sweet red peppers
- ½ cup marinated quartered artichoke hearts, drained
- ¼ pound thinly sliced hard salami, julienned
- ¼ pound sliced deli ham, julienned
- ¼ cup minced fresh basil

1. Place the crust on an ungreased pizza pan. Spread sauce over crust; sprinkle with 1 cup cheese. Top with red peppers, artichokes, salami and ham; sprinkle with remaining cheese.

2. Bake at 450° for 10-12 minutes or until the cheese is melted. Sprinkle with basil.

FREEZER OPTION *Before baking, wrap pizza; freeze for up to 2 months. To use frozen pizza, unwrap and place on a pizza pan; thaw in refrigerator. Bake at 450° for 10-12 minutes or until cheese is melted. Sprinkle with basil.*

Marinated Pork with Caramelized Fennel

With a flavorful marinade, these tenderloins are juicy and delicious. Caramelized fennel on the side makes for a delightfully different entree everyone will remember.

—GILDA LESTER MILLSBORO, DE

PREP: 20 MIN. • **BAKE:** 30 MIN. • **MAKES:** 6 SERVINGS

- ¼ cup olive oil
- 1 tablespoon reduced-sodium soy sauce
- 2 garlic cloves, minced
- 2 teaspoons grated lemon peel
- 1 teaspoon ground cumin
- 1 teaspoon fennel seed, crushed
- ½ teaspoon salt
- ½ teaspoon pepper
- ½ teaspoon ground allspice
- 2 pork tenderloins (¾ pound each)

FENNEL
- 2 medium fennel bulbs, halved and cut into ½-inch slices
- 4½ teaspoons plus 1 tablespoon olive oil, divided
- ¼ teaspoon salt
- ¼ teaspoon pepper
  Fennel fronds, optional

1. In a large resealable plastic bag, combine the first nine ingredients; add pork. Seal bag and turn to coat. Refrigerate for 8 hours or overnight.

2. Place fennel in a large bowl; drizzle with 4½ teaspoons oil. Sprinkle with salt and pepper; toss to coat. Transfer to an ungreased 15x10x1-in. baking pan. Bake at 450° for 30-35 minutes or until tender, stirring once.

3. Meanwhile, drain and discard the marinade. In a large ovenproof skillet, brown pork in remaining oil on all sides. Place skillet in oven; bake pork for 18-22 minutes or until a thermometer reads 145°.

4. Let stand for 5 minutes before slicing. Serve with the roasted fennel. Garnish with fennel fronds if desired.

Meat Lover's Pizza

START TO FINISH: 30 MIN. • **MAKES:** 8 SLICES

- 2 packages (6½ ounces each) pizza crust mix
- 1 tablespoon olive oil
- 1½ teaspoons garlic powder, divided
- ¼ pound ground beef
- ½ teaspoon onion powder
- ⅔ cup spaghetti sauce
- 1 package (3½ ounces) sliced pepperoni
- 6 ounces Canadian bacon, quartered
- ¼ cup sliced fresh mushrooms
- 2 tablespoons sliced ripe olives
- 2 cups (8 ounces) shredded part-skim mozzarella cheese

1. Prepare pizza dough according to package directions. With floured hands, press dough onto a greased 14-in. pizza pan. Bake at 425° for 7-9 minutes or until lightly browned. Combine the oil and 1 teaspoon garlic powder; brush over the crust edges.

2. In a large skillet over medium heat, cook the beef with onion powder and remaining garlic powder until no longer pink, breaking beef into crumbles; drain.

3. Spread the spaghetti sauce over the crust to within 1 in. of edges. Top with the beef mixture, pepperoni, Canadian bacon, mushrooms, olives and cheese.

4. Bake at 425° for 10-15 minutes or until cheese is melted and crust is golden brown.

❝ I'm a fan of Meat Lover's Pizza because it's a complete meal on a crust! The ground beef, Canadian bacon and pepperoni guarantee satisfied appetites. Serve up big slices the next time you host friends to watch the game on TV. ❞

—EDGAR PEAVY OXNARD, CA

Pork Tenderloin with Pear Cream Sauce

When it comes to enhancing the mild taste of pork, I like to use sweet flavors and lots of seasonings. Here's a great example! The pears and herb blend really complement the meat.
—**JOYCE MOYNIHAN** LAKEVILLE, MN

PREP: 25 MIN. • **BAKE:** 20 MIN. • **MAKES:** 4 SERVINGS

- 1 pork tenderloin (1 pound)
- 1 tablespoon herbes de Provence
- ½ teaspoon salt
- ¼ teaspoon pepper
- 4 tablespoons butter, divided
- 4 medium pears, peeled and sliced
- 1 tablespoon sugar
- 4 shallots, chopped
- 1¼ teaspoons dried thyme
- ¼ cup pear brandy or pear nectar
- 1 cup heavy whipping cream
- ⅓ cup pear nectar

1. Preheat oven to 425°. Sprinkle the pork tenderloin with herbes de Provence, salt and pepper. In a large ovenproof skillet, brown the pork in 1 tablespoon butter on all sides. Bake 18-22 minutes or until a thermometer reads 145°. Remove pork from the skillet and keep warm. Let meat stand for 5 minutes before slicing.

2. Meanwhile, in a large skillet, saute the pears and sugar in 2 tablespoons butter until golden brown. Remove from the pan and keep warm. In the same pan, melt the remaining butter. Add shallots; saute until tender. Stir in thyme.

3. Remove from the heat. Add brandy; cook over medium heat until liquid is almost evaporated, stirring to loosen browned bits from pan. Add cream and nectar; cook and stir until slightly thickened. Slice pork; serve with pears and cream sauce.

NOTE *Look for herbes de Provence in the spice aisle.*

The Best Derned Southwestern Casserole

Want to add a little spice to life—and to mealtime? Serve up this hearty main dish featuring chorizo sausage. Every bite gives you layer after layer of Tex-Mex goodness.
—**VALERIE IGAL** OAK HILL, VA

PREP: 35 MIN. • **BAKE:** 45 MIN. + STANDING • **MAKES:** 12 SERVINGS

- 1½ pounds uncooked chorizo or bulk spicy pork sausage
- 1 small onion, chopped
- 1 can (15 ounces) black beans, rinsed and drained
- 1 can (15 ounces) tomato sauce
- 1 can (11 ounces) Mexicorn, drained
- 2 cans (4 ounces each) chopped green chilies
- 1 cup salsa
- ¼ cup minced fresh cilantro
- 3 teaspoons each ground cumin, chili powder and paprika
- 2 teaspoons garlic powder
- 12 corn tortillas (6 inches)
- 2 large tomatoes, sliced
- 2 cups (8 ounces) shredded Monterey Jack or cheddar-Monterey Jack cheese

1. Preheat oven to 375°. Crumble the chorizo into a large skillet; add the onion. Cook over medium heat until meat is fully cooked; drain. Add beans, tomato sauce, corn, chilies, salsa, cilantro and seasonings; heat through.

2. Place six tortillas in the bottom of a greased 13x9x2-in. baking dish. Layer with 3½ cups meat mixture, tomatoes and 1 cup cheese. Top with the remaining tortillas, meat mixture and cheese.

3. Cover casserole and bake 40 minutes. Uncover; bake 5-10 minutes longer or until heated through. Let stand 10 minutes before cutting.

Tangy Ribs and Onions

We raised hogs on our family farm when I was a child, and our saucy sparerib recipe was a dinnertime mainstay.

—**MARGARET JESTRAB** PROTIVIN, IA

PREP: 10 MIN. • **BAKE:** 1¾ HOURS • **MAKES:** 4 SERVINGS

- 4 **pounds spareribs, cut into serving-size pieces**
- 1 **teaspoon salt**
- ½ **teaspoon pepper**
- 2 **medium onions, sliced**
- 1 **cup ketchup**
- ¾ **cup water**
- 2 **tablespoons vinegar**
- 2 **tablespoons Worcestershire sauce**
- 1 **teaspoon chili powder**
- 1 **teaspoon paprika**
- ½ **teaspoon cayenne pepper**

1. Place spareribs in a shallow roasting pan; sprinkle with salt and pepper. Top with onions. Cover and bake at 350° for 30 minutes; drain.

2. Combine the remaining ingredients; mix well. Pour over the spareribs. Cover and bake for 1 hour. Uncover and bake 15 minutes longer.

Southwestern Potpie with Cornmeal Biscuits

Brimming with pinto beans, chilies, jalapeno pepper and more, this spiced-up potpie is a surefire winner anytime. Cornmeal gives the cheesy biscuits on top a pleasant crunch.

—**ANDREA BOLDEN** UNIONVILLE, TN

PREP: 35 MIN. + SIMMERING • **BAKE:** 15 MIN. + STANDING **MAKES:** 12 SERVINGS

- ¼ **cup all-purpose flour**
- 1½ **pounds boneless pork loin roast, cut into ½-inch cubes**
- 2 **tablespoons butter**
- 1 **jalapeno pepper, seeded and chopped**
- 2 **garlic cloves, minced**
- 2 **cups beef broth**
- 1 **can (14½ ounces) diced tomatoes, undrained**
- 1 **teaspoon ground cumin**
- ½ **teaspoon chili powder**
- ¼ **to ½ teaspoon ground cinnamon**
- 1 **can (15¼ ounces) whole kernel corn, drained**
- 1 **can (15 ounces) pinto beans, rinsed and drained**
- 1 **can (4 ounces) chopped green chilies**

BISCUITS
- 3 **cups biscuit/baking mix**
- ¾ **cup cornmeal**
- ½ **cup shredded cheddar cheese**
- 4½ **teaspoons sugar**
- 1 **cup 2% milk**

1. Place the flour in a large resealable plastic bag. Add the pork roast, a few pieces at a time, and shake to coat. In a Dutch oven, brown the pork roast in butter in batches. Remove and set aside.

2. In same pan, saute the jalapeno and garlic in drippings 1 minute. Stir in the broth, tomatoes, cumin, chili powder, cinnamon and pork. Bring to a boil. Reduce the heat; cover and simmer 1 hour or until pork is tender.

3. Preheat oven to 400°. Add the corn, beans and chilies; heat through. Transfer to a greased 13x9x2-in. baking dish.

4. In a large bowl, combine biscuit mix, cornmeal, cheese and sugar; stir in milk just until moistened. Turn onto a lightly floured surface; knead 8-10 times.

5. Pat or roll out to ½-in. thickness; cut with a floured 2½-in. biscuit cutter. Arrange over mixture. Bake 15-18 minutes or until golden brown. Let stand 10 minutes before serving.

NOTE *Wear disposable gloves when cutting hot peppers; the oils can burn skin. Avoid touching your face.*

Marinated Pork Medallions

Gather just five simple ingredients, and you'll be well on your way to enjoying a mouthwatering entree from the grill.

—**MELANIE MILLER** BASCOM, OH

PREP: 15 MIN. + MARINATING • **GRILL:** 10 MIN. • **MAKES:** 5 SERVINGS

- ½ **cup packed brown sugar**
- ½ **cup Italian salad dressing**
- ¼ **cup unsweetened pineapple juice**
- 3 **tablespoons soy sauce**
- 2 **pork tenderloins (1 pound each), cut into ¾-inch slices**

1. In a small bowl, combine brown sugar, dressing, juice and soy sauce. Pour ½ cup marinade into a large resealable plastic bag. Add pork; seal bag and turn to coat. Refrigerate overnight. Cover and refrigerate remaining marinade.

2. Drain and discard the marinade. Moisten a paper towel with cooking oil; using long-handled tongs, rub on grill rack to coat lightly.

3. Grill the pork, covered, over medium heat or broil 4 in. from the heat for 5-7 minutes on each side or until a thermometer reads 145°, basting occasionally with the reserved marinade. Let stand 5 minutes before serving.

Sausage Spinach Pasta Bake, page 128

116

127

125

Poultry Entrees

When it comes to chicken and turkey dishes, why settle for ordinary? Serve up some **real showstoppers**—cheesy Italian pasta, bubbling casseroles, grilled tenderloins and more!

GRAND PRIZE

Chicken Florentine Meatballs

Served with noodle-like strands of spaghetti squash and a chunky tomato sauce, these tender meatballs add heartiness and savory flavor to a low-calorie Italian meal.

—DIANE NEMITZ LUDINGTON, MI

PREP: 40 MIN. • **COOK:** 20 MIN. • **MAKES:** 6 SERVINGS

- 2 eggs, lightly beaten
- 1 package (10 ounces) frozen chopped spinach, thawed and squeezed dry
- ½ cup dry bread crumbs
- ¼ cup grated Parmesan cheese
- 1 tablespoon dried minced onion
- 1 garlic clove, minced
- ¼ teaspoon salt
- ⅛ teaspoon pepper
- 1 pound ground chicken
- 1 medium spaghetti squash

SAUCE
- ½ pound sliced fresh mushrooms
- 2 teaspoons olive oil
- 1 can (14½ ounces) diced tomatoes, undrained
- 1 can (8 ounces) tomato sauce
- 2 tablespoons minced fresh parsley
- 1 garlic clove, minced
- 1 teaspoon dried oregano
- 1 teaspoon dried basil

1. In a large bowl, combine the first eight ingredients. Crumble chicken over mixture and mix well. Shape into 1½-in. balls.

2. Place the meatballs on a rack in a shallow baking pan. Bake, uncovered, at 400° for 20-25 minutes or until no longer pink. Meanwhile, cut squash in half lengthwise; discard the seeds. Place the squash cut side down on a microwave-safe plate. Microwave, uncovered, on high for 15-18 minutes or until tender.

3. For sauce, in a large nonstick skillet, saute mushrooms in oil until tender. Stir in the remaining ingredients. Bring to a boil. Reduce heat; simmer, uncovered, for 8-10 minutes or until slightly thickened. Add meatballs and heat through.

4. When the squash is cool enough to handle, use a fork to separate strands. Serve with meatballs and sauce.

NOTE *This recipe was tested in a 1,100-watt microwave.*
PER SERVING *303 cal., 12 g fat (3 g sat. fat), 123 mg chol., 617 mg sodium, 31 g carb., 7 g fiber, 22 g pro. Diabetic Exchanges: 3 lean meat, 2 starch, ½ fat.*

Thai Chicken Pasta

START TO FINISH: 25 MIN. • **MAKES:** 2 SERVINGS

- 3   ounces uncooked whole wheat linguine
- ½   cup salsa
- 2   tablespoons reduced-fat creamy peanut butter
- 1   tablespoon orange juice
- 1½ teaspoons honey
- 1   teaspoon reduced-sodium soy sauce
- 1   cup cubed cooked chicken breast
- 1   tablespoon chopped unsalted peanuts
- 1   tablespoon minced fresh cilantro

1. Cook the linguine according to the package directions.
2. Meanwhile, in a microwave-safe dish, combine the salsa, creamy peanut butter, orange juice, honey and soy sauce. Cover and microwave on high for 1 minute; stir. Add the chicken; heat through.
3. Drain linguine. Serve with chicken mixture. Garnish with peanuts and cilantro.
NOTE *This recipe was tested in a 1,100-watt microwave.*

Chicken in Wine Sauce

Plum wine and fresh mushrooms elevate this main course to a company-special entree. It's so quick and easy to fix, you can make it on a moment's notice when unexpected guests drop in.
—**KATHLEEN VALLE** PHILADELPHIA, PA

START TO FINISH: 25 MIN. • **MAKES:** 4 SERVINGS

- 4   boneless skinless chicken breast halves (5 ounces each)
- 1   egg
- 1   tablespoon water
- ¾   cup all-purpose flour
- ½   teaspoon salt
- ½   teaspoon pepper
- ¾   pound sliced fresh mushrooms
- ⅔   cup plum wine

1. Flatten chicken to ¼-in. thickness. In a shallow bowl, whisk the egg and water. In another shallow bowl, combine the flour, salt and pepper. Dip chicken in egg mixture, then coat with flour mixture.
2. In a large nonstick skillet coated with cooking spray, cook chicken over medium heat for 4-5 minutes on each side or until juices run clear. Remove and keep warm.
3. In the same skillet, saute the mushrooms until tender. Add the plum wine, stirring to loosen browned bits from the pan. Bring to a boil; cook until the liquid is reduced by half. Serve with the chicken.

Mediterranean Chicken with Spaghetti Squash

Brimming with classic Mediterranean ingredients, this recipe replaces pasta with strands of spaghetti squash.
—**JAYNE MARTIN** STRATHCLAIR, MB

PREP: 35 MIN. • **COOK:** 35 MIN. • **MAKES:** 6 SERVINGS

- 1 **medium spaghetti squash**
- 1½ **pounds boneless skinless chicken breasts, cut into ½-inch cubes**
- 5 **center-cut bacon strips, chopped**
- 1 **medium leek (white portion only), coarsely chopped**
- 4 **garlic cloves, minced**
- 3 **tablespoons all-purpose flour**
- 1 **cup reduced-sodium chicken broth**
- ½ **cup white wine or additional reduced-sodium chicken broth**
- ⅓ **cup half-and-half cream**
- 2 **plum tomatoes, chopped**
- 1 **can (2¼ ounces) sliced ripe olives, drained**
- ⅓ **cup grated Parmesan cheese**
- 1½ **teaspoons minced fresh sage or ½ teaspoon rubbed sage**
- 1 **teaspoon minced fresh thyme or ¼ teaspoon dried thyme**
- ½ **teaspoon salt**
- ⅛ **teaspoon pepper**

1. Cut the squash in half lengthwise; discard seeds. Place squash cut side down on a microwave-safe plate. Microwave, uncovered, on high for 15-18 minutes or until tender.
2. Meanwhile, in a large nonstick skillet coated with cooking spray, cook chicken over medium heat until no longer pink; drain. Remove from skillet.
3. In the same skillet, cook bacon and leek over medium heat until the bacon is crisp. Using a slotted spoon, remove the bacon mixture to paper towels. Add the garlic; cook for 1 minute. Stir in the flour until blended; gradually add the chicken broth, wine and cream. Bring to a boil; cook and stir for 1-2 minutes or until thickened. Stir in the remaining ingredients. Add chicken and bacon mixture; heat through.

4. When the squash is cool enough to handle, use a fork to separate strands. Serve with chicken mixture.
PER SERVING *340 cal., 12 g fat (4 g sat. fat), 82 mg chol., 656 mg sodium, 27 g carb., 5 g fiber, 30 g pro.* **Diabetic Exchanges:** *4 lean meat, 2 fat, 1½ starch.*

Louisiana Red Beans and Rice

Enjoy a slow-cooked version of a traditional New Orleans dish. Pepper flakes give it a nice zip, but if your family prefers a little extra heat, offer red pepper sauce at the table.
—**JULIA BUSHREE** COMMERCE CITY, CO

PREP: 20 MIN. • **COOK:** 8 HOURS • **MAKES:** 8 SERVINGS

- 4 **cans (16 ounces each) kidney beans, rinsed and drained**
- 1 **can (14½ ounces) diced tomatoes, undrained**
- 1 **package (14 ounces) smoked turkey sausage, sliced**
- 3 **celery ribs, chopped**
- 1 **large onion, chopped**
- 1 **cup chicken broth**
- 1 **medium green pepper, chopped**
- 1 **small sweet red pepper, chopped**
- 6 **garlic cloves, minced**
- 1 **bay leaf**
- ½ **teaspoon crushed red pepper flakes**
- 2 **green onions, chopped**
  Hot cooked rice

1. In a 4- or 5-qt. slow cooker, combine the first 11 ingredients. Cook, covered, on low 8-10 hours or until the vegetables are tender.
2. Stir before serving. Remove the bay leaf. Serve with green onions and rice.
FREEZE OPTION *Discard bay leaf and freeze cooled bean mixture in freezer containers. To use, partially thaw in refrigerator overnight. Heat through in a saucepan, stirring occasionally and adding a little broth or water if necessary. Serve as directed.*

Jerk Turkey Tenderloins

I think the tangy salsa for this turkey is best with fresh pineapple, but on really busy days, I've used canned tidbits with good results. The fruit flavor blends so well with the peppers, onion and garlic.

—**HOLLY BAUER** WEST BEND, WI

START TO FINISH: 30 MIN. • **MAKES:** 5 SERVINGS (2 CUPS SALSA)

- 1 **package (20 ounces) turkey breast tenderloins**
- ½ **teaspoon seasoned salt**
- 2 **tablespoons olive oil**
- 1 **tablespoon dried rosemary, crushed**
- 1 **tablespoon Caribbean jerk seasoning**
- 1 **tablespoon brown sugar**

SALSA

- 1½ **cups cubed fresh pineapple**
- 1 **medium sweet red pepper, chopped**
- ¼ **cup chopped red onion**
- ¼ **cup minced fresh cilantro**
- 1 **jalapeno pepper, seeded and minced**
- 2 **tablespoons lime juice**
- 2 **garlic cloves, minced**
- ¼ **teaspoon salt**
- ⅛ **teaspoon pepper**

1. Sprinkle the tenderloins with seasoned salt. Combine the oil, rosemary, jerk seasoning and brown sugar. Rub over the tenderloins. Broil 3-4 in. from the heat for 7-9 minutes on each side or until a thermometer reads 170°.

2. Meanwhile, in a large bowl, combine salsa ingredients. Serve with turkey.

NOTE *Wear disposable gloves when cutting hot peppers; the oils can burn skin. Avoid touching your face.*

PER SERVING *216 cal., 7 g fat (1 g sat. fat), 56 mg chol., 503 mg sodium, 12 g carb., 2 g fiber, 27 g pro.* ***Diabetic Exchanges:*** *3 lean meat, 1 vegetable, 1 fat, ½ fruit.*

FRUITY FLAIR

When I wanted a change of pace from traditional homemade salsa, I replaced the tomatoes with pitted fresh cherries that I coarsely chopped in the food processor. My family loves this fruit-filled variation served with our favorite chicken and pork dishes.

—**MARY ANN HENSINGER** OXFORD, MD

Chicken Stuffed with Walnuts, Apples & Brie

One afternoon when I was wondering what to make for dinner, I decided to try stuffed chicken. It turned out better than I expected! Now I pull out the recipe not only on weekdays, but on holidays when we want something a little different.

—NICOLE PAVELICH LEXINGTON, KY

PREP: 20 MIN. • **COOK:** 25 MIN.
MAKES: 2 SERVINGS

- ¼ cup chopped onion
- 3 tablespoons butter, divided
- ½ cup chopped peeled apple
- 2 tablespoons chopped walnuts, toasted
- ⅛ teaspoon dried rosemary, crushed
  Dash plus ¼ teaspoon salt, divided
  Dash plus ¼ teaspoon pepper, divided
- 2 boneless skinless chicken breast halves (6 ounces each)
- ⅛ teaspoon garlic powder
- 2 ounces Brie cheese, cubed
- ¼ cup cider vinegar
- ¾ cup unsweetened apple juice, divided
- 1½ teaspoons cornstarch

1. In a large skillet, saute the onion in 1 tablespoon butter for 1 minute. Add the apple; cook 2-3 minutes longer or until apple is golden brown. Remove from the heat; add walnuts, rosemary, and a dash of salt and pepper.

2. Flatten chicken to ¼-in. thickness; sprinkle with the garlic powder and remaining salt and pepper. Place the apple mixture and Brie on half of each chicken breast; fold the chicken over. Secure with toothpicks if necessary.

3. In the same skillet, brown chicken in remaining butter. Stir in the cider vinegar and ¼ cup apple juice. Bring to a boil. Reduce the heat; cover and cook for 15-20 minutes or until a thermometer reads 170°.

4. Remove the chicken to a serving platter; discard toothpicks. Combine the cornstarch and remaining apple juice; add to the pan. Bring to a boil; cook and stir for 2 minutes or until thickened. Serve with chicken.

BBQ Chicken Baked Potatoes

These baked potatoes are meals in themselves. The smoky barbecue taste is guaranteed to make mouths water! Top off each spud with crumbled blue cheese and green onions.

—**AMBER MASSEY** ARGYLE, TX

PREP: 15 MIN. • **COOK:** 6 HOURS
MAKES: 10 SERVINGS

- 4½ **pounds bone-in chicken breast halves, skin removed**
- 2 **tablespoons garlic powder**
- 1 **large red onion, sliced into thick rings**
- 1 **bottle (18 ounces) honey barbecue sauce**
- 1 **cup Italian salad dressing**
- ½ **cup packed brown sugar**
- ½ **cup cider vinegar**
- ¼ **cup Worcestershire sauce**
- 2 **tablespoons liquid smoke, optional**
- 10 **medium potatoes, baked**
  Crumbled blue cheese and chopped green onions, optional

1. Place the chicken in a greased 5- or 6-qt. slow cooker; sprinkle with garlic powder and top with red onion. Combine the barbecue sauce, salad dressing, brown sugar, cider vinegar, Worcestershire sauce and liquid smoke if desired; pour over chicken.
2. Cover; cook on low for 6-8 hours or until the chicken is tender. When cool enough to handle, remove the chicken from the bones; discard the bones and onion. Skim the fat from the cooking juices.
3. Shred the meat with two forks and return to slow cooker; heat through. Serve with potatoes, blue cheese and green onions if desired.

Margarita Chicken

The three-ingredient marinade for this grilled entree blends margarita mix, garlic and a splash of lime juice.

—**KELLY BRUNEMAN** CEDAR PARK, TX

PREP: 10 MIN. + MARINATING
GRILL: 10 MIN. • **MAKES:** 4 SERVINGS

- 1 **can (10 ounces) frozen non-alcoholic margarita mix, thawed**
- 3 **tablespoons lime juice**
- 3 **garlic cloves, minced**
- 4 **boneless skinless chicken breast halves (6 ounces each)**
- ¼ **teaspoon salt**
- ¼ **teaspoon pepper**

1. In a small bowl, combine the margarita mix, lime juice and garlic. Pour 1 cup marinade into a large resealable plastic bag. Add chicken; seal bag and turn to coat. Refrigerate for 2-4 hours. Cover and refrigerate remaining marinade.
2. Drain and discard the marinade. Sprinkle chicken with salt and pepper. Using long-handled tongs, moisten a paper towel with cooking oil and lightly coat the grill rack.
3. Grill the chicken, covered, over medium heat or broil 4 in. from the heat for 5-7 minutes on each side or until a thermometer reads 160°, basting frequently with the reserved marinade.
PER SERVING *251 cal., 4 g fat (1 g sat. fat), 94 mg chol., 230 mg sodium, 19 g carb., trace fiber, 34 g pro.* **Diabetic Exchanges:** *5 lean meat, 1 starch.*

[GRAND PRIZE]

Chicken Alfredo Stuffed Shells

Three kinds of cheese, hearty portobello mushrooms, a rich sauce—it's no wonder everyone loves these shells! To complete the meal, I add a simple green salad.

—MICHELE SHEPPARD MASONTOWN, PA

PREP: 45 MIN. • **BAKE:** 40 MIN.
MAKES: 10 SERVINGS

- 1 **package (12 ounces) jumbo pasta shells**
- 1½ **pounds boneless skinless chicken breasts, cut into ½-inch cubes**
- 2 **tablespoons olive oil, divided**
- ½ **pound sliced baby portobello mushrooms**
- 1 **egg, lightly beaten**
- 1 **carton (15 ounces) ricotta cheese**
- 3¼ **cups grated Parmesan cheese, divided**
- 1 **cup (4 ounces) shredded part-skim mozzarella cheese**
- 1 **teaspoon dried parsley flakes**
- ¾ **teaspoon salt**
- ½ **teaspoon pepper**
- ½ **cup butter, cubed**
- 2 **garlic cloves, minced**
- 2 **cups heavy whipping cream**

1. Cook the pasta according to the package directions.

2. Meanwhile, in a large skillet, brown chicken in 1 tablespoon oil. Remove and set aside. In the same pan, saute portobello mushrooms in remaining oil until tender; set aside. In a small bowl, combine the egg, ricotta cheese, 1½ cups Parmesan cheese, mozzarella cheese and seasonings.

3. Drain and rinse pasta with cold water; stuff each shell with about 1 tablespoon of cheese mixture. Place in a greased 13x9x2-in. baking dish. Top with chicken and mushrooms.

4. In a large saucepan over medium heat, melt the butter. Add the garlic; cook and stir for 1 minute. Add the cream; cook 5 minutes longer. Add 1½ cups Parmesan cheese; cook and stir until thickened.

5. Pour the sauce over the casserole. Sprinkle with remaining Parmesan. Cover and bake at 350° for 30 minutes. Uncover; bake 10-15 minutes longer or until bubbly.

FREEZE OPTION *Cover and freeze unbaked shells for up to 1 month. To use frozen shells, thaw in refrigerator. Let stand at room temperature for 30 minutes. Bake as directed.*

Spanish Turkey Tenderloins

If you're craving warm-weather fare, try this. The grilled turkey and colorful relish have the look and taste of summer.

—ROXANNE CHAN ALBANY, CA

PREP: 20 MIN. • **GRILL:** 15 MIN.
MAKES: 6 SERVINGS

- 1 **package (20 ounces) turkey breast tenderloins**
- 1 **tablespoon olive oil**
- ½ **teaspoon salt**
- ½ **teaspoon pepper**
- ¼ **teaspoon paprika**

RELISH

- 1 **plum tomato, chopped**
- 1 **large navel orange, peeled, sectioned and chopped**
- ¼ **cup sliced pimiento-stuffed olives**
- 1 **green onion, finely chopped**
- 2 **tablespoons minced fresh oregano or 2 teaspoons dried oregano**
- 2 **tablespoons sliced almonds**
- 2 **tablespoons minced fresh parsley**
- 1 **large garlic clove, minced**
- 1 **tablespoon capers, drained**
- 1 **teaspoon lemon juice**
- ½ **teaspoon grated lemon peel**
- ¼ **teaspoon salt**

1. Rub turkey with oil; sprinkle with salt, pepper and paprika.

2. Grill turkey, covered, over medium heat or broil 4 in. from the heat for 15-20 minutes or until a thermometer reads 170°, turning occasionally. Let stand for 5 minutes before slicing.

3. Meanwhile, in a small bowl, combine the relish ingredients. Serve with turkey.

PER SERVING *163 cal., 6 g fat (1 g sat. fat), 46 mg chol., 510 mg sodium, 6 g carb., 1 g fiber, 23 g pro.* **Diabetic Exchanges:** *3 lean meat, ½ starch, ½ fat.*

Mixed Paella

Feel free to skip the side dishes! Packed with chunks of chicken, shrimp, rice, tomatoes, peas and stuffed olives, paella will satisfy even the heartiest appetites at your table.

—LIBBY WALP CHICAGO, IL

START TO FINISH: 30 MIN.
MAKES: 6 SERVINGS

- 1¼ **pounds boneless skinless chicken breasts, thinly sliced**
- 2 **tablespoons olive oil**
- 1 **medium onion, chopped**
- 2 **garlic cloves, minced**
- 2¼ **cups chicken broth**
- 1 **cup uncooked long grain rice**
- 1 **teaspoon dried oregano**
- ½ **teaspoon ground turmeric**
- ½ **teaspoon paprika**
- ¼ **teaspoon salt**
- ¼ **to ½ teaspoon pepper**
- 1 **pound cooked medium shrimp, peeled and deveined**
- 1 **can (14½ ounces) diced tomatoes, undrained**
- ¾ **cup frozen peas, thawed**
- ½ **cup sliced pimiento-stuffed olives**

1. In a large skillet, saute chicken in oil until no longer pink. Remove and keep warm. In the same skillet, saute onion until tender. Add garlic; cook 1 minute longer. Stir in chicken broth, rice and seasonings. Bring to a boil. Reduce heat; cover and simmer for 15-18 minutes or until rice is tender.

2. Stir in the shrimp, tomatoes, peas, olives and chicken; cover and cook for 3-4 minutes or until heated through.

Smothered Home-Style Chicken

Gather your family around the table and dig in to a down-home supper of skillet chicken, rice and vegetables. With a creamy sauce on top, it's impossible to resist.

—BILLY HENSLEY MOUNT CARMEL, TN

START TO FINISH: 30 MIN. • **MAKES:** 5 SERVINGS

- ⅓ **cup all-purpose flour**
- 1 **teaspoon salt**
- 1 **teaspoon garlic powder**
- 1 **teaspoon Cajun seasoning**
- 1 **teaspoon pepper**
- 5 **boneless skinless chicken thighs (about 1½ pounds)**
- 3 **tablespoons olive oil, divided**
- 2 **medium carrots, chopped**
- 1 **small onion, chopped**
- ½ **cup chopped green pepper**
- 2 **garlic cloves, minced**
- ½ **cup white wine or chicken broth**
- 1 **can (10¾ ounces) condensed cream of chicken soup, undiluted**
- ½ **cup chicken broth**
  Hot cooked rice

1. In a large resealable plastic bag, combine the flour, salt, garlic powder, Cajun seasoning and pepper. Add chicken thighs, one at a time, and shake to coat. In a large skillet, brown the chicken in 2 tablespoons oil in batches. Remove and keep warm.
2. In same skillet, saute carrots, onion and green pepper in remaining oil until tender. Add the garlic; cook 1 minute. Add wine, stirring to loosen browned bits from pan. Stir in soup and broth.
3. Return chicken to skillet. Bring to a boil. Reduce heat; cover and simmer for 10-15 minutes or until a thermometer reads 165°. Serve with rice.

One-Pot Chili Penne

Here's one of my mainstays on busy weeknights. I love the fact that I don't have to make the pasta separately—it cooks right in the chili. And that means one less pot to wash!

—DAWN FORSBERG ST. JOSEPH, MO

PREP: 25 MIN. • **COOK:** 15 MIN. • **MAKES:** 6 SERVINGS (2 QUARTS)

- 1 **pound lean ground turkey**
- 1 **small onion, chopped**
- ¼ **cup chopped green pepper**
- 1 **teaspoon olive oil**
- 2 **cups water**
- 1 **can (15 ounces) pinto beans, rinsed and drained**
- 1 **can (14½ ounces) reduced-sodium beef broth**
- 1 **can (14½ ounces) diced tomatoes with mild green chilies, undrained**
- 1 **can (8 ounces) no-salt-added tomato sauce**
- 2 **teaspoons chili powder**
- 1 **teaspoon ground cumin**
- ½ **teaspoon dried oregano**
- 2 **cups uncooked multigrain penne pasta**
- ¼ **cup reduced-fat sour cream**
- ¼ **cup minced fresh cilantro**

1. In a large saucepan coated with cooking spray, cook the turkey, onion and pepper in the oil over medium heat until meat is no longer pink, breaking meat into crumbles; drain.
2. Stir in the water, beans, broth, tomatoes, tomato sauce, chili powder, cumin and oregano. Bring to a boil. Add pasta; cook for 15-20 minutes or until tender, stirring occasionally. Serve with sour cream; sprinkle with cilantro.
PER SERVING *384 cal., 10 g fat (2 g sat. fat), 64 mg chol., 598 mg sodium, 47 g carb., 8 g fiber, 25 g pro.* **Diabetic Exchanges:** *3 starch, 2 lean meat, 1 vegetable.*

Potato-Crusted Chicken Casserole

Thinly sliced potatoes form the bottom layer of this comforting vegetable-filled casserole. For the finishing touch, I sprinkle on a crunchy bread-crumb topping that bakes up golden brown. The bonus? Each serving has fewer than 350 calories!

—**BECKY MATHENY** STRASBURG, VA

PREP: 30 MIN. • **BAKE:** 40 MIN. • **MAKES:** 6 SERVINGS

- 1 large potato, thinly sliced
- 1 tablespoon olive oil
- ½ teaspoon salt
- ¼ teaspoon pepper

FILLING

- 1½ pounds chicken tenderloins, cut into ½-inch cubes
- 2 teaspoons olive oil
- 1 medium onion, chopped
- 1 tablespoon butter
- 2 tablespoons all-purpose flour
- 1½ cups fat-free milk
- ¼ cup shredded part-skim mozzarella cheese
- ¼ cup grated Parmesan cheese
- 2 tablespoons shredded reduced-fat cheddar cheese
- 2 cups frozen peas and carrots
- ½ teaspoon salt
- ½ teaspoon dried thyme
- ¼ teaspoon dried basil
  Dash rubbed sage

CRUMB TOPPING

- 1 cup soft bread crumbs
- 1 tablespoon butter, melted
- ½ teaspoon garlic powder

1. In a large bowl, toss the potato slices with oil, salt and pepper. Arrange the slices onto the bottom and sides of an 11x7-in. baking dish coated with cooking spray. Bake at 400° for 20-25 minutes or until potatoes are tender. Reduce the heat to 350°.

2. Meanwhile, for the filling, in a large skillet over medium heat, cook the chicken in oil until no longer pink. Remove from the skillet. In the same skillet, saute onion in butter. Stir in the flour until blended; gradually add milk. Bring to a boil; cook and stir for 2 minutes or until thickened. Reduce the heat; stir in mozzarella, Parmesan and cheddar cheeses until melted. Stir in vegetables, seasonings and chicken. Spoon into potato crust.

3. Combine the topping ingredients; sprinkle over chicken mixture. Bake, uncovered, for 40-45 minutes or until bubbly and topping is golden brown.

PER SERVING 340 cal., 11 g fat (4 g sat. fat), 85 mg chol., 674 mg sodium, 28 g carb., 3 g fiber, 35 g pro. **Diabetic Exchanges:** 4 lean meat, 2 starch, 1 fat.

Saucy Garlic Chicken

When I'm having dinner guests, I rely on this go-to recipe. I can assemble it ahead of time and pop it into the oven when my company arrives. With roasted garlic, spinach and a bed of pasta, the meal-in-one entree always goes over well.

—**JOANNA JOHNSON** FLOWER MOUND, TX

PREP: 40 MIN. + COOLING • **BAKE:** 35 MIN. • **MAKES:** 6 SERVINGS

- 4 whole garlic bulbs
- 2 tablespoons olive oil, divided
- 1 package (9 ounces) fresh baby spinach
- ¾ teaspoon salt, divided
- ½ teaspoon coarsely ground pepper, divided
- 6 boneless skinless chicken breast halves (6 ounces each)
- 6 tablespoons butter, cubed
- 6 tablespoons all-purpose flour
- 3 cups 2% milk
- 2½ cups grated Parmesan cheese, divided
- ⅛ teaspoon nutmeg
  Hot cooked pasta
  Chopped tomato and minced fresh parsley, optional

1. Remove the papery outer skin from the garlic (do not peel or separate the cloves). Cut the tops off the garlic bulbs; brush the bulbs with 1 tablespoon oil. Wrap each bulb in heavy-duty foil. Bake at 425° for 30-35 minutes or until softened. Cool for 10-15 minutes.

2. Meanwhile, place the spinach in a greased 13x9x2-in. baking dish; sprinkle with ¼ teaspoon each of salt and pepper. In a large skillet, brown the chicken in remaining oil on both sides; place over spinach.

3. In a large saucepan, melt the butter. Stir in flour until smooth; gradually add milk. Bring to a boil; cook and stir for 1-2 minutes or until thickened. Stir in 2 cups Parmesan cheese, nutmeg and remaining salt and pepper.

4. Transfer to a blender; squeeze the softened garlic into the blender. Cover and process until smooth. Pour mixture over the chicken.

5. Cover and bake at 425° for 30-35 minutes or until a thermometer reads 170° and the sauce is bubbly. Uncover; sprinkle with remaining Parmesan cheese. Bake 5 minutes longer. Serve with the pasta. Sprinkle with tomato and parsley if desired.

Jamaica-Me-Crazy Chicken Tropicale

PREP: 25 MIN. • **COOK:** 5 HOURS
MAKES: 4 SERVINGS

- 3 **medium sweet potatoes, peeled and cut into 2-inch pieces**
- 1 **can (8 ounces) sliced water chestnuts, drained**
- 1 **cup dried cranberries**
- 1 **can (20 ounces) unsweetened pineapple tidbits**
- 2 **pounds bone-in chicken breast halves, skin removed**
- 2 **tablespoons Caribbean jerk seasoning**
- ¼ **cup dried minced onion**
- 3 **tablespoons minced fresh gingerroot**
- 2 **tablespoons Worcestershire sauce**
- 1 **tablespoon grated lime peel**
- 1 **teaspoon cumin seeds, crushed**
- 3 **fresh thyme sprigs**
  Hot cooked rice

1. Place the sweet potatoes in a 4- or 5-qt. slow cooker. Add water chestnuts and dried cranberries. Drain the pineapple, reserving the juice; add the pineapple to the slow cooker. Top with chicken. Sprinkle jerk seasoning over the chicken.

2. Combine minced onion, ginger, Worcestershire sauce, lime peel, cumin seeds and reserved pineapple juice. Pour over the chicken. Top with thyme sprigs.

3. Cover; cook on low for 5-6 hours or until chicken and vegetables are tender. Serve with rice.

"About half an hour before my Jamaican-style supper comes out of the slow cooker, I sample the sauce and add seasonings to taste. If you like, thicken it a bit with a tablespoon of cornstarch."

—**MARY LOUISE LEVER** ROME, GA

Chicken Casserole Supreme

One of my favorite comfort foods on a chilly day is chicken casserole. I tossed in some golden raisins and chopped apple once on a whim, and now I add those ingredients all the time.

—**JUDY WILSON** SUN CITY WEST, AZ

PREP: 40 MIN. • **BAKE:** 20 MIN.
MAKES: 6 SERVINGS

- 1 cup reduced-sodium chicken broth
- 1 medium apple, peeled and chopped
- ½ cup golden raisins
- 1 tablespoon butter
- 1 package (6 ounces) reduced-sodium stuffing mix
- 1 pound boneless skinless chicken breasts, cubed
- ¼ teaspoon salt
- ¼ teaspoon pepper
- 1 cup sliced fresh mushrooms
- 1 small onion, chopped
- 1 tablespoon olive oil
- 3 garlic cloves, minced

- 1½ cups (12 ounces) fat-free sour cream
- 1 can (10¾ ounces) reduced-fat reduced-sodium condensed cream of mushroom soup, undiluted
- 4 cups frozen broccoli florets, thawed

1. In a large saucepan, combine the broth, apple and raisins. Bring to a boil. Reduce heat; simmer, uncovered, for 3-4 minutes or until the apple is tender. Stir in butter and stuffing mix. Remove from the heat; cover and let stand for 5 minutes.

2. Sprinkle chicken with salt and pepper. In a large skillet, cook the chicken, mushrooms and onion in oil over medium heat until chicken is no longer pink. Add garlic; cook 1 minute longer. Remove from the heat. Stir in sour cream and soup.

3. Transfer to a 13x9x2-in. baking dish coated with cooking spray. Layer with broccoli and stuffing mixture. Bake, uncovered, at 350° for 20-25 minutes or until heated through.

Hungarian Chicken

Looking through an old church cookbook, I discovered this hearty home-style recipe. It's become a popular choice for both weeknights and special occasions.

—**CRYSTAL GARZA** SHAMROCK, TX

PREP: 10 MIN. • **COOK:** 1 HOUR
MAKES: 4-6 SERVINGS

- 6 tablespoons all-purpose flour
  Salt and pepper to taste
- 1 broiler/fryer chicken (about 3½ pounds), cut up
- ¼ cup butter, divided
- 1 large onion, chopped
- ⅔ cup tomato juice
- 1 to 2 tablespoons paprika
- 1 teaspoon sugar
- 1 teaspoon salt
- 1 bay leaf
- ⅔ cup chicken broth
- ⅔ cup sour cream
  Hot cooked egg noodles

1. Combine the flour, salt and pepper in a large resealable plastic bag. Add the chicken, a few pieces at a time, and shake to coat.

2. Melt 1 tablespoon butter in a large skillet. Add the onion and cook until tender. Remove from the pan and set aside. In the same skillet, melt the remaining butter and brown chicken on all sides.

3. Combine the tomato juice, paprika, sugar and salt; add to the chicken. Add the bay leaf, chicken broth and onion. Cover and simmer 45-60 minutes or until chicken is tender.

4. Remove chicken to a platter; keep warm. Reduce the heat to low, remove the bay leaf and stir in the sour cream. Heat through (do not boil). Pour sauce over chicken. Serve with noodles.

Bacon & Rosemary Chicken

Bacon makes just about everything better! Combined with lots of fresh garlic, rosemary, red pepper and lemon juice, it lends fantastic flavor to this 30-minute skillet entree.

—**YVONNE STARLIN** HERMITAGE, TN

START TO FINISH: 30 MIN. • **MAKES:** 4 SERVINGS

- 4 **boneless skinless chicken breast halves (5 ounces each)**
- ½ **teaspoon salt**
- ¼ **teaspoon pepper**
- ¼ **cup all-purpose flour**
- 5 **bacon strips, chopped**
- 1 **tablespoon butter**
- 4 **garlic cloves, thinly sliced**
- 1 **tablespoon minced fresh rosemary or 1 teaspoon dried rosemary, crushed**
- ⅛ **teaspoon crushed red pepper flakes**
- 1 **cup reduced-sodium chicken broth**
- 2 **tablespoons lemon juice**

1. Pound the chicken breasts slightly with a meat mallet to uniform thickness; sprinkle with salt and pepper. Place flour in a shallow bowl. Dip chicken in flour to coat both sides; shake off excess.

2. In a large skillet, cook bacon over medium heat until crisp, stirring occasionally. Remove with a slotted spoon; drain on paper towels. Discard bacon drippings, reserving 2 tablespoons in pan. Cook chicken in butter and reserved drippings 4-6 minutes on each side or until a thermometer reads 165°. Remove and keep warm.

3. Add the garlic, rosemary and red pepper flakes to the skillet; cook and stir 1 minute. Add the chicken broth and lemon juice; bring to a boil. Cook until the liquid is reduced by half. Return chicken and bacon to skillet; heat through.

Grilled Caesar Chicken Breasts

This recipe was a big hit when I served it to my foodie friends, who were surprised to discover it requires just five ingredients. Marinated overnight in a creamy blend featuring Caesar salad dressing, the meat grills up juicy and delicious.

—**MARCIA WALLENFELDT** KENT, OH

PREP: 10 MIN. + MARINATING • **GRILL:** 15 MIN. • **MAKES:** 4 SERVINGS

- ½ **cup creamy Caesar salad dressing**
- 3 **tablespoons olive oil**
- 3 **tablespoons Dijon mustard**
- 6 **garlic cloves, minced**
- 4 **boneless skinless chicken breast halves (5 ounces each)**

1. In a large resealable plastic bag, combine the Caesar salad dressing, olive oil, Dijon mustard and garlic. Add the chicken; seal the bag and turn to coat. Refrigerate for 8 hours or overnight.

2. Drain and discard marinade. Grill chicken, covered, over medium heat or broil 4 in. from the heat for 6-8 minutes on each side or until a thermometer reads 170°.

Quick Chicken and Dumplings

I love the versatility and convenience of frozen biscuits. They make short work of preparing chicken and dumplings.

—**LAKEYA ASTWOOD** SCHENECTADY, NY

START TO FINISH: 30 MIN. • **MAKES:** 6 SERVINGS

- 6 **individually frozen biscuits**
- ¼ **cup chopped onion**
- ¼ **cup chopped green pepper**
- 1 **tablespoon olive oil**
- 4 **cups shredded rotisserie chicken**
- 2 **cans (14½ ounces each) reduced-sodium chicken broth**
- 1 **can (4 ounces) mushroom stems and pieces, drained**
- 1 **teaspoon chicken bouillon granules**
- 1 **teaspoon minced fresh parsley**
- ½ **teaspoon dried sage leaves**
- ¼ **teaspoon dried rosemary, crushed**
- ¼ **teaspoon pepper**

1. Cut each biscuit into fourths and set aside. In a large saucepan, saute the onion and green pepper in oil until tender. Stir in the shredded rotisserie chicken, chicken broth, mushrooms, chicken bouillon granules, parsley, sage, rosemary and pepper.

2. Bring to a boil. Reduce the heat; add the biscuits for the dumplings. Cover and simmer for 10 minutes or until a toothpick inserted near the center of a dumpling comes out clean (do not lift cover while simmering).

Sausage Spinach Pasta Bake

Sometimes I add green beans, summer squash, zucchini or mushrooms to this cheesy casserole. You could also replace the turkey sausage with chicken sausage, ground pork or veal.

—KIM FORNI LACONIA, NH

PREP: 35 MIN. • **BAKE:** 25 MIN.
MAKES: 10 SERVINGS

- 1 **package (16 ounces) whole wheat spiral pasta**
- 1 **pound Italian turkey sausage links, casings removed**
- 1 **medium onion, chopped**
- 5 **garlic cloves, minced**
- 1 **can (28 ounces) crushed tomatoes**
- 1 **can (14½ ounces) diced tomatoes, undrained**
- 1 **teaspoon dried oregano**
- 1 **teaspoon dried basil**
- ¼ **teaspoon pepper**
- 1 **package (10 ounces) frozen chopped spinach, thawed and squeezed dry**
- ½ **cup half-and-half cream**
- 2 **cups (8 ounces) shredded part-skim mozzarella cheese**
- ½ **cup grated Parmesan cheese**

1. Preheat oven to 350°. Cook the whole wheat spiral pasta according to the package directions.

2. Meanwhile, in a large skillet, cook turkey and onion over medium heat until meat is no longer pink. Add garlic. Cook 1 minute longer; drain. Stir in tomatoes, oregano, basil and pepper. Bring to a boil. Reduce heat; simmer, uncovered, 10 minutes.

3. Drain pasta; stir into turkey mixture. Add spinach and cream; heat through. Transfer to a 13x9x2-in. baking dish coated with cooking spray. Sprinkle with the cheeses. Bake, uncovered, 25-30 minutes or until golden brown.

PER SERVING *377 cal., 11 g fat (5 g sat. fat), 50 mg chol., 622 mg sodium, 45 g carb., 8 g fiber, 25 g pro.* **Diabetic Exchanges:** *3 lean meat, 2 starch, 2 vegetable, ½ fat.*

Deep-Dish Chicken Pizza

I've been making this deep-dish pizza for my family for decades. It's the only one we eat! For a delicious pie that's a little bit lighter, try it meatless.

—**EDWARD SMULSKI** LYONS, IL

PREP: 20 MIN. + RISING
BAKE: 25 MIN. + STANDING
MAKES: 12 PIECES

- 1 **package (16 ounces) hot roll mix**
- 1 **pound boneless skinless chicken breasts, cut into ½-inch cubes**
- 2 **tablespoons olive oil, divided**
- ½ **pound sliced fresh mushrooms**
- 1 **large sweet red pepper, cut into strips**
- 1 **large green pepper, cut into strips**
- 1 **medium onion, sliced**
- ½ **teaspoon Italian seasoning**
- ¼ **teaspoon dried basil**
- ¼ **teaspoon dried oregano**
- ¼ **teaspoon pepper**
- 1 **jar (14 ounces) pizza sauce**
- 2 **cups (8 ounces) shredded part-skim mozzarella cheese**
- 1 **cup grated Parmesan cheese**

1. Prepare mix according to package directions. Meanwhile, in a large skillet over medium heat, cook chicken in 1 tablespoon oil until no longer pink. Remove chicken and keep warm.
2. In same skillet, saute mushrooms, peppers, onion and seasonings in the remaining oil until the vegetables are tender. Return chicken to pan.
3. Roll the dough into a 17x12-in. rectangle. Transfer dough to a greased 15x10x1-in. baking pan; build up edges slightly. Spread the sauce over dough. Top with chicken mixture and cheeses.
4. Wrap and freeze for up to 2 months or bake at 375° for 25-30 minutes or until the crust and cheeses are lightly browned. Let stand for 10 minutes before serving.

TO USE FROZEN PIZZA *Thaw in the refrigerator. Uncover; bake at 375° for 25-30 minutes or until golden brown. Let stand for 10 minutes before serving.*
PER SERVING *328 cal., 12 g fat (5 g sat. fat), 60 mg chol., 598 mg sodium, 33 g carb., 2 g fiber, 21 g pro.* **Diabetic Exchanges:** *2 starch, 2 medium-fat meat, 1 fat.*

Peanut Chicken Stir-Fry

Here's a wonderful alternative to takeout. The colorful, satisfying stir-fry is ready to enjoy in just half an hour.

—**LISA ERICKSON** RIPON, WI

START TO FINISH: 30 MIN.
MAKES: 6 SERVINGS

- 8 **ounces uncooked thick rice noodles**
- ⅓ **cup water**
- ¼ **cup reduced-sodium soy sauce**
- ¼ **cup peanut butter**
- 4½ **teaspoons brown sugar**
- 1 **tablespoon lemon juice**
- 2 **garlic cloves, minced**
- ½ **teaspoon crushed red pepper flakes**
- 1 **pound boneless skinless chicken breasts, cut into ½-inch strips**
- 2 **tablespoons canola oil, divided**
- 1 **bunch broccoli, cut into florets**
- ½ **cup shredded carrot**

1. Cook the rice noodles according to the package directions. Meanwhile, in a small bowl, combine the water, soy sauce, peanut butter, brown sugar, lemon juice, garlic and red pepper flakes; set aside.
2. In a large skillet or wok, stir-fry chicken in 1 tablespoon oil until no longer pink. Remove and keep warm. Stir-fry the broccoli and carrot in the remaining oil for 4-6 minutes or until the vegetables are crisp-tender. Stir the sauce mixture; add the sauce and chicken to the skillet. Return chicken to skillet. Drain the noodles; toss with chicken mixture.

PER SERVING *361 cal., 13 g fat (2 g sat. fat), 42 mg chol., 525 mg sodium, 40 g carb., 5 g fiber, 24 g pro.* **Diabetic Exchanges:** *2 starch, 2 lean meat, 2 fat, 1 vegetable.*

Chicken in Puff Pastry

I've prepared this easy entree countless times, but I still marvel at how just puff pastry and a handful of other ingredients can create such a special dish. It's always an impressive, delicious main course.

—**GINA HOBBS** TIFTON, GA

PREP: 15 MIN. • **BAKE:** 20 MIN.
MAKES: 4 SERVINGS

4	**chicken tenderloins**
⅛	**teaspoon salt**
⅛	**teaspoon pepper**
1	**sheet frozen puff pastry, thawed**
½	**cup spreadable spinach and artichoke cream cheese**
4	**slices Muenster cheese, halved**
1	**egg**
1	**tablespoon water**

1. Sprinkle chicken with salt and pepper; set aside. On a lightly floured surface, roll puff pastry into a 14-in. square. Cut into four squares.
2. Spoon 2 tablespoons cream cheese into the center of each square; top with Muenster cheese and chicken.
3. Whisk egg and water; lightly brush over edges. Bring opposite corners of pastry over each bundle; pinch seams to seal. Place seam side down on a greased baking sheet; brush with remaining egg mixture.
4. Bake at 400° for 18-22 minutes or until golden brown.

GRAND PRIZE WINNER

GRAND PRIZE

Stuffed-Crust Chicken Pizza

If you've wanted to try making your own stuffed-crust pizza at home, here's the recipe for you! Convenient string cheese is the ooey-gooey secret ingredient.

—**PAM BROOKS** SOUTH BERWICK, ME

PREP: 35 MIN. • **BAKE:** 10 MIN.
MAKES: 12 PIECES

2	**tubes (13.8 ounces each) refrigerated pizza crust**
10	**pieces string cheese**
½	**pound boneless skinless chicken breasts, cut into ½-inch cubes**
1	**small onion, chopped**
2	**tablespoons olive oil**
3	**garlic cloves, minced**
½	**cup oil-packed sun-dried tomatoes, julienned**
1	**teaspoon dried rosemary, crushed**
½	**teaspoon salt**
½	**teaspoon pepper**
¾	**cup pizza sauce**
2	**cups (8 ounces) shredded part-skim mozzarella cheese**
½	**cup pitted ripe olives, chopped**

1. Preheat oven to 425°. Unroll both pizza crusts and place in a greased 15x10x1-in. baking pan, letting dough drape 1 in. over the edges. Pinch center seam to seal.
2. Place string cheese around edges of pan. Fold dough over cheese; pinch to seal. Bake 5 minutes.
3. Meanwhile, in a large skillet, saute the chicken and onion in the oil until chicken is no longer pink. Add garlic; cook 1 minute longer. Stir in tomatoes, rosemary, salt and pepper.
4. Spread pizza sauce over the crust. Top with chicken mixture. Sprinkle with mozzarella and olives.
5. Bake 10-15 minutes or until cheese is melted and crust is golden brown.

Chicken Enchilada Casserole

PREP: 30 MIN. • **BAKE:** 30 MIN.
MAKES: 6 SERVINGS

- 1 large onion, chopped
- 1 medium green pepper, chopped
- 1 teaspoon butter
- 3 cups shredded cooked chicken breast
- 2 cans (4 ounces each) chopped green chilies
- ¼ cup all-purpose flour
- 1½ to 2 teaspoons ground coriander
- 2½ cups reduced-sodium chicken broth
- 1 cup (8 ounces) reduced-fat sour cream
- 1 cup (4 ounces) reduced-fat Monterey Jack or reduced-fat Mexican cheese blend, divided
- 12 corn tortillas (6 inches), warmed

1. In a small skillet, saute onion and green pepper in butter until tender. In a large bowl, combine the chicken, green chilies and onion mixture.

2. In a small saucepan, combine the flour and coriander. Add the broth; stir until smooth. Cook and stir over medium heat until the mixture comes to a boil. Cook and stir 1-2 minutes longer or until thickened. Remove from the heat; stir in the sour cream and ½ cup cheese. Stir ¾ cup sauce into chicken mixture.

3. Place ⅓ cup chicken mixture down the center of each corn tortilla. Roll up the corn tortillas and place seam side down in a 13x9x2-in. baking dish coated with cooking spray. Pour the remaining sauce over top; sprinkle with remaining cheese. Bake, uncovered, at 350° for 30-35 minutes or until heated through.

PER SERVING *383 cal., 12 g fat (6 g sat. fat), 82 mg chol., 710 mg sodium, 37 g carb., 5 g fiber, 33 g pro.* **Diabetic Exchanges:** *4 lean meat, 2 starch, 1 fat.*

"Love Mexican food but looking to cut fat and calories? Chicken Enchilada Casserole is a little bit lighter but has all the spicy, saucy, cheesy goodness you crave."

—**AMY JOHNSON** NEW BRAUNFELS, TX

Chicken Mole Ole

PREP: 40 MIN. • **COOK:** 4 HOURS • **MAKES:** 6 SERVINGS

- 2 dried ancho chilies
- 1½ pounds tomatillos, husks removed, halved
- 2 medium onions, sliced, divided
- 1 serrano pepper, halved and seeded
- 3 garlic cloves, peeled
- 3 pounds bone-in chicken breast halves, skin removed
- 1 tablespoon canola oil
- 2 teaspoons ground cumin, divided
- 1½ teaspoons chili powder
- 1 teaspoon pepper
- ¼ teaspoon ground cinnamon
- 2 whole cloves
- ½ cup almonds
- 1 ounce unsweetened chocolate, chopped
- 1 tablespoon lime juice
- 1 teaspoon salt
- 1½ cups (6 ounces) shredded cheddar-Monterey Jack cheese
- ½ cup minced fresh cilantro

1. Place chilies in a small bowl. Cover with boiling water; let stand for 20 minutes. Drain. Remove stems and seeds. Coarsely chop; set aside. Place the tomatillos, 1 onion, serrano pepper and garlic in a greased 15x10x1-in. baking pan. Bake, uncovered, at 400° for 10-15 minutes or until tender, stirring once.

2. In a large skillet, brown the chicken in oil. Transfer to a 4-qt. slow cooker. In the same skillet, saute the remaining onion until tender. Add 1 teaspoon cumin, chili powder, pepper, cinnamon, cloves and hydrated chilies; cook 1 minute longer. Discard cloves.

3. Place the almonds in a food processor; cover and process until ground. Add spiced onion mixture and unsweetened chocolate; cover and process until blended. Transfer to a small bowl.

4. Place tomatillo mixture, lime juice, salt and remaining cumin in food processor; cover and process until chopped. Stir into almond mixture. Pour over chicken. Cover and cook on low for 4 to 5 hours or until chicken is tender. Sprinkle each serving with cheese and cilantro.

NOTE *Wear disposable gloves when cutting hot peppers; the oils can burn skin. Avoid touching your face.*

Chicken with Cranberry-Balsamic Sauce

GRAND PRIZE

With a sauce of cranberries and balsamic vinegar, this entree is especially nice during fall and winter. Sometimes I serve polenta or a scoop of brown or wild rice on the side.

—**SUSAN CORTESI** NORTHBROOK, IL

PREP: 20 MIN. • **BAKE:** 15 MIN. • **MAKES:** 4 SERVINGS

- 4 boneless skinless chicken breast halves (6 ounces each)
- 1¼ teaspoons salt, divided
- ½ teaspoon pepper
- 1 tablespoon olive oil
- 1 cup cranberry juice
- ⅓ cup balsamic vinegar
- ¼ cup whole-berry cranberry sauce
- 2 tablespoons finely chopped shallot
- 3 tablespoons butter

1. Sprinkle chicken with 1 teaspoon salt and the pepper. In a large skillet, brown the chicken in oil on both sides. Transfer to a greased 13x9x2-in. baking pan. Bake at 425° for 12-15 minutes or until a thermometer reads 170°.

2. Add the cranberry juice, vinegar, cranberry sauce and shallot to the skillet, stirring to loosen browned bits from pan. Bring to a boil; cook until liquid is reduced to about ½ cup. Stir in butter and remaining salt until butter is melted. Serve with chicken.

GRAND PRIZE
WINNER
★ ★ ★ ★

Greek Pizzas

Top herbed flatbread wraps with feta cheese, Greek vinaigrette, chicken and more, then pop the pies into the oven. Pizza night may never be the same!
—**CATHI SCHUETT** OMAHA, NE

START TO FINISH: 20 MIN.
MAKES: 4 SERVINGS

 2 **Italian herb flatbread wraps**
 1 **tablespoon Greek vinaigrette**
 ½ **cup crumbled feta cheese**
 ¼ **cup grated Parmesan cheese**
 ½ **cup pitted Greek olives, sliced**
 ½ **cup water-packed artichoke hearts, rinsed, drained and chopped**
 ½ **cup ready-to-use grilled chicken breast strips, chopped**
 ⅛ **teaspoon dried oregano**
 ⅛ **teaspoon dried basil**
    Dash pepper
 1 **cup (4 ounces) shredded part-skim mozzarella cheese**

1. Place the flatbread wraps on an ungreased baking sheet; brush with the Greek vinaigrette. Layer with the remaining ingredients.
2. Bake at 400° for 8-10 minutes or until the cheese is melted.

Chicken & Vegetable Stir-Fry

When you want a light but satisfying one-dish meal, it's hard to beat a stir-fry. This recipe is loaded with different tastes and textures. Adjust the amount of pepper flakes to suit your heat preference.
—**SAMUEL ONIZUK** ELKTON, MD

PREP: 20 MIN. • **COOK:** 15 MIN.
MAKES: 5 SERVINGS

 4 **teaspoons cornstarch**
 1 **cup reduced-sodium chicken broth**
 2 **tablespoons reduced-sodium soy sauce**
 1 **pound boneless skinless chicken breasts, cut into ¼-inch strips**
 2 **tablespoons olive oil, divided**
 1½ **cups fresh cauliflowerets**
 1½ **cups fresh broccoli florets**
 2 **medium carrots, sliced**
 1 **small sweet red pepper, julienned**
 1 **small onion, halved and sliced**
 1 **garlic clove, minced**
 ½ **teaspoon salt**
 ½ **teaspoon pepper**
 ¼ to ½ **teaspoon crushed red pepper flakes**
 2½ **cups hot cooked rice**
    Minced fresh cilantro

1. Combine the cornstarch, broth and soy sauce until smooth; set aside.
2. In a large nonstick skillet or wok, stir-fry the chicken in 1 tablespoon oil until no longer pink. Remove chicken and keep warm.
3. Stir-fry the cauliflower, broccoli, carrots, red pepper and onion in the remaining oil until crisp-tender. Add the garlic, salt, pepper and red pepper flakes; cook 1 minute longer.
4. Stir cornstarch mixture and add to the pan. Bring to a boil; cook and stir for 2 minutes or until thickened. Add chicken; heat through. Serve with rice. Sprinkle each serving with cilantro.
PER SERVING *297 cal., 8 g fat (1 g sat. fat), 50 mg chol., 670 mg sodium, 32 g carb., 3 g fiber, 23 g pro.* **Diabetic Exchanges:** *2 lean meat, 1½ starch, 1 vegetable, 1 fat.*

Poblanos Stuffed with Chipotle Turkey Chili

As an emergency room doctor, I stay pretty busy. At home, I like to unwind by cooking dishes that are healthy but full of flavor. My chili featuring lean ground turkey gets a nice boost from adobo sauce and two kinds of hot peppers.

—**SONALI RUDER** NEW YORK, NY

PREP: 35 MIN. • **BAKE:** 10 MIN.
MAKES: 4 SERVINGS

- 8 **poblano peppers**
- 1 **package (20 ounces) lean ground turkey**
- 1 **medium onion, chopped**
- 3 **garlic cloves, minced**
- 2 **teaspoons olive oil**
- 1 **can (14½ ounces) fire-roasted diced tomatoes, undrained**
- 1 **can (8¾ ounces) whole kernel corn, drained**
- 1 **tablespoon minced chipotle pepper in adobo sauce**
- 2 **teaspoons adobo sauce**
- ½ **teaspoon salt**
- ½ **teaspoon ground cumin**
- ½ **teaspoon chili powder**
- ¼ **teaspoon pepper**
- 3 **tablespoons minced fresh cilantro, divided**
- 1 **cup (4 ounces) shredded Mexican cheese blend**
- ½ **cup reduced-fat sour cream**

1. Broil the poblano peppers 4 in. from the heat until the skins blister, about 5 minutes. With tongs, rotate the peppers a quarter turn. Broil and rotate until all sides are blistered and blackened. Immediately place the peppers in a large bowl; cover and let stand for 20 minutes.

2. Meanwhile, in a large nonstick skillet over medium heat, cook the turkey, onion and garlic in oil until the meat is no longer pink, breaking meat into crumbles; drain. Add the fire-roasted tomatoes, corn, chipotle, adobo sauce, salt, cumin, chili powder and pepper; heat through. Remove from the heat; stir in 2 tablespoons cilantro. Set aside.

3. Peel off and discard the charred skins from the poblano peppers. Cut a lengthwise slit down each pepper, leaving the stem intact; remove the membranes and seeds. Fill each pepper with ½ cup turkey mixture.

4. Place the poblano peppers in a greased 13x9x2-in. baking dish. Sprinkle with the Mexican cheese blend. Bake, uncovered, at 375° for 10-15 minutes or until the cheese is melted. Sprinkle with the remaining cilantro. Serve with sour cream.

HOT, HOT, HOT!

Chili peppers come in many sizes, shapes and heat levels. Most of the capsaicin—the compound that makes peppers fiery—is found in the seeds and membranes. Here are some of the most common chili peppers, from the hottest at the top to the mildest at the bottom:

- Habanero pepper
- Cayenne pepper
- Serrano pepper
- Chipotle pepper (smoked jalapeno)
- Jalapeno pepper
- Poblano pepper
- Anaheim pepper
- Cubanelle pepper
- Sweet bell pepper

Creole Jambalaya, page 139

138

141

143

Seafood &
More Entrees

This catchall chapter offers a **variety of choices**, from surefire shrimp dishes to meatless mainstays. But all of these recipes have one thing in common—they're bona fide **contest winners!**

Black Bean Veggie Burritos

Sweet potatoes give these baked burritos seasonal appeal and extra nutrition, too.

—**CARISSA SUMNER** WASHINGTON, DC

PREP: 30 MIN. • **BAKE:** 25 MIN.
MAKES: 8 SERVINGS

- 1   large sweet potato, peeled and cut into ½-inch cubes
- 1   medium onion, finely chopped
- 1   tablespoon water
- 1   can (15 ounces) black beans, rinsed and drained
- 1   cup frozen corn
- 1   medium green pepper, chopped
- 2   tablespoons lemon juice
- 3   garlic cloves, minced
- 1   tablespoon chili powder
- 2   teaspoons dried oregano
- 1   teaspoon ground cumin
- 8   whole wheat tortillas (8 inches), warmed
- 2   cups (8 ounces) shredded Monterey Jack cheese
- ½   cup fat-free plain yogurt
- ½   cup salsa

1. In a large microwave-safe bowl, combine the sweet potato, onion and water. Cover; microwave on high for 4-5 minutes or until potato is almost tender. Stir in the beans, corn, pepper, lemon juice, garlic and seasonings.

2. Spoon a heaping ½ cup filling off center on each tortilla. Sprinkle with ¼ cup cheese. Fold sides and ends over filling and roll up.

3. Place seam side down in a 13x9x2-in. baking dish coated with cooking spray. Cover; bake at 350° for 25-30 minutes or until heated through. Serve with yogurt and salsa.

Shrimp and Pineapple Fried Rice

Love fried rice? Put a tropical spin on it with tangy pineapple chunks and plenty of shrimp. You'll have a restaurant-quality dinner everyone will enjoy.

—**LYNNE VAN WAGENEN** SALT LAKE CITY, UT

START TO FINISH: 30 MIN.
MAKES: 6 SERVINGS

- 2   eggs
- 1   small onion, chopped
- 1   teaspoon canola oil
- 3   garlic cloves, minced
- 3   cups cooked instant brown rice
- 1   can (20 ounces) unsweetened pineapple chunks, drained
- ½   pound cooked medium shrimp, peeled and deveined
- ½   cup chopped cashews
- ½   cup frozen peas, thawed
- 2   green onions, sliced
- 3   tablespoons reduced-sodium soy sauce
- 1   tablespoon hoisin sauce
- 1   teaspoon sugar
- 1   teaspoon sesame oil
- ¼   teaspoon pepper

1. In a small bowl, whisk the eggs. Heat a large nonstick skillet coated with cooking spray over medium heat. Add the eggs. Cook and stir until set; remove from skillet and keep warm.

2. In the same skillet, saute the onion in oil until tender. Add the garlic; cook 1 minute longer. Stir in the brown rice, pineapple chunks, shrimp, cashews, peas and green onions; heat through. Combine the soy sauce, hoisin sauce, sugar, sesame oil and pepper; stir into rice mixture. Stir in eggs.

Creole Jambalaya

Creole jambalaya, also known as red jambalaya, is a traditional Louisiana dish with deep roots in French and Spanish cuisines. Most recipes call for chicken or sausage in addition to the seafood, but mine uses ham for a bit of a twist.

—**RUBY WILLIAMS** BOGALUSA, LA

PREP: 20 MIN. • **COOK:** 35 MIN.
MAKES: 8 SERVINGS

- ¾ cup chopped onion
- ½ cup chopped celery
- ¼ cup chopped green pepper
- 2 tablespoons butter
- 2 garlic cloves, minced
- 2 cups cubed fully cooked ham
- 1 can (28 ounces) diced tomatoes, undrained
- 1 can (10½ ounces) condensed beef broth, undiluted
- 1 cup uncooked long grain white rice
- 1 cup water
- 1 teaspoon sugar
- 1 teaspoon dried thyme
- ½ teaspoon chili powder
- ¼ teaspoon pepper
- 1½ pounds fresh or frozen uncooked shrimp, peeled and deveined
- 1 tablespoon minced fresh parsley

1. In a Dutch oven, saute the onion, celery and green pepper in butter until tender. Add the garlic; cook 1 minute longer. Add the next nine ingredients; bring to a boil. Reduce heat; cover and simmer until the rice is tender, about 25 minutes.

2. Add shrimp and parsley; simmer, uncovered, for 7-10 minutes or until shrimp turn pink.

PER SERVING *310 cal., 8 g fat (0 sat. fat), 154 mg chol., 464 mg sodium, 28 g carb., 0 fiber, 31 g pro.* **Diabetic Exchanges:** *3 lean meat, 1½ starch, 1 vegetable.*

Salmon Spirals with Cucumber Sauce

When I serve this salmon, my guests are doubly impressed—by both the delicious taste and the elegant presentation.

—**ROSALIND POPE** GREENSBORO, NC

PREP: 20 MIN. + MARINATING
GRILL: 10 MIN.
MAKES: 4 SKEWERS (1⅓ CUPS SAUCE)

- 1 salmon fillet (1 pound)
- 8 fresh dill sprigs
- ¼ cup lime juice
- 1 tablespoon olive oil
- 2 teaspoons Dijon mustard

SAUCE

- 1 cup (8 ounces) fat-free plain yogurt
- ¼ cup fat-free mayonnaise
- 2 tablespoons finely chopped seeded peeled cucumber
- 2 tablespoons snipped fresh dill
- 1 tablespoon lemon juice

1. Remove the skin from the fillet and discard. Cut fillet lengthwise into four strips. Place two dill sprigs on each strip; roll up. Thread the salmon onto four metal or soaked wooden skewers.

2. In a large resealable plastic bag, combine the lime juice, olive oil and Dijon mustard; add the salmon. Seal the bag and turn to coat; refrigerate for 30 minutes, turning occasionally.

3. Drain and discard the marinade. Using long-handled tongs, moisten a paper towel with cooking oil and lightly coat the grill rack. Grill salmon, covered, over high heat or broil 3-4 in. from heat for 4-5 minutes on each side or until fish flakes easily with a fork.

4. Meanwhile, in a small bowl, combine sauce ingredients. Serve with the salmon.

Shrimp and Fontina Casserole

Indulge in a seafood casserole that tastes like gourmet cooking. You'll love the roasted red peppers and three different cheeses.

—**EMORY DOTY** JASPER, GA

PREP: 35 MIN. • **BAKE:** 15 MIN. + STANDING • **MAKES:** 8 SERVINGS

- ½ cup all-purpose flour
- 1 tablespoon Cajun seasoning
- ½ teaspoon pepper
- 2 pounds uncooked large shrimp, peeled and deveined
- 2 tablespoons olive oil
- 4 thin slices prosciutto or deli ham, cut into thin strips
- ½ pound medium fresh mushrooms, quartered
- 2 tablespoons butter
- 4 green onions, chopped
- 2 garlic cloves, minced
- 1 cup heavy whipping cream
- 8 ounces fontina cheese, cubed
- 1 jar (7 ounces) roasted sweet red peppers, drained and chopped
- ¼ cup grated Parmigiano-Reggiano cheese
- ¼ cup grated Romano cheese

1. Preheat oven to 350°. In a large resealable plastic bag, combine flour, Cajun seasoning and pepper. Add shrimp, a few at a time, and shake to coat.

2. In a large skillet over medium heat, cook shrimp in oil in batches until golden brown. Drain on paper towels. Transfer to an ungreased 13x9x2-in. baking dish; top with prosciutto. Set aside.

3. In same skillet, saute mushrooms in butter until tender. Add onions and garlic; cook 1 minute longer. Add cream and fontina cheese; cook and stir until cheese is melted. Remove from heat; stir in peppers. Pour over prosciutto. Sprinkle with remaining cheeses.

4. Bake, uncovered, 15-20 minutes or until bubbly and cheese is melted. Let stand 10 minutes before serving.

Grilled Veggie Pizza

Grilling the veggies before piling them on the pizza really brings out their flavor. For extra flair, add some olives or pine nuts.

—**SUSAN MARSHALL** COLORADO SPRINGS, CO

PREP: 30 MIN. • **BAKE:** 10 MIN. • **MAKES:** 6 SERVINGS

- 8 small fresh mushrooms, halved
- 1 small zucchini, cut into ¼-inch slices
- 1 small sweet yellow pepper, sliced
- 1 small sweet red pepper, sliced
- 1 small onion, sliced
- 1 tablespoon white wine vinegar
- 1 tablespoon water
- 4 teaspoons olive oil, divided
- 2 teaspoons minced fresh basil or ½ teaspoon dried basil
- ¼ teaspoon salt
- ¼ teaspoon pepper
- 1 prebaked 12-inch thin whole wheat pizza crust
- 1 can (8 ounces) pizza sauce
- 2 small tomatoes, chopped
- 2 cups (8 ounces) shredded part-skim mozzarella cheese

1. In a large bowl, combine mushrooms, zucchini, peppers, onion, vinegar, water, 3 teaspoons olive oil and seasonings. Transfer to a grill wok or basket. Grill, covered, over medium heat for 8-10 minutes or until tender, stirring once.

2. Prepare the grill for indirect heat. Brush the crust with the remaining oil; spread with the pizza sauce. Top with the grilled vegetables, tomatoes and cheese. Grill, covered, over indirect medium heat for 10-12 minutes or until edges are lightly browned and cheese is melted. Rotate pizza halfway through cooking to ensure an evenly browned crust.

NOTE *If you do not have a grill wok or basket, use a disposable foil pan. Poke holes in the bottom of the pan with a meat fork to allow liquid to drain.*

PER SERVING *274 cal., 11 g fat (5 g sat. fat), 22 mg chol., 634 mg sodium, 30 g carb., 5 g fiber, 17 g pro.* **Diabetic Exchanges:** *2 starch, 2 medium-fat meat, 1 vegetable.*

Classic Cottage Pie

The perfect comfort food? To me, it's a hearty ground lamb or beef filling smothered with a bubbling, cheesy layer of mashed potatoes. This classic pie warms me body and soul!

—**SHANNON ARTHUR** WHEELERSBURG, OH

PREP: 45 MIN. • **BAKE:** 20 MIN. • **MAKES:** 6 SERVINGS

- 1 **pound ground lamb or beef**
- 2 **medium carrots, finely chopped**
- 1 **medium onion, finely chopped**
- 2 **tablespoons all-purpose flour**
- 2 **tablespoons minced fresh parsley**
- 1 **tablespoon Italian seasoning**
- ¾ **teaspoon salt**
- ¼ **teaspoon pepper**
- 1½ **cups reduced-sodium beef broth**
- 2 **tablespoons dry red wine or additional reduced-sodium beef broth**
- 1 **tablespoon tomato paste**
- 1 **teaspoon brown sugar**
- ½ **cup frozen peas**

TOPPING
- 4 **medium potatoes, peeled and cubed**
- ½ **cup 2% milk**
- ¼ **cup butter, cubed**
- ¾ **cup shredded cheddar cheese, divided**
- ¼ **teaspoon salt**
- ⅛ **teaspoon pepper**

1. In a large skillet, cook the lamb, carrots and onion over medium heat until meat is no longer pink and vegetables are tender, breaking meat into crumbles; drain. Stir in flour, parsley, Italian seasoning, salt and pepper until blended.

Gradually add beef broth and wine; stir in the tomato paste and brown sugar. Bring to a boil. Reduce the heat; simmer, uncovered, 10-15 minutes or until thickened, stirring occasionally. Stir in peas.

2. Meanwhile, place potatoes in a large saucepan and cover with water. Bring to a boil. Reduce the heat; cover and cook 10-15 minutes or until tender.

3. Preheat oven to 400°. Transfer the meat mixture into a greased 9-in. deep-dish pie plate. Drain potatoes; mash with milk and butter. Stir in ½ cup cheese, salt and pepper. Spread over meat mixture; sprinkle with remaining cheese.

4. Place pie plate on a foil-lined baking sheet (plate will be full). Bake 20-25 minutes or until the top is golden brown.

Orange-Glazed Salmon

The first time I made this citrusy glazed salmon, my husband said it was his new favorite entree. And that's really saying something because all his previous favorites were beef!

—**TAMMY HAYDEN** QUINCY, MI

START TO FINISH: 20 MIN. • **MAKES:** 4 SERVINGS

- 2 **tablespoons Cajun seasoning**
- 1 **teaspoon brown sugar**
- 4 **salmon fillets (6 ounces each), skin removed**
- ½ **cup orange marmalade**
- ¼ **cup lime juice**

Combine Cajun seasoning and brown sugar; rub over fillets. In a large nonstick skillet coated with cooking spray, cook fillets over medium heat for 3-4 minutes on each side or until fish flakes easily with a fork. Add marmalade and lime juice to the skillet; heat through.

Tater Crust Tuna Pie

My husband and I especially like this tuna pie's homemade pastry crust flavored with mashed potato flakes.

—**CYNTHIA KOLBERG** SYRACUSE, IN

PREP: 15 MIN. • **BAKE:** 30 MIN.
MAKES: 6-8 SERVINGS

CRUST

- 1 **cup all-purpose flour**
- ½ **cup mashed potato flakes**
- ½ **cup cold butter**
- 3 **to 4 tablespoons ice water**
- 1 **can (2.8 ounces) french-fried onions, divided**

FILLING

- 1 **egg**
- 1 **can (10¾ ounces) reduced-fat reduced-sodium condensed cream of mushroom soup, undiluted**
- 1 **cup (4 ounces) shredded cheddar cheese, divided**
- ¾ **cup mashed potato flakes**
- 1 **can (6½ ounces) light water-packed tuna, drained and flaked**
- 2 **tablespoons chopped pimiento-stuffed green olives**

1. In a small bowl, combine flour and potato flakes; cut in butter until crumbly. Add the water, 1 tablespoon at a time, until dough is moist enough to hold together. Press pastry over bottom and up sides of an ungreased 9-in. pie plate. Flute edge. Set aside ½ cup onions for topping. Sprinkle remaining onions into pastry shell.

2. In a large bowl, combine egg, soup, ½ cup cheese, potato flakes, tuna and olives. Spoon into pastry crust.

3. Bake at 350° for 25 minutes or until the crust is golden. Sprinkle with the remaining cheese and reserved onions; bake 5-10 minutes longer or until cheese is melted. Let stand for 5 minutes before serving.

KEEP IT COOL

When making pastry dough for a crust, make sure your butter is cold and the water is icy. The cold helps prevent the fat in the pastry from melting or softening.

Vegetable Pad Thai

Skip the expense of having popular pad thai in a restaurant—whip up your own specialty dish right at home!
—**SARA LANDRY** BROOKLINE, MA

PREP: 25 MIN. • **COOK:** 15 MIN.
MAKES: 6 SERVINGS

- 1 package (12 ounces) whole wheat fettuccine
- ¼ cup rice vinegar
- 3 tablespoons reduced-sodium soy sauce
- 2 tablespoons brown sugar
- 2 tablespoons fish sauce or additional reduced-sodium soy sauce
- 1 tablespoon lime juice
  Dash Louisiana-style hot sauce
- 1 package (12 ounces) extra-firm tofu, drained and cut into ½-inch cubes
- 3 teaspoons canola oil, divided
- 2 medium carrots, grated
- 2 cups fresh snow peas, halved
- 3 garlic cloves, minced
- 2 eggs, lightly beaten
- 2 cups bean sprouts
- 3 green onions, chopped
- ½ cup minced fresh cilantro
- ¼ cup unsalted peanuts, chopped

1. Cook the fettuccine according to the package directions. Meanwhile, in a small bowl, combine the vinegar, soy sauce, brown sugar, fish sauce, lime juice and hot sauce until smooth; set aside.

2. In a large skillet or wok, stir-fry tofu in 2 teaspoons oil until golden brown. Remove and keep warm. Stir-fry the carrots and snow peas in remaining oil for 1-2 minutes. Add garlic; cook 1 minute longer or until vegetables are crisp-tender. Add the eggs; cook and stir until set.

3. Drain pasta; add to the vegetable mixture. Stir the vinegar mixture and add to skillet. Bring to a boil. Add the tofu, bean sprouts and green onions; heat through. Sprinkle with cilantro and peanuts.

Chicken Shrimp Creole

Living in coastal Alaska, we put out our own shrimp pots. Our fresh catch always tastes great in this satisfying dinner.
—**BONNIE ROHER** WRANGELL, AK

PREP: 20 MIN. • **COOK:** 35 MIN.
MAKES: 6 SERVINGS

- 2 bacon strips
- ½ pound boneless skinless chicken breasts, cut into 1-inch cubes
- 1 medium onion, chopped
- 1 small green pepper, chopped
- 1 celery rib, chopped
- 1 garlic clove, minced
- 1 can (14½ ounces) diced tomatoes, undrained
- 1 bay leaf
- ½ teaspoon salt
- ¼ teaspoon pepper
- ¼ teaspoon Worcestershire sauce
- ¼ teaspoon hot pepper sauce
- 1 pound uncooked medium shrimp, peeled and deveined
- 3 cups cooked brown rice

1. In a large skillet, cook bacon over medium heat until crisp. Remove to paper towels; drain, reserving 1 tablespoon drippings. Crumble bacon and set aside. Saute chicken, onion, green pepper and celery in drippings for 5-6 minutes or until chicken is no longer pink. Add garlic; cook 1 minute longer.

2. Stir in tomatoes, bay leaf, salt, pepper, Worcestershire and pepper sauce. Bring to a boil. Reduce the heat; cover and simmer for 20 minutes. Add shrimp and reserved bacon; return to a boil. Reduce heat; cover and simmer 5 minutes or until shrimp turn pink. Discard bay leaf. Serve with rice.

Grilled Shrimp with Cilantro Dipping Sauce

I came up with this entree when my daughter grew a beautiful jalapeno plant in our garden. I already had some cilantro, so I used those two ingredients for a yummy dipping sauce.

—ELIZABETH LUBIN HUNTINGTON BEACH, CA

PREP: 25 MIN. + MARINATING • **GRILL:** 5 MIN. • **MAKES:** 4 SERVINGS

- 2 **tablespoons minced fresh cilantro**
- 2 **tablespoons olive oil**
- 1 **tablespoon minced fresh chives**
- 1 **garlic clove, minced**
- 1 **pound uncooked medium shrimp, peeled and deveined**

DIPPING SAUCE

- 1 **cup fresh cilantro leaves**
- 1 **cup fat-free mayonnaise**
- 1 **jalapeno pepper, seeded**
- 1 **garlic clove, peeled**
- 1 **tablespoon white vinegar**
- 1 **teaspoon sugar**
  Dash cayenne pepper

1. In a large resealable plastic bag, combine the cilantro, oil, chives and garlic. Add the shrimp; seal bag and turn to coat. Cover and refrigerate for 1 hour.

2. In a blender, combine the sauce ingredients; cover and process until blended. Chill until serving.

3. Thread the shrimp onto four metal or soaked wooden skewers. Grill, covered, over medium heat for 2-3 minutes on each side or until the shrimp turn pink. Serve with the sauce for dipping.

NOTE *Wear disposable gloves when cutting hot peppers; the oils can burn skin. Avoid touching your face.*

Risotto-Stuffed Portobellos

PREP: 45 MIN. • **BAKE:** 20 MIN. • **MAKES:** 4 SERVINGS

- 1 **can (14½ ounces) reduced-sodium chicken or vegetable broth**
- 1 **cup water**
- 2 **celery ribs, finely chopped**
- 2 **medium carrots, finely chopped**
- 1 **large onion, finely chopped**
- 1 **tablespoon olive oil**
- 1 **cup uncooked arborio rice**
- ½ **cup chopped shallots**
- 1 **garlic clove, minced**
- 1 **cup dry white wine or additional broth**
- ½ **cup grated Parmesan cheese**
- 4 **green onions, finely chopped**
- 4 **large portobello mushrooms (4 to 4½ inches), stems removed**
  Cooking spray
- ¼ **teaspoon salt**
- ⅛ **teaspoon pepper**
- ¼ **cup shredded part-skim mozzarella cheese**

1. In a small saucepan, heat the broth and water and keep warm. In a large nonstick skillet coated with cooking spray, saute the celery, carrots and onion in oil until crisp-tender. Add the arborio rice, shallots and garlic; cook and stir for 2-3 minutes. Reduce heat; stir in wine. Cook and stir until all of the liquid is absorbed.

2. Add heated broth mixture, ½ cup at a time, stirring constantly. Allow the liquid to absorb between additions. Cook just until risotto is creamy and rice is almost tender. (Cooking time is about 20 minutes.) Remove from the heat; add the Parmesan cheese and green onions. Stir until the cheese is melted.

3. Spritz the portobello mushrooms with cooking spray; sprinkle with salt and pepper. Fill each mushroom with 1 cup risotto mixture and sprinkle with the mozzarella cheese. Place in a 13x9x2-in. baking dish coated with cooking spray.

4. Bake, uncovered, at 350° for 20-25 minutes or until mushrooms are tender and cheese is melted.

> ❝One day when I was having last-minute dinner guests, I rushed to the local farm stand for some produce. The result? Risotto-Stuffed Portobellos. My friends still ask for the recipe!❞

—RIAN MACDONALD POWDER SPRINGS, GA

Baked Strawberry Salmon

PREP: 10 MIN. + MARINATING
BAKE: 15 MIN. • **MAKES:** 4 SERVINGS

- ¾ **cup soy sauce**
- 2 **tablespoons lemon juice**
- 1 **tablespoon Dijon mustard**
- ¼ **teaspoon pepper**
- 4 **salmon fillets (6 ounces each), skin removed**
- ⅔ **cup strawberry preserves**

1. In a large resealable plastic bag, combine the soy sauce, lemon juice, mustard and pepper. Add the salmon; seal bag and turn to coat. Refrigerate for 30 minutes.

2. Drain and discard the marinade. Place salmon in a greased 13x9x2-in. baking dish; spoon preserves over fillets. Bake, uncovered, at 375° for 15-20 minutes or until salmon flakes easily with a fork.

Scallop Mac & Cheese

Seafood lovers go crazy for this jazzed-up variation of macaroni and cheese.
—**LAURIE LUFKIN** ESSEX, MA

PREP: 35 MIN. • **BAKE:** 15 MIN.
MAKES: 5 SERVINGS

- 2 **cups uncooked medium pasta shells**
- ½ **cup butter, divided**
- 1 **cup French bread baguette crumbs**
- 1 **pound bay scallops**
- 1 **cup sliced fresh mushrooms**
- 1 **small onion, chopped**
- 3 **tablespoons all-purpose flour**
- ¾ **teaspoon dried thyme**
- ¼ **teaspoon salt**
- ⅛ **teaspoon pepper**
- 2 **cups whole milk**
- ½ **cup white wine or chicken broth**
- 2 **tablespoons sherry or chicken broth**
- 1 **cup (4 ounces) shredded Swiss cheese**
- 1 **cup (4 ounces) shredded sharp cheddar cheese**

1. Cook the pasta shells according to the package directions. Meanwhile, in a small skillet, melt 4 tablespoons butter. Add bread crumbs; cook and stir until lightly toasted.

2. In a large skillet over medium heat, melt 2 tablespoons butter. Add scallops; cook and stir for 2 minutes or until firm and opaque. Remove and keep warm. Melt the remaining butter in the pan; add the mushrooms and onion. Cook and stir until tender. Stir in the flour, thyme, salt and pepper until blended.

3. Gradually add the milk, white wine and sherry. Bring to a boil; cook and stir for 1-2 minutes or until thickened. Stir in the cheeses until melted. Drain the pasta; stir the pasta and scallops into the sauce.

4. Divide among five 10-oz. ramekins or custard cups. Sprinkle with bread crumbs. Place ramekins on a baking sheet. Bake, uncovered, at 350° for 15-20 minutes or until heated through. Spoon onto plates if desired.

Zesty Herbed Lamb Chops

The refreshing sauce in this recipe is just as good with seared scallops and grilled fish as it is with lamb. I've also made a version with basil instead of mint, and I sometimes use thyme in place of oregano.

—CORA ANDERSON SEATTLE, WA

START TO FINISH: 30 MIN.
MAKES: 4 SERVINGS

- ½ cup fresh mint leaves
- ¼ cup minced fresh oregano
- ¼ cup packed fresh parsley sprigs, stems removed
- ¼ cup lemon juice
- 3 tablespoons water
- 6 garlic cloves
- 1 tablespoon olive oil
- ¼ teaspoon salt
  Dash pepper

LAMB CHOPS

- 8 lamb loin chops (3 ounces each)
- ½ teaspoon salt
- ½ teaspoon pepper
- 1 tablespoon olive oil

1. In a food processor, combine the first nine ingredients; cover and pulse until blended. Set aside half of the sauce. Brush the remaining sauce over the lamb chops; sprinkle with the salt and pepper.

2. In a large skillet coated with cooking spray, cook the lamb chops in the olive oil over medium heat for 7-10 minutes on each side or until the meat reaches desired doneness (for medium-rare, a thermometer should read 145°; medium, 160°; well-done, 170°). Serve chops with the reserved mint sauce.

Seafood Pasta Alfredo

I created a crab-and-shrimp pasta Alfredo one night by tossing together ingredients I had on hand. Luckily, I wrote down what I did. My husband loved it!

—REBEKAH BEYER SABETHA, KS

START TO FINISH: 30 MIN.
MAKES: 6 SERVINGS

- 8 ounces uncooked linguine
- 1 small zucchini, quartered and sliced
- 1 cup julienned carrots
- 1 small onion, chopped
- 1 tablespoon olive oil
- 1 garlic clove, minced
  Dash crushed red pepper flakes
- 1 cup heavy whipping cream
- ½ cup grated Parmesan cheese
- 2 tablespoons butter
- ½ teaspoon salt
- ⅛ teaspoon pepper
- 1 pound cooked medium shrimp, peeled and deveined
- 2 plum tomatoes, chopped
- 1 can (6 ounces) crab, drained
- 4 ounces imitation crabmeat, chopped
- 3 green onions, sliced

1. Cook linguine according to the package directions. Meanwhile, in a large skillet, saute zucchini, carrots and onion in oil until crisp-tender. Add garlic and pepper flakes; cook 1 minute longer. Stir in the cream, cheese, butter, salt and pepper.

2. Bring to a gentle boil; cook for 1-2 minutes or until slightly thickened. Add the shrimp, tomatoes, crabmeat and green onions. Drain the linguine; toss with shrimp mixture.

Spicy Shrimp Pizza

Let the kids have the pepperoni pie and treat the grown-ups to a sophisticated blend of tender shrimp, zippy seasonings and white wine. This distinctive pizza is not only special enough for company, but also easy enough to assemble on a weeknight.

—**DEBRA UDDEN** COLORADO SPRINGS, CO

PREP: 30 MIN. • **BAKE:** 10 MIN. • **MAKES:** 6 SLICES

- 1 pound uncooked medium shrimp, peeled and deveined
- ½ to ¾ teaspoon crushed red pepper flakes
- 2 tablespoons olive oil
- 1 medium onion, chopped
- 5 garlic cloves, minced
- 12 cherry tomatoes, halved
- 1 can (15 ounces) crushed tomatoes, undrained
- 1 cup white wine or chicken broth
- ½ teaspoon dried oregano
- ⅛ teaspoon pepper
- 3 tablespoons minced fresh parsley
- 1 prebaked 12-inch thin pizza crust
- 1 cup (4 ounces) shredded Italian cheese blend
- 1 cup (4 ounces) shredded Parmesan or Parmigiano-Reggiano cheese

1. In a large skillet over medium heat, cook shrimp and pepper flakes in oil for 2-3 minutes or until shrimp turn pink. Remove and keep warm.

2. In the same skillet, saute onion until tender. Add garlic; cook 1 minute longer. Add the cherry tomatoes, crushed tomatoes, wine, oregano and pepper. Bring to a boil; cook until liquid is reduced, stirring occasionally. Add shrimp and parsley; heat through.

3. Place pizza crust on an ungreased pizza pan. Spread the shrimp mixture over crust to within ½ in. of edges; sprinkle with cheeses.

4. Bake at 450° for 8-10 minutes or until cheese is melted and edges are lightly browned.

Sauerbraten Lamb Shanks

PREP: 1 HOUR + MARINATING • **COOK:** 2 HOURS
MAKES: 6 SERVINGS (ABOUT 6 CUPS GRAVY)

- 7½ cups water
- 2 cups white vinegar
- 1 large onion, sliced
- 1 medium lemon, sliced
- ½ cup sugar
- 3 bay leaves
- 1½ teaspoons whole peppercorns
- 5 whole allspice

LAMB SHANKS

- 6 lamb shanks (20 ounces each)
- 3 garlic cloves, sliced
- 6 tablespoons all-purpose flour
- ⅓ cup plus 2 tablespoons canola oil, divided
- 2 large onions, thinly sliced
- 3 medium carrots, sliced
- 9 gingersnap cookies, crushed
- 1 tablespoon beef bouillon granules
- 6 tablespoons cornstarch
- ⅓ cup cold water

1. In a Dutch oven, combine the first eight ingredients. Bring to a boil. Reduce the heat; simmer, uncovered, for 2 minutes. Cool completely. Strain half of the marinade; cover and refrigerate.

2. Cut slits into each lamb shank; insert the garlic slices. Place in a large shallow nonmetallic bowl; add remaining marinade. Cover and refrigerate overnight.

3. Drain and discard marinade from lamb. Place flour in a shallow bowl; coat lamb shanks with flour. In a stockpot, brown shanks on all sides in ⅓ cup oil in batches. Remove and set aside.

4. In the same pan, saute the onions in the remaining oil. Add reserved marinade. Return shanks to pan. Bring to a boil. Reduce heat; cover and simmer for 1¾ hours. Add carrots and return to a boil. Reduce heat; cover and simmer 15-20 minutes longer or until carrots are tender.

5. Remove the shanks to a cutting board. Skim fat from the cooking juices. Stir in cookies and bouillon. In a small bowl, combine cornstarch and water until smooth; gradually stir into juices. Bring to a boil; cook and stir for 1-2 minutes or until thickened. Return meat to gravy; heat through.

❝The return of chilly fall weather is the perfect time to rediscover slow-cooked meats. Sauerbraten Lamb Shanks marinate overnight and have a rich, tangy gravy.❞

—**SANDY MCKENZIE** BRAHAM, MN

Fresh Tomato Pasta Toss

When my parents and I had an abundance of garden tomatoes, I put the harvest to good use in a fresh-tasting pasta dish.

—CHERYL TRAVAGLIANTE
INDEPENDENCE, OH

START TO FINISH: 30 MIN.
MAKES: 8 SERVINGS

- 3 pounds ripe fresh tomatoes
- 1 package (16 ounces) uncooked penne pasta
- 2 garlic cloves, minced
- 1 tablespoon canola oil
- 1 tablespoon minced fresh parsley or 1 teaspoon dried parsley flakes
- 1 tablespoon minced fresh basil or 1 teaspoon dried basil
- 2 teaspoons minced fresh oregano or ¾ teaspoon dried oregano
- 1 teaspoon salt
- ¼ teaspoon sugar
- ⅛ teaspoon pepper
- ¼ cup heavy whipping cream
- ¼ cup shredded Parmesan or Romano cheese

1. To remove peels from tomatoes, fill a large saucepan with water and bring to a boil. Place tomatoes, one at a time, in boiling water for 30 seconds. Immediately plunge in ice water. Peel the skins with a sharp paring knife and discard. Chop pulp; set aside.

2. Cook pasta according to package directions. In a large skillet, cook the garlic in the oil over medium heat for 1 minute or until tender. Add parsley, basil, oregano, salt, sugar, pepper and reserved tomato pulp. Bring to a boil; reduce heat. Add cream; heat through.

3. Drain pasta; transfer to a serving bowl. Pour tomato sauce over pasta; toss to coat. Sprinkle with cheese.

RIPE AND READY

To ripen green garden tomatoes, I put them in brown paper bags, making sure to avoid bruising by not stacking too many in one bag. I check them every few days and remove the ripe ones.

—DELIA KENNEDY DEER PARK, WA

Mediterranean Shrimp Couscous

My family loves the lightness and elegance of this Mediterranean-flavored couscous.

—HEATHER CARROLL
COLORADO SPRINGS, CO

PREP: 20 MIN. • **COOK:** 25 MIN.
MAKES: 6 SERVINGS

- 1½ pounds uncooked medium shrimp, peeled and deveined
- 1 tablespoon chopped shallot
- 2 garlic cloves, minced
- 3 tablespoons olive oil, divided
- 1 cup chopped zucchini
- ½ cup white wine or reduced-sodium chicken broth
- ¼ cup chopped sun-dried tomatoes (not packed in oil)
- 2 tablespoons capers, drained
- 3 cups fresh baby spinach
- 1½ cups reduced-sodium chicken broth
- 1½ cups uncooked couscous
- 2 tablespoons lemon juice
- 2 tablespoons balsamic vinegar
- ½ cup crumbled feta cheese, divided
- ½ teaspoon dried oregano
- ¼ teaspoon salt
- ¼ teaspoon pepper

1. In a large skillet, saute the shrimp, shallot and garlic in 1 tablespoon oil until shrimp turn pink. Remove and keep warm.

2. In the same skillet, cook and stir the zucchini, wine, tomatoes and capers until the zucchini is tender. Add spinach; cook just until wilted. Add broth and bring to a boil. Stir in couscous. Cover and remove from the heat; let stand for 5 minutes or until liquid is absorbed. Fluff with a fork.

3. Whisk the lemon juice, vinegar and remaining oil; add to pan. Stir in ¼ cup cheese, the seasonings and reserved shrimp mixture; cook and stir over low heat until heated through. Sprinkle with remaining cheese.

PER SERVING *385 cal., 11 g fat (2 g sat. fat), 143 mg chol., 619 mg sodium, 41 g carb., 3 g fiber, 28 g pro.* **Diabetic Exchanges:** *3 lean meat, 2½ starch, 2 fat.*

Individual Tuna Casseroles

This deliciously updated, fun-to-eat tuna casserole bakes in individual ramekins.

—**CHERYL WOODSON** LIBERTY, MO

PREP: 30 MIN. • **BAKE:** 25 MIN.
MAKES: 6 SERVINGS

- 1½ cups uncooked whole wheat penne pasta
- 1 can (12 ounces) albacore white tuna in water
- 1 can (10¾ ounces) reduced-fat reduced-sodium condensed cream of mushroom soup, undiluted
- 1¼ cups water-packed artichoke hearts, rinsed, drained and chopped
- ½ cup reduced-fat sour cream
- ¼ cup roasted sweet red peppers, drained and chopped
- 3 tablespoons chopped onion
- 3 tablespoons sun-dried tomatoes (not packed in oil), chopped
- 2 tablespoons Greek olives, chopped
- 1 tablespoon snipped fresh dill or 1 teaspoon dill weed
- 1 tablespoon capers, drained
- 2 garlic cloves, minced
- 1 teaspoon grated lemon peel
- ½ teaspoon crushed red pepper flakes
- ½ cup dry bread crumbs
- ¼ cup grated Parmesan cheese
- ½ teaspoon Italian seasoning

1. Cook the penne pasta according to the package directions.

2. Meanwhile, In a large bowl, combine tuna, cream of mushroom soup, artichokes, sour cream, roasted sweet red peppers, onion, sun-dried tomatoes, Greek olives, dill, capers, garlic, lemon peel and pepper flakes. Drain penne pasta; stir into the tuna mixture. Divide among six 10-oz. ramekins or custard cups.

3. In a small bowl, combine the dry bread crumbs, Parmesan cheese and Italian seasoning. Sprinkle over the tuna mixture. Place the ramekins on a baking sheet. Bake, uncovered, at 350° for 25-30 minutes or until golden brown.

Southwest Spinach Strata

I've prepared my strata with pinto and cannellini beans instead of black beans, and I think it's just as good. Thanks to all the reduced-fat ingredients, every cheesy bite is guilt-free.

—**DEBORAH BIGGS** OMAHA, NE

PREP: 20 MIN. • **BAKE:** 45 MIN. + STANDING
MAKES: 6 SERVINGS

- 2½ cups cubed day-old white bread
- 2½ cups cubed day-old whole wheat bread
- ⅔ cup black beans, rinsed and drained
- 1 package (10 ounces) frozen chopped spinach, thawed and squeezed dry
- 1½ cups (6 ounces) shredded reduced-fat cheddar cheese, divided
- 1 cup Southwestern-style egg substitute
- 2 cups fat-free milk
- ¼ cup minced fresh cilantro
- ¼ teaspoon salt
- 6 tablespoons reduced-fat sour cream
- 6 tablespoons salsa

1. Place half of the bread cubes in an 8-in.-square baking dish coated with cooking spray. Layer with the black beans, spinach and half of the cheese. Top with remaining bread cubes.

2. In a large bowl, whisk the egg substitute, milk, cilantro and salt. Pour over top. Let stand for 5 minutes.

3. Bake, uncovered, at 350° for 40 minutes. Sprinkle with remaining cheese. Bake 5 minutes longer or until cheese is melted and a knife inserted near the center comes out clean. Let stand for 10 minutes before cutting. Serve with sour cream and salsa.

PER SERVING *264 cal., 9 g fat (5 g sat. fat), 27 mg chol., 736 mg sodium, 28 g carb., 4 g fiber, 20 g pro.* **Diabetic Exchanges:** *2 starch, 2 lean meat, ½ fat.*

Asian Quinoa, page 171

167

169

165

Sides, Breads & Condiments

A winning main course calls for sides that are **just as special**.
Serve up a completely memorable meal with the veggie casseroles,
fresh-baked breads and other **amazing accompaniments** here.

Glazed Pearl Onions

START TO FINISH: 15 MIN.
MAKES: 6 SERVINGS

- 1 package (16 ounces) frozen pearl onions, thawed
- 2 tablespoons butter
- 2 tablespoons plus 1½ teaspoons brown sugar
- 1 tablespoon Dijon mustard
- 2 tablespoons minced fresh parsley

In a large skillet, saute the onions in butter until tender. Add brown sugar and mustard; cook 2 minutes longer. Sprinkle with parsley.

PER SERVING *91 cal., 4 g fat (2 g sat. fat), 10 mg chol., 92 mg sodium, 14 g carb., 1 g fiber, 1 g pro.* **Diabetic Exchanges:** *1 starch, 1 fat.*

> ❝I tried Glazed Pearl Onions at a restaurant I went to in Florida, and the chef's assistant gave me the recipe. I've been putting it on my menus ever since.❞

—DIXIE TERRY GOREVILLE, IL

> What do you get when you combine three kinds of berries, a peach, jerk seasoning and lime? A bold, savory salsa—and a fabulous way to dress up grilled meat.
>
> **—CHERYL PERRY** HERTFORD, NC

Caribbean Four-Fruit Salsa

START TO FINISH: 20 MIN.
MAKES: 12 SERVINGS

- 1 medium peach, chopped
- ½ cup each fresh blackberries, blueberries and raspberries
- ¼ cup chopped red onion
- ¼ cup chopped sweet red pepper
- 2 green onions, thinly sliced
- ¼ cup minced fresh cilantro
- 2 tablespoons lime juice
- 1 jalapeno pepper, seeded and minced
- 1½ teaspoons Caribbean jerk seasoning
- 1 teaspoon minced fresh gingerroot
- ½ teaspoon grated lime peel
- ⅛ teaspoon salt

In a large bowl, combine all ingredients. Chill salsa until serving. Serve with grilled meat, fish or poultry.

NOTE *Wear disposable gloves when cutting hot peppers; the oils can burn skin. Avoid touching your face.*

PER SERVING *16 cal., trace fat (trace sat. fat), 0 chol., 61 mg sodium, 4 g carb., 1 g fiber, trace pro.* **Diabetic Exchange:** *Free food.*

Oven Parmesan Chips

My husband and I tend to avoid any foods that are fried, but we enjoy potatoes so much that we eat them almost every day. To keep our meals exciting, I'm constantly on the lookout for new ideas. These sliced spuds get nice and crispy in the oven and require only basic ingredients.
—MARY LOU KELLY SCOTTDALE, PA

START TO FINISH: 25 MIN.
MAKES: 2 SERVINGS

- 2 **medium potatoes**
- ¼ **cup butter, melted**
- 1 **tablespoon finely chopped onion**
- ½ **teaspoon salt**
- ⅛ **teaspoon pepper**
  Dash paprika
- 2 **tablespoons grated Parmesan cheese**

1. Preheat oven to 425°. Cut potatoes into ¼-in. slices; arrange in a single layer on two greased baking sheets. In a small bowl, mix butter, onion, salt, pepper and paprika; brush over both sides of potatoes.
2. Roast 15-20 minutes or until the potatoes are tender and golden, turning occasionally. Sprinkle with Parmesan cheese.

POTATO PRIMER

FINGERLINGS Finger-shaped potato with tan skin, 2-4 inches long. Waxy, firm and flavorful.
NEW POTATOES Small potato with tan or red tender skin. Fresh from the garden.
ROUND REDS Round-shaped potato with smooth red skin. Waxy or low starch.
ROUND WHITES Round-shaped potato with light to medium-brown skin. Waxy or low starch.
RUSSETS Oblong potato with a rough, reddish-brown skin. High starch, low moisture.
YELLOW-FLESHED Round potato with golden-colored skin and flesh that has a buttery flavor. All-purpose potato.

Potato and Mushroom Gratin

Rich and decadent, this creamy gratin recipe dresses up plain potatoes and mushrooms with a splash of Marsala wine, basil and two kinds of cheese. Keep it in mind the next time you need a contribution to a potluck get-together or party—just don't count on having any leftovers when you get home!

—LAURIE LACLAIR NORTH RICHLAND HILLS, TX

PREP: 20 MIN. • **BAKE:** 55 MIN. • **MAKES:** 8 SERVINGS

- 2 **jars (4½ ounces each) sliced mushrooms, drained**
- 3 **shallots, finely chopped**
- 1 **tablespoon olive oil**
- 2 **tablespoons Marsala wine**
- 3 **large potatoes (about 1½ pounds), peeled and thinly sliced**
- 1 **cup (4 ounces) shredded Swiss cheese**
- ½ **cup shredded Parmesan cheese**
- 2 **tablespoons minced fresh basil or 2 teaspoons dried basil**
- 1½ **cups heavy whipping cream**
- 1 **tablespoon butter, cubed**
- ⅛ **teaspoon salt**
- ⅛ **teaspoon pepper**

1. In a large skillet, saute the mushrooms and shallots in the olive oil until tender. Add the Marsala wine; cook and stir for 2 minutes.

2. Arrange a third of the potatoes in a greased 10-in. round shallow baking dish. Layer with half of the mushroom mixture, cheeses, basil and another third of the potatoes. Repeat the layers. Pour cream over top. Dot with butter; sprinkle with salt and pepper.

3. Bake, uncovered, at 350° for 55-65 minutes or until potatoes are tender.

Crispy Pub Rings

My husband brews his own beer. When we decided to throw a beer-tasting party for friends, I came up with my own onion rings and dipping sauce to serve as a snack.
—**JENNIFER RODRIGUEZ** WEST JORDAN, UT

PREP: 40 MIN. • **COOK:** 5 MIN./BATCH • **MAKES:** 4 SERVINGS

- ½ cup sour cream
- ½ cup mayonnaise
- ½ cup crumbled blue cheese
- 2 green onions, finely chopped
- 1 tablespoon dried parsley flakes
- 1 garlic clove, minced
- ½ teaspoon hot pepper sauce
- ¼ teaspoon garlic salt

RINGS

- 1¼ cups all-purpose flour
- 1 teaspoon salt
- 1 teaspoon baking powder
- 1 egg
- 1 cup 2% milk
- 1½ teaspoons hot pepper sauce
- 1 garlic clove, minced
- ¾ cup dry bread crumbs
- 1 teaspoon garlic powder
- 1 teaspoon seasoned salt
- 1 large sweet onion, sliced and separated into rings
  Oil for deep-fat frying

1. In a small bowl, combine the first eight ingredients; chill until serving.
2. In a large shallow bowl, combine the flour, salt and baking powder. In another shallow bowl, whisk the egg, milk, pepper sauce and minced garlic. In a third bowl, combine the bread crumbs, garlic powder and seasoned salt. Coat onions in flour mixture, dip in egg mixture, then roll in crumbs.
3. In a deep fryer or electric skillet, heat the oil to 375°. Drop the onion rings, a few at a time, into the hot oil. Fry for 2-3 minutes or until golden brown. Drain on paper towels. Serve with sauce.

Whole Wheat Butterhorns

Store-bought roll dough just can't compare to the homemade kind. It takes a little extra time to make but is well worth it!
—**MARY JANE MULLINS** LIVONIA, MO

PREP: 30 MIN. + RISING • **BAKE:** 10 MIN. • **MAKES:** 18-24 ROLLS

- 2¾ cups all-purpose flour, divided
- 2 packages (¼ ounce each) active dry yeast
- 1¾ cups water
- ⅓ cup packed brown sugar
- ½ cup butter, divided
- 2 tablespoons honey
- 2 teaspoons salt
- 2 cups whole wheat flour

1. In a large bowl, combine 1½ cups all-purpose flour and the yeast.
2. Heat water, brown sugar, 3 tablespoons butter, honey and salt to 120°-130°; add to flour mixture. Beat on low for 30 seconds with electric mixer; increase speed to high and continue beating 3 minutes. Stir in whole wheat flour and enough remaining all-purpose flour to form a soft dough.
3. Turn out onto a lightly floured surface and knead until smooth and elastic, about 6-8 minutes. Place in a greased bowl, turning once to grease the top. Cover with plastic wrap and let rise in a warm place until doubled, about 1½ hours. Punch the dough down and divide into thirds. Shape each into a ball; cover and let rest 10 minutes.
4. On a lightly floured surface, roll the balls into three 12-in. circles. Cut each circle into 6-8 wedges. Roll wedges into crescent shapes, starting at the wide end. Place on greased baking sheets. Cover and let rise in a warm place until doubled, about 1 hour. Melt remaining butter and brush some on each crescent.
5. Bake at 400° for 10-15 minutes or until golden brown. Brush again with butter while hot.

Potato and Fennel Gratin

Fennel adds a snappy undertone to this velvety gratin without being overpowering. It balances the richness of the cheese.
—**NANCY ROTH** SAINT JOSEPH, IL

PREP: 20 MIN. • **BAKE:** 65 MIN. + STANDING
MAKES: 8 SERVINGS

- 1 small fennel bulb, sliced
- 2 teaspoons olive oil
- 3 tablespoons butter
- 3 tablespoons all-purpose flour
- ½ teaspoon salt
- ¼ teaspoon pepper
- ¼ teaspoon ground nutmeg
- 1½ cups whole milk
- 1½ cups (6 ounces) shredded Gruyere or Swiss cheese
- 3 medium potatoes, thinly sliced
- ½ cup soft bread crumbs

1. In a large skillet, saute the fennel in oil until tender.
2. Meanwhile, in a small saucepan, melt butter. Stir in the flour, salt, pepper and nutmeg until smooth; gradually add milk. Bring to a boil; cook and stir for 1-2 minutes or until thickened. Stir in cheese until melted.
3. Layer half of the potatoes, fennel and sauce in a greased 2-qt. baking dish; repeat layers. Cover and bake at 375° for 55 minutes. Uncover and sprinkle with the bread crumbs; bake 10-15 minutes longer or until golden brown and bubbly. Let stand for 10 minutes before serving.

Kathy's Herbed Corn

My husband and I agreed that the corn recipe we had needed a little jazzing up, so I mixed a bit of dried thyme and zippy cayenne pepper into the herbed butter to suit our taste. Now fresh cobs make a regular appearance on our grill.
—**KATHY VONKORFF** NORTH COLLEGE HILL, OH

START TO FINISH: 30 MIN. • **MAKES:** 8 SERVINGS

- ½ cup butter, softened
- 2 tablespoons minced fresh parsley
- 2 tablespoons minced fresh chives
- 1 teaspoon dried thyme
- ½ teaspoon salt
- ½ teaspoon cayenne pepper
- 8 ears sweet corn, husked

1. In a small bowl, beat the first six ingredients until blended. Spread 1 tablespoon mixture over each ear of corn. Wrap corn individually in heavy-duty foil.
2. Grill corn, covered, over medium heat 10-15 minutes or until tender, turning occasionally. Open foil carefully to allow steam to escape.

SILKY SMOOTH

I use a crumpled paper towel to gently brush the silk from corn. For me, this works better than a vegetable brush, and the towel isn't abrasive to the kernels.

—**HILDA NEWCOMER** HAGERSTOWN, MD

Spinach-Topped Tomatoes

These pretty tomatoes smothered with a blend of spinach, melted Parmesan and golden bread crumbs always go over big with my daughter. Because the prep time is just 20 minutes and the baking time is even shorter, I can fix them often.

—ILA MAE ALDERMAN GALAX, VA

PREP: 20 MIN. • **BAKE:** 15 MIN.
MAKES: 6 SERVINGS

- 1 package (10 ounces) frozen chopped spinach
- 2 chicken bouillon cubes
  Salt
- 3 large tomatoes, halved
- 1 cup soft bread crumbs
- ½ cup grated Parmesan cheese
- ½ cup chopped onion
- ½ cup butter, melted
- 1 egg, lightly beaten
- 1 garlic clove, minced
- ¼ teaspoon pepper
- ⅛ teaspoon cayenne pepper
  Shredded Parmesan cheese, optional

1. In a large saucepan, cook the spinach according to the package directions with the chicken bouillon; drain well. Cool slightly; press out the excess liquid.

2. Lightly salt the tomato halves; place with the cut side down on a paper towel for 15 minutes to absorb excess moisture.

3. Meanwhile, in a small bowl, combine the spinach, soft bread crumbs, grated Parmesan cheese, onion, butter, egg, garlic, pepper and cayenne pepper.

4. Place the tomato halves, cut side up, in a shallow baking dish. Divide the spinach mixture over tomatoes. Sprinkle with the shredded cheese if desired. Bake at 350° for about 15 minutes or until heated through.

Fresh Vegetable Casserole

I gave an old recipe an update and liked it so much, I fixed it for our church potluck.

—AUDREY THIBODEAU GILBERT, AZ

PREP: 20 MIN. • **BAKE:** 30 MIN.
MAKES: 6-8 SERVINGS

- 2 **cups fresh broccoli florets**
- 1½ **cups sliced carrots**
- 1 **cup mayonnaise**
- 1 **cup (4 ounces) shredded cheddar cheese**
- 3 **to 4 drops hot pepper sauce**
- ¼ **teaspoon pepper**
- ¼ **cup sherry or dry white wine, optional**
- 1½ **cups sliced zucchini**
- 1 **cup sliced celery**
- ½ **cup diced green pepper**
- ½ **cup diced onion**
- 1 **tablespoon minced fresh parsley**
- 1 **tablespoon minced fresh basil**
- 3 **tablespoons butter**
- 12 **saltines, crushed**
- ⅓ **cup grated Parmesan cheese**

1. Steam broccoli and carrots until crisp-tender; drain and set aside.
2. In a large bowl, combine the mayonnaise, cheddar cheese, pepper sauce, pepper and sherry if desired. Add the broccoli, carrots, remaining vegetables, parsley and basil; stir gently to combine.
3. Spoon into a greased 2-qt. baking dish. Melt butter in a small saucepan. Add the crushed saltines; stir until browned. Remove from the heat and stir in cheese; sprinkle over vegetables.
4. Bake, uncovered, at 350° for 30-40 minutes or until heated through.

GRAND PRIZE WINNER ★★★★

GRAND PRIZE

Pepper Jack Mac

Here's comfort food at its finest! Every rich, creamy bite tastes like a treat.

—RIANNA STYX LIBERTYVILLE, IL

PREP: 35 MIN. • **BAKE:** 20 MIN.
MAKES: 6 SERVINGS

- 2 **cups uncooked elbow macaroni**
- ¼ **cup butter, cubed**
- ¼ **cup all-purpose flour**
- ½ **teaspoon salt**
- ½ **teaspoon ground mustard**
- ½ **teaspoon pepper**
- ½ **teaspoon Worcestershire sauce**
- 1½ **cups milk**
- ½ **cup heavy whipping cream**
- 3 **cups (12 ounces) shredded pepper jack cheese**
- 1 **package (8 ounces) cream cheese, cubed**
- 1 **cup (4 ounces) shredded sharp cheddar cheese**
- ½ **cup shredded Asiago cheese**

TOPPING
- ¾ **cup panko (Japanese) bread crumbs**
- 4 **bacon strips, cooked and crumbled**
- ¼ **cup grated Parmesan cheese**
- 1 **cup cheddar French-fried onions, crushed**

1. Cook macaroni according to the package directions; drain and set aside.
2. In a large saucepan, melt butter. Stir in the flour, salt, ground mustard, pepper and Worcestershire sauce until smooth; gradually add the milk and heavy whipping cream. Bring to a boil; cook and stir for 1 minute or until thickened. Stir in the cheeses until melted. Stir the macaroni into the cheese mixture.
3. Transfer to a greased 2-qt. baking dish. Sprinkle with the panko bread crumbs, bacon, Parmesan cheese and French-fried onions. Bake, uncovered, at 350° for 20-25 minutes or until bubbly and golden brown.

Sweet Potato Delight

"Delight" is the perfect name for this dish. It's so popular, I prepare it at least once a month. The fluffy texture, subtle orange flavor and crunchy nuts make it a standout no matter what else I'm serving.

—**MARLENE KROLL** CHICAGO, IL

PREP: 25 MIN. • **BAKE:** 30 MIN.
MAKES: 10 SERVINGS

- 4 large sweet potatoes, peeled and quartered
- ½ cup orange marmalade
- ½ cup orange juice
- ¼ cup packed brown sugar
- ½ teaspoon almond extract
- 3 egg whites
- ¼ cup slivered almonds

1. Place the sweet potatoes in a Dutch oven; cover with water. Bring to a boil. Reduce the heat; cover and cook for 15-20 minutes or just until tender. Drain potatoes; place in a large bowl and mash. Stir in orange marmalade, orange juice, brown sugar and almond extract. Cool slightly.

2. In a small bowl, beat the egg whites until stiff peaks form. Fold into sweet potato mixture. Transfer to a 2½-qt. baking dish coated with cooking spray. Sprinkle with slivered almonds. Bake, uncovered, at 350° for 30-35 minutes or until a thermometer reads 160°.
PER SERVING *174 cal., 1 g fat (trace sat. fat), 0 chol., 36 mg sodium, 38 g carb., 3 g fiber, 3 g pro.* **Diabetic Exchange:** *2 starch.*

Cheddar Cheese Batter Bread

As a dairy farmer, I always try to promote our products. Cheese takes center stage in my golden batter bread.

—**JEANNE KEMPER** BAGDAD, KY

PREP: 30 MIN. + RISING
BAKE: 25 MIN. + COOLING
MAKES: 2 LOAVES (16 SLICES EACH)

- 2 packages (¼ ounce each) active dry yeast
- ¾ cup warm water (110° to 115°)
- 3 cups (12 ounces) shredded cheddar cheese

- ¾ cup shredded Parmesan cheese
- 2 cups warm 2% milk (110° to 115°)
- 3 tablespoons sugar
- 1 tablespoon butter, melted
- 2 teaspoons salt
- 6 to 6½ cups all-purpose flour
- 1 egg white, beaten
- 1 tablespoon water

TOPPING
- ½ cup finely shredded cheddar cheese
- 1 garlic clove, minced
- ½ teaspoon sesame seeds
- ½ teaspoon poppy seeds
- ½ teaspoon paprika
- ¼ teaspoon celery seed

1. In a large bowl, dissolve the yeast in the warm water. Add cheeses, milk, sugar, butter, salt and 3 cups flour. Beat on medium speed for 3 minutes. Stir in enough remaining flour to form a firm dough.
2. Do not knead. Cover and let rise in a warm place until doubled, about 1½ hours.
3. Stir dough down; transfer to two greased 9x5-in. loaf pans. Cover; let rise until doubled, about 30 minutes.
4. Preheat oven to 375°. In a small bowl, combine egg white and water. In another bowl, combine topping ingredients. Brush the loaves with the egg white mixture; sprinkle with topping. Bake for 25-30 minutes or until golden brown. Remove from pans to wire racks to cool.
PER SERVING *155 cal., 5 g fat (3 g sat. fat), 17 mg chol., 266 mg sodium, 21 g carb., 1 g fiber, 7 g pro.* **Diabetic Exchanges:** *1½ starch, 1 fat.*

Parsnips & Turnips au Gratin

A delicious au gratin without any potatoes? Yes! I always include parsnips but sometimes substitute rutabaga for the turnips. Either way, it's a dish I'm proud to serve.

—**PRISCILLA GILBERT** INDIAN HARBOUR BEACH, FL

PREP: 20 MIN. • **BAKE:** 15 MIN. • **MAKES:** 8 SERVINGS

- 1½ **pounds parsnips, peeled and sliced**
- 1¼ **pounds turnips, peeled and sliced**
- 1 **can (10¾ ounces) reduced-fat reduced-sodium condensed cream of celery soup, undiluted**
- 1 **cup fat-free milk**
- ½ **teaspoon pepper**
- 1 **cup (4 ounces) shredded sharp cheddar cheese**
- ½ **cup panko (Japanese) bread crumbs**
- 1 **tablespoon butter, melted**

1. Place the parsnips and turnips in a large saucepan; cover with water. Bring to a boil. Reduce heat; simmer, uncovered, for 5-7 minutes or until crisp-tender.

2. Meanwhile, in a small saucepan, combine the soup, milk and pepper. Bring to a boil; reduce the heat to low. Stir in cheese until melted. Drain the vegetables; transfer to an 11x7-in. baking dish coated with cooking spray. Pour sauce over vegetables.

3. Combine the panko bread crumbs and butter; sprinkle over the top. Bake, uncovered, at 400° for 15-20 minutes or until the vegetables are tender and the bread crumbs are golden brown.

PER SERVING *189 cal., 7 g fat (4 g sat. fat), 21 mg chol., 309 mg sodium, 27 g carb., 4 g fiber, 7 g pro.* **Diabetic Exchanges:** *1 starch, 1 high-fat meat, 1 vegetable.*

Fruited Rice Mix

During the holiday season one year, a friend of mine gave me a container of this as a Christmas present. I liked her gift so much that the next year, I gave it to all my friends. Every single one of them asked for the recipe! I have fun putting the mix in mason jars and decorating them for the occasion.

—**LILLIAN JUSTIS** BELLEPLAIN, NJ

PREP: 10 MIN. • **COOK:** 30 MIN.
MAKES: ABOUT 5 CUPS DRY MIX (EACH CUP MAKES 4-6 SERVINGS)

- 3 **cups uncooked long grain rice**
- 1 **cup chopped dried apples**
- ⅓ **cup golden raisins**
- ⅓ **cup slivered almonds**
- ¼ **cup chicken bouillon granules**
- 3 **tablespoons dried minced onion**
- 4½ **teaspoons curry powder**

In a large bowl, combine all ingredients and store in an airtight container.

TO PREPARE RICE MIX *In a large saucepan, combine 1 cup mix with 2 cups water and 2 tablespoons butter. Bring to a boil. Reduce heat; cover and simmer for 25-30 minutes or until water is absorbed.*

Rosemary Roasted Potatoes

I use fresh rosemary instead of the dried variety when possible for my roasted potatoes. Feel free to replace the spuds with carrots if you're in the mood for something different.

—**SHANNON KOENE** BLACKSBURG, VA

PREP: 15 MIN. • **BAKE:** 40 MIN. • **MAKES:** 8 SERVINGS

- 1½ **pounds potatoes, peeled and cut into 1-inch cubes**
- 1½ **pounds sweet potatoes, peeled and cut into 1-inch cubes**
- 1 **large onion, cut into wedges**
- 2 **garlic cloves, minced**
- 3 **tablespoons olive oil**
- 4½ **teaspoons minced fresh rosemary or 1½ teaspoons dried rosemary, crushed**
- 1½ **teaspoons Creole seasoning**
- ¼ **teaspoon salt**
- ¼ **teaspoon pepper**

1. In a large bowl, combine the potatoes, onion and garlic; drizzle with the olive oil. Sprinkle with rosemary, Creole seasoning, salt and pepper; toss to coat. Transfer to a greased 15x10x1-in. baking pan.

2. Bake at 425° for 40-50 minutes or until tender, stirring occasionally.

NOTE *The following spices may be substituted for 1 teaspoon Creole seasoning: ¼ teaspoon each salt, garlic powder and paprika; and a pinch each of dried thyme, ground cumin and cayenne pepper.*

PER SERVING *157 cal., 5 g fat (1 g sat. fat), 0 chol., 206 mg sodium, 26 g carb., 3 g fiber, 2 g pro.* **Diabetic Exchanges:** *1½ starch, 1 fat.*

Blue Cheese Bread Pudding

Use sharp Stilton, saltier Gorgonzola or any other variety of blue cheese you like.

—**CRYSTAL BRUNS** ILIFF, CO

PREP: 30 MIN. + STANDING
BAKE: 40 MIN. + STANDING
MAKES: 12 SERVINGS

- ¼ **cup butter, cubed**
- 1 **medium onion, chopped**
- 3 **garlic cloves, minced**
- 2 **French bread baguettes (10½ ounces each), cut into 1-inch cubes**
- 4 **cups (16 ounces) crumbled blue cheese**
- 5 **eggs**
- 5 **egg yolks**
- 3 **cups heavy whipping cream**
- 1 **teaspoon salt**
- ½ **teaspoon pepper**

1. In a small skillet over medium heat, melt the butter. Add the onion; cook and stir until softened. Reduce the heat to medium-low; cook, stirring occasionally, for 20 minutes or until the onion is golden brown. Add garlic; cook 2 minutes longer.

2. Place half of the bread in a greased 13x9x2-in. baking dish. Layer with the onion mixture and half of blue cheese. Top with remaining bread and cheese.

3. In a large bowl, whisk eggs, yolks, cream, salt and pepper. Pour over the bread; let stand for 15 minutes or until bread is softened.

4. Bake, uncovered, at 375° for 40-45 minutes or until a knife inserted near center comes out clean. Let stand 10 minutes before serving. Serve warm.

GRAND PRIZE WINNER ★★★★

Au Gratin Potato Pancakes `GRAND PRIZE`

START TO FINISH: 25 MIN.
MAKES: 8 POTATO PANCAKES

- 2 **cups mashed potatoes (without added milk and butter)**
- 1 **egg, lightly beaten**
- 1 **tablespoon minced chives**
- 1 **teaspoon minced fresh parsley**
- ¾ **teaspoon salt**
- ⅛ **teaspoon dried minced garlic**
- ⅛ **teaspoon pepper**
  Dash dried rosemary, crushed
- ½ **cup shredded sharp cheddar cheese**
- 4 **tablespoons canola oil, divided**

1. In a large bowl, combine the first eight ingredients. Stir in cheese.

2. Heat 2 tablespoons oil in a large nonstick skillet over medium heat. Drop the batter by ¼ cupfuls into oil; press lightly to flatten. Cook in batches for 2-3 minutes on each side or until golden brown, using remaining oil as needed. Drain on paper towels.

"Everyone who tries these cheesy herbed pancakes raves about them. I think the tasty fried patties could replace almost any potato dish in any meal. I serve them most often with barbecued ribs and chicken."

—**CATHY HALL** LYNDHURST, VA

Rustic Rye Bread

Treat your family and friends to the pure delight of fresh-baked homemade bread. This beautiful, crusty rye loaf gets a touch of sweetness from molasses and brown sugar. With a firm texture, hearty slices hold up well in sandwiches but are also nice just spread with butter.

—**HOLLY WADE** HARRISONBURG, VA

PREP: 20 MIN. + RISING
BAKE: 30 MIN. + COOLING
MAKES: 2 LOAVES (12 SLICES EACH)

- 1 package (¼ ounce) active dry yeast
- 1¾ cups warm water (110° to 115°), divided
- ¼ cup packed brown sugar
- ¼ cup light molasses
- 3 tablespoons caraway seeds
- 2 tablespoons canola oil
- 3 teaspoons salt
- 1¾ cups rye flour
- ¾ cup whole wheat flour
- 1¾ to 2¼ cups all-purpose flour

1. In a large bowl, dissolve yeast in ¼ cup warm water. Add brown sugar, molasses, caraway seeds, oil, salt and remaining water; mix well. Add rye flour, whole wheat flour and 1¾ cups all-purpose flour. Beat until smooth. Stir in enough remaining all-purpose flour to form a firm dough.
2. Turn onto a lightly floured surface; knead until smooth and elastic, about 6-8 minutes. Place in a bowl coated with cooking spray, turning once to coat top. Cover and let rise in a warm place until doubled, about 1 hour.
3. Punch dough down; shape into two round loaves. Place on a baking sheet coated with cooking spray. Cover and let rise until doubled, about 1 hour.
4. Bake at 350° for 30-35 minutes or until golden brown. Remove from pan to wire rack to cool.
PER SERVING *104 cal., 2 g fat (trace sat. fat), 0 chol., 298 mg sodium, 21 g carb., 2 g fiber, 2 g pro.* **Diabetic Exchange:** *1½ starch.*

Pasta with Asparagus

A fantastic side is only 30 minutes away! Featuring bacon, cream and Parmesan, it could even make a main course.

—**BARBARA CALHOUN**
MARQUETTE HEIGHTS, IL

START TO FINISH: 30 MIN.
MAKES: 8 SERVINGS

- 2 pounds fresh asparagus, trimmed and cut diagonally into 1-inch pieces
- 1 package (16 ounces) thin spaghetti
- 8 bacon strips, coarsely chopped
- 4 green onions, sliced
- ½ teaspoon pepper
- ½ cup half-and-half cream
- ½ to ¾ cup grated Parmesan cheese
- ¼ cup butter, cubed

1. In a large saucepan, bring ½ in. of water to a boil. Add the asparagus; cook, covered, 3-5 minutes or until crisp-tender. Drain.
2. In a 6-qt. stockpot, cook spaghetti according to the package directions. Meanwhile, in a large skillet, cook the bacon over medium heat until crisp, stirring occasionally. Remove with a slotted spoon; drain on paper towels. Cook and stir green onions in the bacon drippings 1-2 minutes or until tender. Add asparagus and pepper; heat through.
3. Drain pasta; return to stockpot. Add asparagus mixture, cream, cheese, butter and bacon; toss to combine until butter is melted.

Coconut Twice-Baked Sweet Potatoes

With coconut, maple syrup and just a few other ingredients, it's a breeze to dress up sweet potatoes. These twice-baked spuds look so pretty on the plate, too.

—**NANCY SOBEL** BAY SHORE, NY

PREP: 30 MIN. • **BAKE:** 20 MIN.
MAKES: 8 SERVINGS

- 4 medium sweet potatoes
- ½ cup coconut milk
- 1 tablespoon maple syrup
- 1 teaspoon minced fresh gingerroot
- 1 teaspoon adobo sauce
- ½ teaspoon salt
- ¼ cup chopped pecans
- ¼ cup flaked coconut

1. Scrub and pierce potatoes; place on a microwave-safe plate. Microwave, uncovered, on high for 10-12 minutes or until tender, turning once.
2. When cool enough to handle, cut each potato in half lengthwise. Scoop out the pulp, leaving thin shells. In a large bowl, mash the pulp with the coconut milk. Stir in the maple syrup, ginger, adobo sauce and salt. Spoon into potato shells.
3. Place potatoes on a baking sheet. Sprinkle with pecans and coconut. Bake at 350° for 20-25 minutes or until heated through.
PER SERVING *137 cal., 7 g fat (4 g sat. fat), 0 chol., 175 mg sodium, 18 g carb., 2 g fiber, 2 g pro.* **Diabetic Exchanges:** *1 starch, 1 fat.*

Winter Vegetable Gratin

Here's a rich and creamy dish with all the comfort you crave during chilly weather. I like to use a mandolin cutter on the root vegetables to speed up preparation.

—**RACHEL DUEKER** GERVAIS, OR

PREP: 30 MIN. + COOLING
BAKE: 55 MIN. + STANDING
MAKES: 6 SERVINGS

- 1 small onion, chopped
- 1 tablespoon butter
- 1 garlic clove, minced
- 1½ cups heavy whipping cream
- ½ cup sour cream
- 4½ teaspoons minced fresh rosemary or 1½ teaspoons dried rosemary, crushed
- 1 tablespoon minced fresh basil or 1 teaspoon dried basil
- ½ teaspoon salt
- ½ teaspoon pepper
- ½ teaspoon ground cumin
- 3 medium Yukon Gold potatoes, peeled and thinly sliced
- 2 medium turnips, peeled and thinly sliced
- 1 medium sweet potato, peeled and thinly sliced

1. In a small skillet, saute the onion in butter until tender. Add the garlic; cook 1 minute longer. Stir in whipping cream, sour cream, rosemary, basil, salt, pepper and cumin. Bring to a gentle boil. Remove from the heat; cool for 10 minutes.
2. Layer half of the potatoes, turnips and sweet potato in a greased 8-in. square baking dish; pour half of sauce over the top. Repeat layers.
3. Cover; bake at 350° for 45 minutes. Uncover; bake 10-15 minutes longer or until bubbly and the potatoes are tender. Let stand for 10 minutes before serving.

Zesty Lemon Curd

We have backyard lemon trees, and I'm always looking for new uses for the fruit. This curd keeps well and adds a tangy twist to everything from muffins to ice cream.

—**JEAN GAINES** BULLHEAD CITY, AZ

PREP: 5 MIN. • **COOK:** 20 MIN. + COOLING
MAKES: 3 CUPS

- 3 **eggs, lightly beaten**
- 2 **cups sugar**
- ¾ **cup lemon juice**
- 2 **teaspoons grated lemon peel**
- 1 **cup butter, cubed**

1. In a large heavy saucepan, whisk eggs, sugar, lemon juice and peel until blended. Add the butter; cook over medium heat, whisking constantly, until the mixture is thick enough to coat the back of a metal spoon and a thermometer reads at least 170°. Do not allow to boil. Remove from heat immediately. Transfer to a small bowl; cool. Press plastic wrap onto the surface of curd. Refrigerate until cold.
2. Spread on muffins or rolls, or serve over waffles or ice cream.

Zucchini Fritters

Enjoy your homegrown zucchini in more than cakes or breads! Savory fried fritters flavored with ranch dip mix make a great side for a variety of menus. One of my favorites during summer is barbecued ribs or pork chops with corn on the cob.

—**MARY KAY DIXSON** DECATUR, AL

START TO FINISH: 30 MIN.
MAKES: 1½ TO 2 DOZEN

-   **Vegetable oil**
- ½ **cup milk**
- 1 **egg, lightly beaten**
- 1 **cup all-purpose flour**
- 1½ **teaspoons baking powder**
- ½ **of 1-ounce package ranch-style dip mix**
- 2 **cups (8 ounces) shredded zucchini**

1. Fill a deep-fat fryer or skillet with oil to a 2-in. depth. Heat to 375°.
2. Meanwhile, combine milk and egg in a bowl. Stir together dry ingredients and add to the egg mixture; blend well. Fold in the zucchini. Drop the batter by rounded teaspoonfuls into hot oil. Fry until deep golden brown, turning once. Drain thoroughly on paper towels.

Mission Baked Beans

PREP: 10 MIN. • **BAKE:** 1 HOUR
MAKES: 8-10 SERVINGS

- 8 slices bacon, cooked and crumbled
- 1 can (28 ounces) pork and beans, drained
- 1 can (16 ounces) chili beans, drained
- ¾ cup finely chopped onion
- ½ cup packed dark brown sugar
- 1 can (10 ounces) enchilada sauce
- 1 tablespoon all-purpose flour
- 2 teaspoons chili powder
- 1 teaspoon ground cumin
- ⅛ teaspoon garlic powder
- 1 cup (4 ounces) shredded Monterey Jack cheese

1. In a bowl, combine the first 10 ingredients. Transfer bean mixture to a greased 2-qt. baking dish. Bake, uncovered, at 450° for 15 minutes.
2. Reduce the heat to 375°; bake 35 minutes longer, stirring occasionally. Sprinkle with Monterey Jack cheese; bake 15 minutes more.

“My friends and relatives are always happy to see Mission Baked Beans, a favorite I've been making for over 20 years. Delicious paired with corn bread or tortillas, it's also hearty enough to eat as an entree with a salad.”

—MRS. CHARLES LEWIS YUCAIPA, CA

Company Vegetable Casserole

A neighbor shared this recipe with me, and now I get requests for it all the time. The cheesy casserole has become my go-to choice for everything from family dinners to reunions and potlucks.
—**LEORA CLARK** LINCOLN, NE

PREP: 10 MIN. • **BAKE:** 35 MIN.
MAKES: 6-8 SERVINGS

- 1 can (14½ ounces) cut green beans, drained, or 2 cups frozen cut green beans, thawed
- 1 can (15¼ ounces) whole kernel corn, drained, or 2 cups cooked fresh or frozen whole kernel corn
- 1 can (10¾ ounces) condensed cream of celery soup, undiluted
- ½ cup sour cream
- ½ cup shredded cheddar cheese
- ½ cup chopped onion
- ¼ cup butter, melted
- ¾ cup saltine crumbs
- ¼ cup sliced almonds, toasted

1. In a large bowl, combine the green beans, corn, cream of celery soup, sour cream, cheese and onion. Pour into an ungreased 2-qt. baking dish.
2. Combine the butter, saltine crumbs and sliced almonds; sprinkle over the vegetables. Bake, uncovered, at 350° for 35-40 minutes or until bubbly.

Rice and Barley Pilaf

A trio of whole grains, wild and brown rice, barley...it all adds up to a dish that's packed with nutrition. A little grated Parmesan cheese and half-and-half cream lend richness.

—**BARB TEMPLIN** NORWOOD, MN

PREP: 20 MIN. • **COOK:** 1 HOUR
MAKES: 6 SERVINGS

- 3 cups reduced-sodium chicken broth
- ¼ cup uncooked wild rice
- ¼ cup medium pearl barley
- ¼ cup uncooked brown rice
- ½ pound baby portobello mushrooms, chopped
- 1 small onion, chopped
- 1 celery rib, finely chopped
- 1 tablespoon butter
- 1 tablespoon olive oil
- 3 garlic cloves, minced
- ¼ cup grated Parmesan cheese
- ¼ cup half-and-half cream
- ⅛ teaspoon pepper

1. In a large saucepan, combine the chicken broth and wild rice. Bring to a boil. Reduce heat; cover and simmer for 10 minutes. Stir in the barley and brown rice; cover and simmer for 40-45 minutes or until grains are tender and liquid is absorbed.

2. Meanwhile, in a large nonstick skillet, saute portobello mushrooms, onion and celery in butter and oil until tender. Add the garlic; cook 1 minute longer. Stir in rice mixture, Parmesan cheese, half-and-half cream and pepper; heat through.

PER SERVING *176 cal., 7 g fat (3 g sat. fat), 13 mg chol., 363 mg sodium, 23 g carb., 3 g fiber, 7 g pro.* **Diabetic Exchanges:** *1½ fat, 1 starch, 1 vegetable.*

Rosemary-Garlic Focaccia Bread

You know you're in for a treat when you smell this bread baking! I make it mostly during summer when I have herbs in my garden, but I also enjoy it at holiday time using rosemary from the store.

—**TAMMY BOLLMAN** MINATARE, NE

PREP: 30 MIN. + RISING • **BAKE:** 15 MIN.
MAKES: 1 LOAF (12 WEDGES)

- ¾ cup warm fat-free milk (70° to 80°)
- ¼ cup water (70° to 80°)

- ¼ cup butter, softened
- 1 egg
- 2¾ cups bread flour
- 2 tablespoons sugar
- 2 teaspoons kosher salt, divided
- 2 teaspoons active dry yeast
- 4 teaspoons olive oil
- 4 garlic cloves, minced
- 1 tablespoon minced fresh rosemary

1. In bread machine pan, place the milk, water, butter, egg, bread flour, sugar, 1 teaspoon salt and yeast in order suggested by manufacturer. Select the dough setting (check the dough after 5 minutes of mixing; add 1 to 2 tablespoons of water or flour if needed).

2. When the cycle is completed, turn dough onto a lightly floured surface. Punch dough down. Cover and let rest for 10 minutes. Shape into an 11-in. circle; place on a baking sheet coated with cooking spray. Cover and let rise until doubled, about 30 minutes. Using the end of a wooden spoon handle, make several ¼-in. indentations in the dough.

3. Brush with oil. Sprinkle with garlic, rosemary and remaining salt. Bake at 400° for 15-20 minutes or until golden brown. Cut into wedges.

NOTE *We recommend you do not use a bread machine's time-delay feature for this recipe.*

PER SERVING *162 cal., 6 g fat (3 g sat. fat), 28 mg chol., 353 mg sodium, 24 g carb., 1 g fiber, 5 g pro.* **Diabetic Exchanges:** *1½ starch, 1 fat.*

Spiced Rhubarb Sauce

Just about any cut of pork will get a tangy boost from this unusual sauce. A great way to use up your homegrown rhubarb, the relish-like condiment also pairs well with roasted, baked or grilled chicken.
—KARA HAWKE POLK, PA

PREP: 20 MIN. • **COOK:** 50 MIN.
MAKES: 2½ CUPS

- 4 cups chopped fresh or frozen rhubarb, thawed
- 2 large onions, chopped
- 1 medium green pepper, chopped
- ¾ cup packed brown sugar
- ¾ cup cider vinegar
- ¼ cup reduced-sodium soy sauce
- 2 teaspoons steak seasoning
- 1 garlic clove, minced
- ½ teaspoon celery seed
- ½ teaspoon ground coriander
- ½ teaspoon ground cinnamon
- ½ teaspoon ground allspice

RHUBARB READY

Store unwashed rhubarb in the refrigerator for up to 1 week. Sliced rhubarb may be frozen for up to 9 months. When preparing rhubarb, always trim and discard any leaves, which contain oxalic acid and are toxic. Thick stalks can be peeled with a vegetable peeler to remove fibrous strings. One pound of rhubarb equals about 3 cups chopped raw or 2 cups cooked rhubarb.

In a large saucepan, combine all ingredients. Bring to a boil. Reduce the heat; simmer, uncovered, for 45-50 minutes or until thickened. Serve warm with chicken or pork. Refrigerate leftovers.

NOTES *If using frozen rhubarb, measure rhubarb while still frozen, then thaw completely. Drain in a colander, but do not press the liquid out. This recipe was tested with McCormick's Montreal Steak Seasoning. Look for it in the spice aisle.*

PER SERVING *48 cal., trace fat (trace sat. fat), 0 chol., 195 mg sodium, 11 g carb., 1 g fiber, 1 g pro.* **Diabetic Exchange:** *1 starch.*

Green Beans Provencale

Garlic, tomatoes and olive oil are often found in Southern French cooking. Here, they complement green beans perfectly.
—PAULA WHARTON EL PASO, TX

START TO FINISH: 30 MIN.
MAKES: 5 SERVINGS

- 1 pound fresh green beans, trimmed and cut into 2-inch pieces
- 4 green onions, sliced
- 2 tablespoons minced shallot
- 4 garlic cloves, minced
- 2 teaspoons minced fresh rosemary or ½ teaspoon dried rosemary, crushed
- 1 tablespoon olive oil
- 1½ cups grape tomatoes, halved
- 2 tablespoons minced fresh or 2 teaspoons dried basil
- ½ teaspoon salt
- ¼ teaspoon pepper

1. Place the green beans in a steamer basket; place in a large saucepan over 1 in. of water. Bring to a boil; cover and steam for 4-5 minutes or until beans are crisp-tender.
2. Meanwhile, in a large skillet, saute the green onions, shallot, garlic and rosemary in oil until the vegetables are tender. Add beans, tomatoes, basil, salt and pepper; saute 2-3 minutes longer or until heated through.

PER SERVING *70 cal., 3 g fat (trace sat. fat), 0 chol., 248 mg sodium, 10 g carb., 4 g fiber, 2 g pro.* **Diabetic Exchanges:** *2 vegetable, ½ fat.*

Asian Quinoa

Whether you cook with quinoa frequently or have never tasted it, you'll want to try this delicious side dish. Ginger and plum sauce lend wonderful Asian flavor. For a change of pace, I add a scrambled egg or replace the rice vinegar with soy sauce.

—SONYA LABBE WEST HOLLYWOOD, CA

PREP: 20 MIN. • **COOK:** 20 MIN. + STANDING
MAKES: 4 SERVINGS

- 1   **cup water**
- 2   **tablespoons rice vinegar**
- 2   **tablespoons plum sauce**
- 2   **garlic cloves, minced**
- 1   **teaspoon minced fresh gingerroot**
- 1   **teaspoon sesame oil**
- ¼   **teaspoon salt**
- ¼   **teaspoon crushed red pepper flakes**
- ½   **cup quinoa, rinsed**
- 1   **medium sweet red pepper, chopped**
- ½   **cup sliced water chestnuts, chopped**
- ½   **cup fresh sugar snap peas, trimmed and halved**
- 2   **green onions, thinly sliced**

1. In a large saucepan, combine the first eight ingredients; bring to a boil. Add quinoa. Reduce heat; cover and simmer for 12-15 minutes or until the water is absorbed.

2. Remove from the heat. Add the red pepper, water chestnuts, peas and onions; fluff with a fork. Cover and let stand for 10 minutes.

NOTE *Look for quinoa in the cereal, rice or organic food aisle.*

Creamy Caramels, page 189

179

174

188

Cookies, Bars & Candies

Sweeten any occasion with the top-rated treats in this chapter. Friends and family are sure to **snatch up delights** like tempting truffles, chunky brownies, festive cutouts and luscious fudge.

Touch-of-Gold Christmas Trees

I use pearl dust to add a little glitz to my spritz sandwich cookies, but they look pretty with any kind of sprinkles.
—**LINDA SWEET** CORNWALL, NY

PREP: 40 MIN. • **BAKE:** 10 MIN./BATCH • **MAKES:** 5½ DOZEN

- 1½ **cups butter, softened**
- 1 **cup sugar**
- 1 **egg**
- 2 **tablespoons 2% milk**
- 1 **teaspoon almond extract**
- 1 **teaspoon vanilla extract**
- 3½ **cups all-purpose flour**
- 1 **teaspoon baking powder**
- ⅔ **cup Nutella**
  Gold pearl dust

1. In a large bowl, cream the butter and sugar until light and fluffy. Beat in the egg, milk and extracts. Combine the flour and baking powder; gradually add to creamed mixture and mix well.

2. Using a cookie press fitted with the Christmas tree disk, press the dough 2 in. apart onto ungreased baking sheets. Bake at 375° for 8-10 minutes or until set (do not brown). Remove to wire racks to cool completely.

3. Spread the Nutella on the bottoms of half of the cookies; top with the remaining cookies. Brush tops with pearl dust. Store in an airtight container.

NOTE *Pearl dust is available from Wilton Industries. Call 800-794-5866 or visit* wilton.com.

PER SERVING *1 cookie equals 89 cal., 5 g fat (3 g sat. fat), 14 mg chol., 38 mg sodium, 10 g carb., trace fiber, 1 g pro. Diabetic Exchanges: 1 fat, ½ starch.*

Double-Decker Fudge

Thanks to the convenience of microwaving, this twice-as-nice fudge is just the thing when you need an easy holiday treat.
—**SHERRI MELOTIK** OAK CREEK, WI

PREP: 15 MIN. + CHILLING • **MAKES:** ABOUT 1½ POUNDS

- 1 **teaspoon butter**
- 1 **cup peanut butter chips**
- 1 **can (14 ounces) sweetened condensed milk, divided**
- 1 **teaspoon vanilla extract, divided**
- 1 **cup (6 ounces) semisweet chocolate chips**

1. Line an 8-in.-square pan with foil; butter the foil and set aside.

2. In a microwave-safe bowl, combine the peanut butter chips and ⅔ cup milk. Microwave on high for 1 minute; stir. Microwave at additional 15-second intervals, stirring until smooth. Stir in ½ teaspoon vanilla. Pour into prepared pan. Refrigerate for 10 minutes.

3. Meanwhile, in a microwave-safe bowl combine the chocolate chips and remaining milk. Microwave on high for 1 minute; stir. Microwave at additional 15-seconds intervals, stirring until smooth. Stir in remaining vanilla. Spread over peanut butter layer.

4. Refrigerate for 1 hour or until firm. Using foil, remove fudge from pan. Cut into 1-in. squares.

PER SERVING *One 1-in. square equals 47 cal., 2 g fat (1 g sat. fat), 2 mg chol., 15 mg sodium, 6 g carb., trace fiber, 1 g pro. Diabetic Exchange: ½ starch.*

Nutty Chocolate Batons

Buttery, chocolaty, crunchy—these fun little batons have it all! An added bonus is that their delightfully different shape and pistachio coating make them real standouts on a Christmas platter.

—ANGELA LEINENBACH
MECHANICSVILLE, VA

PREP: 45 MIN. + CHILLING
BAKE: 10 MIN./BATCH + COOLING
MAKES: 8 DOZEN

- ¾ **cup butter, softened**
- ⅓ **cup sugar**
- ⅓ **cup almond paste**
- 1 **egg yolk**
- 1⅔ **cups all-purpose flour**
- 1 **cup (6 ounces) semisweet chocolate chips**
- ½ **cup pistachios, finely chopped and toasted**

1. In a small bowl, cream the butter, sugar and almond paste until light and fluffy. Beat in egg yolk. Gradually add flour and mix well. Shape into a ball, then flatten into a disk. Wrap in plastic wrap and refrigerate for 2 hours or until easy to handle.

2. Divide the dough into eight equal portions; divide each portion in half. On a lightly floured surface, roll each half into a 12-in. rope; cut each rope into 2-in. lengths. Place 2 in. apart on greased baking sheets. Bake at 350° for 6-8 minutes or until the edges are lightly browned. Remove to wire racks to cool completely.

3. In a microwave, melt the chocolate chips; stir until smooth. Dip the ends of each cookie in chocolate, then in pistachios. Let stand on waxed paper until set. Store in an airtight container.

PER SERVING *1 cookie equals 39 cal., 3 g fat (1 g sat. fat), 6 mg chol., 13 mg sodium, 4 g carb., trace fiber, 1 g pro.* ***Diabetic Exchange:*** *½ starch.*

I came up with Chocolate Toffee Delights using my go-to shortbread recipe and some ingredients I had on hand. The flavor reminds me of my favorite Girl Scout cookies.

—**SHANNON KOENE** BLACKSBURG, VA

Chocolate Toffee Delights

PREP: 15 MIN. • **BAKE:** 30 MIN. + COOLING • **MAKES:** 3 DOZEN

- 1 **cup butter, softened**
- ½ **cup plus 2 tablespoons sugar, divided**
- ¾ **teaspoon almond extract**
- ½ **teaspoon coconut extract**
- 2 **cups all-purpose flour**
- ¼ **teaspoon salt**
- ¼ **teaspoon baking powder**
- ½ **cup flaked coconut**
- ½ **cup sliced almonds, toasted and cooled**
- 1 **jar (12¼ ounces) caramel ice cream topping**
- ¾ **cup dark chocolate chips**

1. Preheat oven to 350°. In a small bowl, cream butter and ½ cup sugar until light and fluffy. Beat in extracts. Combine the flour, salt and baking powder; gradually add to creamed mixture and mix well.

2. Press the dough into a greased 13x9-in. baking pan. Bake 10 minutes. Prick the crust with a fork; sprinkle with the remaining sugar. Bake 15 minutes longer or until set.
3. Meanwhile, place the coconut and almonds in a food processor; cover and process until finely chopped. Transfer to a small bowl; stir in caramel ice cream topping. Spread over the crust. Bake 5-10 minutes or until edges are bubbly. Cool on a wire rack.
4. In a microwave, melt chocolate chips; stir until smooth. Drizzle over caramel mixture. Let stand until the chocolate is set. Cut into bars. Store in an airtight container.

PER SERVING *1 bar equals 149 cal., 8 g fat (5 g sat. fat), 13 mg chol., 92 mg sodium, 19 g carb., trace fiber, 2 g pro. Diabetic Exchanges: 1½ fat, 1 starch.*

Mini Cinnamon Roll Cookies

These spiced spirals are a cross between a snickerdoodle and a cinnamon roll. I think they're best with a cup of coffee, so save a few for your morning or afternoon break. You just might be tempted to grab some for breakfast, too!

—**MARY GAUNTT** DENTON, TX

PREP: 1 HOUR • **BAKE:** 10 MIN./BATCH + COOLING
MAKES: ABOUT 2½ DOZEN

- 1 **cup butter, softened**
- 1¾ **cups sugar, divided**
- 3 **egg yolks**
- 1 **tablespoon plus 1 teaspoon honey, divided**
- 1 **teaspoon vanilla extract**
- 2½ **cups all-purpose flour**
- 1 **teaspoon baking powder**
- ½ **teaspoon salt**
- ½ **teaspoon cream of tartar**
- 1 **tablespoon ground cinnamon**
- 8 **ounces white baking chocolate, chopped**

1. In a large bowl, cream the butter and 1¼ cups sugar until light and fluffy. Beat in the egg yolks, 1 tablespoon honey and vanilla. Combine the flour, baking powder, salt and cream of tartar; gradually add to the creamed mixture and mix well.
2. Shape a heaping tablespoonful of dough into a 6-in. log. In a shallow bowl, combine the cinnamon and remaining sugar; roll the log in cinnamon-sugar. Loosely coil the log into a spiral shape; place on a greased baking sheet. Repeat, placing the cookies 1 in. apart. Sprinkle with the remaining cinnamon-sugar.
3. Bake at 350° for 8-10 minutes or until set. Remove to wire racks to cool completely. In a small bowl, melt the baking chocolate with remaining honey; stir until smooth. Drizzle over the cookies. Let stand until set. Store in an airtight container.

PER SERVING *1 cookie equals 189 cal., 9 g fat (6 g sat. fat), 38 mg chol., 105 mg sodium, 25 g carb., trace fiber, 2 g pro. Diabetic Exchanges: 1½ starch, 1½ fat.*

Cuccidati

Cuccidati are Italian cookies traditionally served during the Christmas season, and this is my favorite version. It features dough cut into diagonal strips, a sweet glaze and a classic filling of dried figs, raisins, dates, oranges and nuts.

—**CAROLYN FAFINSKI** DUNKIRK, NY

PREP: 30 MIN. + CHILLING • **BAKE:** 10 MIN./BATCH + COOLING
MAKES: ABOUT 5 DOZEN

- 2 **cups raisins**
- ¾ **pound pitted dates**
- ¾ **cup sugar**
- 2 **small navel oranges, peeled and quartered**
- ⅓ **pound dried figs**
- ⅓ **cup chopped walnuts**
- ¼ **cup water**

DOUGH
- 1 **cup shortening**
- 1 **cup sugar**
- 2 **eggs**
- ¼ **cup 2% milk**
- 2 **teaspoons vanilla extract**
- 3½ **cups all-purpose flour**
- 1 **teaspoon salt**
- 1 **teaspoon baking powder**
- 1 **teaspoon baking soda**

GLAZE
- 2 **cups confectioners' sugar**
- 2 **to 3 tablespoons 2% milk**

1. Place the first seven ingredients in a food processor; cover and process until finely chopped. Set aside.
2. In a large bowl, cream shortening and sugar until light and fluffy. Beat in the eggs, milk and vanilla. Combine the flour, salt, baking powder and baking soda; gradually add to creamed mixture and mix well. Divide dough into four portions; cover and refrigerate for 1 hour.
3. Roll out each portion of dough between two sheets of waxed paper into a 16x6-in. rectangle. Spread 1 cup filling lengthwise down the center of each. Starting at a long side, fold the dough over filling; fold the other side over the top. Pinch the seams and edges to seal. Cut each rectangle diagonally into 1-in. strips. Place seam side down on parchment paper-lined baking sheets.
4. Bake at 400° for 10-14 minutes or until edges are golden brown. Cool for 10 minutes before removing from pans to wire racks to cool completely. Combine confectioners' sugar and enough milk to achieve desired consistency; drizzle over cookies. Store in an airtight container.

PER SERVING *1 cookie equals 132 cal., 4 g fat (1 g sat. fat), 7 mg chol., 67 mg sodium, 24 g carb., 1 g fiber, 1 g pro.*
Diabetic Exchanges: 1 starch, ½ fruit, ½ fat.

Daria's Best-Ever Sugar Cookies

After years of searching for the best homemade sugar cookies, I stopped looking when I discovered these! Almond paste adds a wonderful layer of flavor to the moist cutouts.

—DARIA BURCAR ROCHESTER, MI

PREP: 2 HOURS + CHILLING • **BAKE:** 10 MIN./BATCH + COOLING
MAKES: ABOUT 13½ DOZEN

- ½ **cup almond paste**
- 4 **egg yolks**
- 2 **cups butter, softened**
- 1¾ **cups sugar**
- ½ **teaspoon salt**
- 3¾ **cups all-purpose flour**
- **FROSTING**
- 3¾ **cups confectioners' sugar**
- 3 **tablespoons meringue powder**
- ⅓ **cup water**
  Food coloring, coarse sugar and assorted sprinkles, optional

1. In a large bowl, beat the almond paste and egg yolks until crumbly. Add the butter, sugar and salt; beat until light and fluffy. Gradually add the flour and mix well. Divide into four portions; shape each into a ball, then flatten into a disk. Wrap each disk in plastic wrap and refrigerate 1-2 hours or until easy to handle.

2. Preheat oven to 375°. On a lightly floured surface, roll one portion of dough to ¼-in. thickness. Cut with a floured 2½-in. cookie cutter. Place 2 in. apart on ungreased baking sheets. Repeat with remaining dough.

3. Bake 6-8 minutes or until the edges begin to brown. Cool 2 minutes before removing from pans to wire racks to cool completely.

4. For frosting, beat the confectioners' sugar, meringue powder and water until fluffy, about 5 minutes. Color the frosting if desired. Frost the cookies; decorate with coarse sugar and sprinkles if desired. Let stand until set. Store in an airtight container.

NOTE *Meringue powder is available from Wilton Industries. Call 800-794-5866 or visit* wilton.com.
PER SERVING *1 cookie equals 55 cal., 3 g fat (1 g sat. fat), 11 mg chol., 25 mg sodium, 7 g carb., trace fiber, 1 g pro.*
Diabetic Exchange: ½ starch.

Gooey Chocolate-Peanut Bars

When I need quick treats for a party, bake sale or other event, I turn to convenient refrigerated dough. I use the chocolate chip kind and just three other ingredients to make ooey-gooey bars.

—ELAINE GRIMME SIOUX FALLS, SD

PREP: 10 MIN. • **BAKE:** 20 MIN. + COOLING • **MAKES:** 2 DOZEN

- 1 **package (16½ ounces) refrigerated chocolate chip cookie dough**
- 2 **cups chocolate-covered peanuts**
- 1 **cup miniature marshmallows**
- ½ **cup butterscotch ice cream topping**

1. Press cookie dough into an ungreased 13x9x2-in. baking pan. Bake at 350° for 14-16 minutes or until edges are lightly browned and center is set. Sprinkle with chocolate-covered peanuts and marshmallows; drizzle with butterscotch ice cream topping.

2. Bake 6-8 minutes longer or until the marshmallows are puffed. Cool completely and cut into bars.

PER SERVING *1 bar equals 175 cal., 8 g fat (3 g sat. fat), 6 mg chol., 71 mg sodium, 24 g carb., 1 g fiber, 3 g pro.* **Diabetic Exchanges:** *2 fat, 1 starch.*

Apricot-Almond Dipped Cookies

These elegant crescents are easier to make than they look. For a twist, substitute milk chocolate for the white candy coating and use walnuts instead of almonds.

—TRISHA KRUSE EAGLE, ID

PREP: 35 MIN. • **BAKE:** 10 MIN./BATCH + COOLING
MAKES: 3 DOZEN

- 1 **cup butter, softened**
- ½ **cup confectioners' sugar**
- ½ **teaspoon almond extract**
- 2 **cups all-purpose flour**
- 1 **cup finely chopped dried apricots**
- 8 **ounces white candy coating, chopped**
- 1 **cup finely chopped almonds, toasted**

1. In a large bowl, cream butter and confectioners' sugar until light and fluffy. Beat in extract. Gradually add flour and mix well. Stir in apricots.

2. Roll 1 tablespoonful of dough into a 2½-in. log; shape into a crescent. Repeat. Place 2 in. apart on greased baking sheets. Bake at 350° for 10-14 minutes or until set. Remove to wire racks to cool completely.

3. In a microwave, melt the white candy coating; stir until smooth. Dip half of each cookie in the melted white candy coating; allow the excess to drip off. Press into almonds; place on waxed paper. Let stand until set. Store in an airtight container.

PER SERVING *1 cookie equals 138 cal., 9 g fat (5 g sat. fat), 13 mg chol., 39 mg sodium, 13 g carb., 1 g fiber, 2 g pro.*
***Diabetic Exchanges:** 1 starch, 1 fat.*

Soft Sugar Cookies

Our recipe for sugar cookies has been passed down to children and grandchildren in the family for decades. Try it—you'll see why it's still our favorite after all these years!

—ARNITA SCHROEDER HOAGLAND, IN

PREP: 20 MIN. + CHILLING • **BAKE:** 10 MIN./BATCH
MAKES: ABOUT 7½ DOZEN

- 4 **cups all-purpose flour**
- 1 **teaspoon baking powder**
- ½ **teaspoon nutmeg**
- 1 **cup butter, softened**
- 1¾ **cups sugar**
- ¾ **teaspoon salt**
- 4 **egg yolks**
- 2 **eggs**
- 1 **teaspoon baking soda**
- 2 **tablespoons hot water**
- 1 **cup (8 ounces) sour cream**
  Optional toppings: colored or granulated sugar and walnut halves

1. In a large bowl, whisk the flour, baking powder and nutmeg. In another bowl, cream the butter, sugar and salt until light and fluffy. Beat in the egg yolks and eggs. Dissolve the baking soda in the hot water. Add the sour cream and dissolved baking soda to the creamed mixture. Gradually beat in flour mixture (dough will be sticky). Refrigerate, covered, overnight.

2. Preheat oven to 350°. Working with one-third of the batch at a time, roll the dough on a well-floured surface to ¼-in. thickness. (Cover and refrigerate remaining dough until ready to roll.) Cut with a floured 2½-in. round or other shaped cookie cutter. Place 1 in. apart on greased baking sheets. If desired, sprinkle tops with sugar and top with walnuts.

3. Bake 8-10 minutes or until the cookies are set but not browned. Remove from pans to wire racks to cool.

White Chocolate Fudge

I whip up my white fudge to give as a gift not only for Christmas, but also for Valentine's Day. The cream cheese gives each little square a wonderfully rich texture, and the lighter color is an interesting contrast to darker candies.

—JAN LUTZ STEVENS POINT, WI

PREP: 15 MIN. + CHILLING • **MAKES:** ABOUT 4 DOZEN

- 1 **package (8 ounces) cream cheese, softened**
- 4 **cups confectioners' sugar**
- 1½ **teaspoons vanilla extract**
- 12 **ounces white baking chocolate**
- ¾ **cup chopped pecans**

In a bowl, beat cream cheese, confectioners' sugar and vanilla until smooth. In a double boiler, melt the white baking chocolate. Fold into cream cheese mixture with pecans. Spread into a greased 8-in.-square pan. Chill until serving. Cut into squares.

Sweet Potato Cheesecake Bars

Your whole house will be filled with the aroma of pumpkin spice when you bake these wonderful cheesecake bars. They're so easy to prepare using a boxed yellow cake mix and canned sweet potatoes, you can whip up a batch anytime.
—**NANCY WHITFORD** EDWARDS, NY

PREP: 20 MIN. • **BAKE:** 25 MIN. + CHILLING
MAKES: 2 DOZEN

- 1 **package yellow cake mix (regular size)**
- ½ **cup butter, softened**
- 1 **egg**

FILLING
- 1 **can (15 ounces) sweet potatoes, drained**
- 1 **package (8 ounces) cream cheese, cubed**
- ½ **cup plus ¼ cup sugar, divided**
- 1 **egg**
- 1½ **teaspoons pumpkin pie spice**
- 1 **cup (8 ounces) sour cream**
- ¼ **teaspoon vanilla extract**

TOPPING
- 1¼ **cups granola without raisins**
- ½ **cup white baking chips**
- ¼ **teaspoon pumpkin pie spice**

1. In a large bowl, beat yellow cake mix, butter and egg until crumbly. Press onto the bottom of a greased 13x9x2-in. baking dish.

2. Place the sweet potatoes, cream cheese, ½ cup sugar, egg and pumpkin pie spice in a food processor; cover and process until blended. Spread over the prepared crust.

3. Bake at 350° for 20-25 minutes or until center is almost set. Meanwhile, in a small bowl, combine sour cream, vanilla and remaining sugar. Spread over filling. Combine the topping ingredients; sprinkle over top. Bake 5-8 minutes longer or just until set. Cool on a wire rack.

4. Refrigerate for at least 2 hours. Cut into bars.

GRAND PRIZE WINNER ★★★★

GRAND PRIZE

Ultimate Double Chocolate Brownies

Chocoholics—here are the brownies for you! Baking cocoa and semisweet chunks in each bite make them doubly decadent. I like to stir in some crunchy chopped pecans, too.
—**CAROL PREWETT** CHEYENNE, WY

PREP: 15 MIN. • **BAKE:** 35 MIN.
MAKES: 3 DOZEN

- ¾ **cup baking cocoa**
- ½ **teaspoon baking soda**
- ⅔ **cup butter, melted, divided**
- ½ **cup boiling water**
- 2 **cups sugar**
- 2 **eggs**
- 1⅓ **cups all-purpose flour**
- 1 **teaspoon vanilla extract**
- ¼ **teaspoon salt**
- ½ **cup coarsely chopped pecans**
- 2 **cups (12 ounces) semisweet chocolate chunks**

1. Preheat oven to 350°. In a large bowl, combine the baking cocoa and baking soda; blend ⅓ cup melted butter. Add the boiling water; stir until well blended. Stir in the sugar, eggs and remaining butter. Add the flour, vanilla and salt. Stir in the pecans and chocolate chunks.

2. Pour into a greased 13x9x2-in. baking pan. Bake 35-40 minutes or until the brownies begin to pull away from the sides of pan. Cool.

Mint and chocolate are always a popular combination. This recipe spices it up with cinnamon for good measure! A drizzled topping and candies add a festive touch.

—**BARBARA ESTABROOK** RHINELANDER, WI

Cinnamon Chocolate Minties

PREP: 45 MIN.
BAKE: 10 MIN./BATCH + COOLING
MAKES: ABOUT 4 DOZEN

- ½ cup butter, softened
- ½ cup sugar
- ½ cup packed brown sugar
- 1 egg
- 1 teaspoon vanilla extract
- 1½ cups all-purpose flour
- ⅓ cup baking cocoa
- 1 teaspoon ground cinnamon
- ¼ teaspoon baking soda
- ⅓ cup coarsely crushed soft peppermint candies
- ⅓ cup dark chocolate chips

DRIZZLE

- ½ cup semisweet chocolate chips
- ½ teaspoon canola oil
- 2 teaspoons finely crushed soft peppermint candies

1. Preheat oven to 350°. In a small bowl, cream butter and sugars until light and fluffy. Beat in egg and vanilla. Combine flour, cocoa, cinnamon and baking soda; gradually add to creamed mixture and mix well. Fold in candies and dark chocolate chips.

2. Shape dough into 1-in. balls; place 1 in. apart on greased baking sheets. Flatten slightly. Bake 6-8 minutes or until set. Remove to wire racks to cool completely.

3. In a small bowl, melt the semisweet chocolate chips with the oil; stir until smooth. Drizzle over cookies. Sprinkle with candies. Let stand until set. Store in an airtight container.

NOTE *This recipe was tested with Bob's Sweet Stripes peppermint candies.*

PER SERVING *1 cookie equals 73 cal., 3 g fat (2 g sat. fat), 9 mg chol., 23 mg sodium, 11 g carb., trace fiber, 1 g pro.*
Diabetic Exchanges: ½ starch, ½ fat.

Orange Taffy

PREP: 20 MIN. • **COOK:** 1 HOUR + COOLING
MAKES: ABOUT 6 DOZEN

- 2 cups sugar
- 2 cups light corn syrup
- 1 can (6 ounces) frozen orange juice concentrate, undiluted
  Pinch salt
- 1 cup half-and-half cream
- ½ cup butter, cubed

1. In a heavy saucepan, combine the first four ingredients. Cook and stir over medium heat until the sugar is dissolved. Bring to a rapid boil and cook until a candy thermometer reads 245° (firm-ball stage). Remove from the heat; gradually add the cream and butter. Return to the heat; cook and stir until mixture reaches 245° again.

2. Pour into a greased 15x10x1-in. pan; cool. When cool enough to handle, roll the taffy into ½-in. logs or 1-in. balls. Wrap individually in foil or waxed paper; twist the ends.

NOTE *We recommend that you test your candy thermometer before each use by bringing water to a boil; the thermometer should read 212°. Adjust your recipe temperature up or down based on your test.*

"To me, Orange Taffy has just the right blend of tart and sweet flavors. Wrapping all the pieces takes a little time, but you can turn it into a fun family project by letting the kids help. It's a great way to get them involved in the kitchen."

—**CHRISTINE OLSON** HORSE CREEK, CA

Winter Squash Squares

Create a yummy treat using your cooked squash! Simply mash and stir it into the batter for these squares. You won't want to skip the from-scratch cream cheese frosting—it's a layer of richness that perfectly complements the mild bars.
—**SHIRLEY MURPHY** JACKSONVILLE, IL

PREP: 15 MIN. • **BAKE:** 25 MIN. + COOLING
MAKES: 4 DOZEN

- 2 **cups all-purpose flour**
- 2 **cups sugar**
- 2 **teaspoons baking powder**
- 1 **teaspoon baking soda**
- ½ **teaspoon ground cinnamon**
- ⅛ **teaspoon salt**
- 4 **eggs, beaten**
- 2 **cups mashed cooked winter squash**
- 1 **cup canola oil**

CREAM CHEESE FROSTING
- 1 **package (3 ounces) cream cheese, softened**
- 2 **cups confectioners' sugar**
- 1 **teaspoon vanilla extract**
- 6 **tablespoons butter, softened**
- 1 **tablespoon milk**

1. In a bowl, combine the flour, sugar, baking powder, baking soda, cinnamon and salt. Stir in the eggs, squash and oil; mix well. Spread into a greased 15x10x1-in. baking pan. Bake at 350° for 25-30 minutes or until a toothpick comes out clean. Cool on a wire rack.
2. Meanwhile, beat cream cheese, confectioners' sugar, vanilla and butter. Add milk; stir until smooth. Frost cooled cake. Cut into squares.

SUPER SQUASH

Members of the gourd family, winter squash have a hard, inedible shell and fully mature seeds. Varieties of winter squash include acorn, spaghetti, turban, butternut, Hubbard, buttercup, sweet dumpling and delicata. Store unwashed winter squash in a cool, dry, well-ventilated area for up to four weeks.

Molasses Cookies with a Kick

This recipe features a spice combination I've used for a long time. The kick comes from just a bit of cayenne pepper. Rolling the balls of dough in golden turbinado sugar before baking gives them a lovely shine and sweet finishing touch.
—**TAMARA RAU** MEDINA, ND

PREP: 40 MIN. + CHILLING
BAKE: 10 MIN./BATCH • **MAKES:** 8 DOZEN

- ¾ **cup butter, softened**
- ½ **cup sugar**
- ½ **cup packed brown sugar**
- ¼ **cup molasses**
- 1 **egg**
- 1½ **teaspoons minced fresh gingerroot**
- 2¼ **cups all-purpose flour**
- 1 **teaspoon ground cinnamon**
- ¾ **teaspoon baking soda**
- ½ **teaspoon ground cloves**
- ¼ **to ½ teaspoon cayenne pepper**
- ¼ **teaspoon salt**
- ¼ **teaspoon ground nutmeg**
- ⅛ **teaspoon each ground white pepper, cardamom and coriander**
- ¾ **cup turbinado (washed raw) sugar**

1. In a large bowl, cream butter and sugars until light and fluffy. Beat in the molasses, egg and ginger. Combine the flour, cinnamon, baking soda, cloves, cayenne pepper, salt, nutmeg, white pepper, cardamom and coriander; gradually add to the creamed mixture and mix well. Cover and refrigerate cookie dough for 1½ hours or until easy to handle.
2. Roll the cookie dough into ½-in. balls; roll in the turbinado sugar. Place 3 in. apart on lightly greased baking sheets.
3. Bake at 350° for 8-10 minutes or until set. Cool for 2 minutes before removing from pans to wire racks. Store in an airtight container.
PER SERVING *1 cookie equals 41 cal., 2 g fat (1 g sat. fat), 6 mg chol., 28 mg sodium, 7 g carb., trace fiber, trace pro.* **Diabetic Exchange:** *½ starch.*

Coconut Almond Bombs

I make my little dipped bombs for holiday parties and weddings. For very special occasions, I take a new small paintbrush and spread a light, shimmery coating of gold pearl dust on the sliced almonds.

—DEB HOLBROOK ABINGTON, MA

PREP: 50 MIN. + CHILLING
BAKE: 15 MIN./BATCH • **MAKES:** 3½ DOZEN

- 1 package (7 ounces) almond paste
- 2 cups confectioners' sugar
- 1 package (14 ounces) flaked coconut
- 3 egg whites
- 1 teaspoon vanilla extract
- 1 carton (8 ounces) Mascarpone cheese
- 2 pounds white candy coating, chopped
- ⅔ cup sliced almonds
  Gold pearl dust

1. Place the almond paste in a food processor; cover and process until small crumbs form. Transfer to a large bowl; add the confectioners' sugar and coconut. Beat until the mixture resembles coarse crumbs. In a small bowl, beat the egg whites and vanilla until stiff peaks form; fold into the coconut mixture.

2. Drop by tablespoonfuls 2 in. apart onto parchment paper-lined baking sheets. Bake at 325° for 14-18 minutes or until lightly browned. Remove to wire racks to cool.

3. Spread about 1 teaspoon cheese over each cookie; refrigerate for 20 minutes or until cheese is firm.

4. In a microwave, melt the candy coating; stir until smooth. Dip cookies in the coating; allow excess to drip off. Place on waxed paper; sprinkle with almonds. Let stand until set. Brush pearl dust over almonds. Store in an airtight container in the refrigerator.
NOTE *Pearl dust is available from Wilton Industries. Call 800-794-5866 or visit* wilton.com.

German Chocolate Thumbprints

Traditional German chocolate cake as a cookie? Yes, please!
—DONNA MARIE RYAN
TOPSFIELD, MA

PREP: 45 MIN.
BAKE: 10 MIN./BATCH + COOLING
MAKES: 4 DOZEN

- ½ cup semisweet chocolate chips
- 1 tablespoon shortening

- ½ cup butter, softened
- ¾ cup sugar
- 1 egg
- 1 tablespoon strong brewed coffee
- 1 teaspoon vanilla extract
- 2 cups all-purpose flour
- 1 tablespoon baking cocoa
- 1 teaspoon baking powder
- ¼ teaspoon salt

FILLING
- ¾ cup flaked coconut, toasted
- ¾ cup chopped pecans, toasted
- 1 teaspoon vanilla extract
- 4 to 6 tablespoons sweetened condensed milk

DRIZZLE
- ½ cup semisweet chocolate chips
- 1 tablespoon shortening

1. In a microwave, melt chips and shortening; stir until smooth. Set aside. In a large bowl, cream butter and sugar until light and fluffy. Beat in the egg, coffee, vanilla and melted chocolate mixture. Combine the flour, cocoa, baking powder and salt; gradually add to the creamed mixture and mix well.

2. Roll into 1-in. balls. Place 2 in. apart on greased baking sheets. Using the end of a wooden spoon handle, make an indentation in the center of each ball. Bake at 350° for 6-8 minutes or until firm. Remove to wire racks to cool completely.

3. Meanwhile, for filling, in a small bowl, combine the coconut, pecans and vanilla. Stir in enough milk to form a stiff mixture. Fill cookies with filling, a rounded teaspoonful in each. Melt chips with shortening; stir until smooth. Drizzle over cookies. Store in an airtight container.

Extra-Special Cashew Crescents

These crescent shortbread cutouts are absolutely scrumptious! They're popular no matter how I present them, whether glazed, sprinkled with cashews or dusted with sugar.
—**PAULA MARCHESI** LENHARTSVILLE, PA

PREP: 15 MIN. + CHILLING
BAKE: 10 MIN./BATCH + COOLING • **MAKES:** 6 DOZEN

- 1⅔ cups lightly salted cashews
- 1 cup butter, softened
- ¾ cup packed brown sugar
- ½ cup sugar
- 2 teaspoons vanilla extract, divided
- 1⅔ cups all-purpose flour
- ¼ teaspoon salt
- 2 cups confectioners' sugar
- 3 tablespoons 2% milk
  Chopped lightly salted cashews and additional confectioners' sugar, optional

1. Place cashews in a food processor; cover and process until finely chopped.
2. In a large bowl, cream the butter and sugars until light and fluffy. Beat in 1 teaspoon vanilla. Combine flour, salt and chopped cashews; gradually add to creamed mixture and mix well.
3. Divide the dough in half; shape each into a ball, then flatten into a disk. Wrap in plastic wrap and refrigerate 30 minutes.
4. Preheat oven to 375°. On a lightly floured surface, roll one portion of dough to ¼-in. thickness. Using a floured scalloped round 3-in. cookie cutter, cut a semicircle from one corner of the dough, forming the inside of a crescent shape. Reposition the cutter 1¼ in. from inside of crescent; cut the cookie, forming a crescent shape 1¼ in. wide at its widest point. Repeat with the remaining dough. Chill and reroll scraps if desired.
5. Place cutouts 1 in. apart on ungreased baking sheets. Bake 6-7 minutes or until the edges begin to brown. Cool 2 minutes before removing from the pans to wire racks to cool completely.
6. Combine the confectioners' sugar, milk and remaining vanilla; spread or drizzle over cookies as desired. Sprinkle with chopped cashews if desired. Leave some cookies plain or sprinkle them with additional sugar if desired. Let iced cookies stand until set. Store in an airtight container.

PER SERVING *1 cookie equals 79 cal., 4 g fat (2 g sat. fat), 7 mg chol., 34 mg sodium, 10 g carb., trace fiber, 1 g pro.* **Diabetic Exchange:** *½ starch.*

Fudge Nut Brownies

PREP: 15 MIN. • **BAKE:** 25 MIN. • **MAKES:** ABOUT 24 BROWNIES

- 1⅓ cups all-purpose flour
- 2 cups sugar
- ¾ cup baking cocoa
- 1 teaspoon baking powder
- ½ teaspoon salt
- ½ cup chopped nuts
- ⅔ cup vegetable oil
- 4 eggs, lightly beaten
- 2 teaspoons vanilla extract
- 1 cup chopped nuts, optional

1. Preheat oven to 350°. In a bowl, combine the first six ingredients. In another bowl, combine oil, eggs and vanilla; add to dry ingredients. Do not overmix.
2. Spread in a 13x9x2-in. baking pan. Sprinkle with nuts if desired. Bake 20-25 minutes or until a toothpick inserted in center comes out clean. Cool in pan on a wire rack.

❝ The recipe for Fudge Nut Brownies came from my husband's grandmother, and I've never tasted a better one. It's easy, too—I can get a pan baking in just 15 minutes. ❞

—**BECKY ALBRIGHT** NORWALK, OH

Italian Sprinkle Cookies

My husband and I have two grown children and used to run an Italian-American restaurant. Our family's glazed cookie recipe goes back for generations. Dressed up with colorful sprinkles, the cute little rounds are festive and yummy.

—**GLORIA CRACCHIOLO** NEWBURGH, NY

PREP: 25 MIN. • **BAKE:** 15 MIN./BATCH + STANDING
MAKES: ABOUT 7 DOZEN

- 6 **eggs**
- 5 **cups all-purpose flour**
- 2 **cups confectioners' sugar**
- 2 **tablespoons plus 1½ teaspoons baking powder**
- 1 **cup shortening**
- 3 **teaspoons almond extract**
- 1½ **teaspoons lemon extract**

GLAZE
- 3¾ **cups confectioners' sugar**
- ½ **cup warm milk**
- 1 **teaspoon almond extract**
- 1 **teaspoon vanilla extract**
  Colored sprinkles

1. Using a heavy-duty mixer, beat the eggs on high speed until light and foamy, about 5 minutes; set aside. In a large bowl, combine the flour, confectioners' sugar and baking powder; on low speed, gradually beat in shortening and extracts until mixture resembles fine crumbs. Gradually add beaten eggs (dough will be stiff).

2. Roll cookie dough into 1-in. balls. Place 2 in. apart on ungreased baking sheets. Bake at 350° for 12-14 minutes (the tops of the cookies will not brown, but the bottoms should brown slightly).

3. Meanwhile, in a small bowl, combine the confectioners' sugar, milk and extracts until smooth. As soon as cookies are removed from oven, quickly dip two or three at a time into glaze. Remove with a slotted spoon or tongs; place on wire racks to drain. Immediately top with sprinkles. Let dry for 24 hours before storing in airtight containers.

Cranberry Orange Truffles

Truffles are a treat we look forward to each Christmas season. These have tart cranberries, rich chocolate, a burst of citrus and almond flavor in every bite. Heavenly!

—**TERRYANN MOORE** VINELAND, NJ

PREP: 1 HOUR + CHILLING • **MAKES:** ABOUT 3 DOZEN

- 12 **ounces bittersweet chocolate, chopped**
- ½ **cup unsalted butter, cubed**
- 4 **egg yolks, beaten**
- 1 **cup dried cranberries, chopped**
- 3 **tablespoons thawed orange juice concentrate**
- 1 **teaspoon almond extract**

COATING
- 12 **ounces white candy coating, chopped**
- 1 **ounce bittersweet chocolate, melted**

1. In a double boiler or metal bowl over simmering water, heat chocolate and butter until melted, stirring frequently. Whisk a small amount of the mixture into the egg yolks. Return all to the heat, whisking constantly. Cook and stir until mixture reaches at least 160° and coats the back of a metal spoon.

2. Remove from the heat; stir in the cranberries, orange juice concentrate and extract. Cool to room temperature, stirring occasionally. Refrigerate for 1 hour or until easy to handle. Shape into 1-in. balls.

3. In a microwave, melt the white candy coating. Dip the truffles in the melted coating; allow the excess to drip off. Place on waxed paper-lined baking sheets and drizzle with bittersweet chocolate. Refrigerate for 2 hours or until firm. Store in an airtight container in the refrigerator.

Creamy Caramels

Years ago, our local newspaper featured directions for creating homemade caramels. They beat out the store-bought variety hands down! We've been enjoying them ever since.

—MARCIE WOLFE WILLIAMSBURG, VA

PREP: 10 MIN. • **COOK:** 30 MIN. + COOLING • **MAKES:** 2½ POUNDS

- 1 **teaspoon plus 1 cup butter, divided**
- 1 **cup sugar**
- 1 **cup dark corn syrup**
- 1 **can (14 ounces) sweetened condensed milk**
- 1 **teaspoon vanilla extract**

1. Line an 8-in.-square pan with foil; grease the foil with 1 teaspoon butter and set aside.

2. In a large heavy saucepan, combine sugar, corn syrup and remaining butter; bring to a boil over medium heat, stirring constantly. Boil slowly for 4 minutes without stirring.

3. Remove from the heat; stir in the milk. Reduce the heat to medium-low and cook until a candy thermometer reads 238° (soft-ball stage), stirring constantly. Remove from the heat; stir in vanilla.

4. Pour into the prepared pan (do not scrape saucepan). Cool. Using the foil, lift the candy out of the pan. Discard the foil; cut candy into 1-in. squares. Wrap individually in waxed paper; twist ends.

NOTE *We recommend that you test your candy thermometer before each use by bringing water to a boil; the thermometer should read 212°. Adjust your recipe temperature up or down based on your test.*

Creamy Peanut Butter Pie, page 199

194

200

198

Cakes & Pies

Saving room for dessert is easy when you know it's a prizewinner! From chocolaty layer cakes and fancy tortes to fruit-fillled pies and ice cream treats, these favorites will **make any meal special**.

Chocolate Malt Shoppe Pie

Both kids and adults dive right into slices of this malted milk-flavored pie.

—BETH WANEK LITTLE CHUTE, WI

PREP: 20 MIN. + FREEZING
MAKES: 6-8 SERVINGS

- 1½ cups chocolate wafer crumbs
- ¼ cup butter, melted
- 1 pint vanilla ice cream, softened
- ½ cup crushed malted milk balls
- 2 tablespoons milk, divided
- 3 tablespoons chocolate malted milk powder
- 3 tablespoons marshmallow creme
- 1 cup heavy whipping cream
  Additional heavy whipping cream, whipped, optional
  Additional malted milk balls, optional

1. Combine the chocolate wafer crumbs and butter; press into an ungreased 9-in. pie pan. Freeze until set. Combine the softened vanilla ice cream, crushed malted milk balls and 1 tablespoon milk; spoon into crust. Freeze for 1 hour.

2. In a large bowl, combine the malted milk powder, marshmallow creme and remaining milk. Add whipping cream; whip until soft peaks form. Spread over the ice cream layer. Freeze for several hours or overnight.

3. Just before serving, garnish each serving with additional whipped cream and malted milk balls if desired.

Lemon-Berry Shortcake

At summer picnics and other get-togethers, you just can't go wrong with a warm-weather classic like strawberry shortcake. My favorite has a twist of lemon, a generous layer of whipped topping and plenty of berries.

—MERYL HERR GRAND RAPIDS, MI

PREP: 30 MIN. • **BAKE:** 20 MIN. + COOLING
MAKES: 8 SERVINGS

- 1⅓ cups all-purpose flour
- ½ cup sugar
- 2 teaspoons baking powder
- ¼ teaspoon salt
- 1 egg
- ⅔ cup buttermilk
- ¼ cup butter, melted
- 1 tablespoon lemon juice
- 1 teaspoon grated lemon peel
- 1 teaspoon vanilla extract
- 1 cup sliced fresh strawberries

TOPPING

- 1½ cups sliced fresh strawberries
- 1 tablespoon lemon juice
- 1 teaspoon sugar
- 2 cups reduced-fat whipped topping

1. In a large bowl, combine the flour, sugar, baking powder and salt. In another bowl, combine the egg, buttermilk, butter, lemon juice, lemon peel and vanilla. Stir into dry ingredients just until moistened. Fold in strawberries. Pour into a greased and floured 9-in. round baking pan.

2. Bake at 350° for 20-25 minutes or until a toothpick inserted near the center comes out clean. Cool for 10 minutes before removing from pan to a wire rack to cool completely.

3. For the topping, in a large bowl, combine strawberries, lemon juice and sugar. Cover and refrigerate until serving. Spread whipped topping over cake. Drain berries; arrange over top.

Chocolate Peanut Butter Cupcakes

I've been baking cakes for years and enjoy coming up with new ideas. These yummy peanut butter cupcakes take a bit of time to assemble, but they're well worth it! I receive lots of compliments.

—RONDA SCHABES VICKSBURG, MI

PREP: 55 MIN. • **BAKE:** 20 MIN. + COOLING
MAKES: 2 DOZEN

- 2 cups sugar
- 1¾ cups all-purpose flour
- ¾ cup baking cocoa
- ½ teaspoon salt
- ½ teaspoon baking soda
- ½ teaspoon baking powder
- 1 cup buttermilk
- 1 cup strong brewed coffee, room temperature
- ½ cup canola oil
- 2 eggs
- 1 teaspoon vanilla extract

FILLING
- ½ cup creamy peanut butter
- 3 tablespoons unsalted butter, softened
- 1 cup confectioners' sugar
- 2 to 4 tablespoons 2% milk

GANACHE
- 2 cups (12 ounces) semisweet chocolate chips
- ½ cup heavy whipping cream

PEANUT BUTTER FROSTING
- 1 cup packed brown sugar
- 4 egg whites
- ¼ teaspoon salt
- ¼ teaspoon cream of tartar
- 1 teaspoon vanilla extract
- 2 cups unsalted butter, softened
- ⅓ cup creamy peanut butter
  Assorted sprinkles

1. Preheat oven to 350°. In a large bowl, combine the first six ingredients. Whisk buttermilk, coffee, oil, eggs and vanilla until blended; add to the dry ingredients until combined. (Batter will be very thin.) Fill paper-lined muffin cups two-thirds full.

2. Bake 18-20 minutes or until a toothpick inserted near the center comes out clean. Cool 10 minutes before removing from pans to wire racks to cool completely.

3. In a small bowl, cream peanut butter, butter, confectioners' sugar and enough milk to achieve piping consistency. Cut a small hole in the corner of a pastry or plastic bag; insert a small round tip. Fill with the peanut butter filling. Insert tip into the top center of each cupcake; pipe about 1 tablespoon filling into each.

4. Place semisweet chocolate chips in a small bowl. In a small saucepan, bring the heavy whipping cream just to a boil. Pour over the chocolate; whisk until smooth. Dip the top of each cupcake into ganache; place on wire racks to set.

5. In a large heavy saucepan, combine the brown sugar, egg whites, salt and cream of tartar over low heat. With a hand mixer, beat on low speed 1 minute. Continue beating on low over low heat until frosting reaches 160°, about 8-10 minutes. Pour into a large bowl; add vanilla. Beat on high until stiff peaks form, about 5 minutes.

6. Add the butter, 1 tablespoon at a time, beating well after each addition. If the mixture begins to look curdled, place frosting bowl in another bowl filled with hot water for a few seconds. Continue adding butter and beating until smooth. Beat in peanut butter 1-2 minutes or until smooth.

7. Place the frosting in a pastry or plastic bag with a large star tip; pipe onto each cupcake. Decorate with sprinkles or additional ganache as desired. Store in an airtight container in the refrigerator. Let stand at room temperature before serving.

Berry-Apple-Rhubarb Pie

I bring this fruit-packed favorite to an annual family get-together, where the recipe is known as Uncle Mike's pie.
—**MICHAEL POWERS** NEW BALTIMORE, VA

PREP: 30 MIN. + CHILLING • **BAKE:** 65 MIN. + COOLING
MAKES: 8 SERVINGS

- 2⅔ cups all-purpose flour
- 1 teaspoon salt
- 1 cup butter-flavored shortening
- 6 to 8 tablespoons cold water

FILLING

- 2 cups thinly sliced peeled tart apples
- 1 tablespoon lemon juice
- 1 teaspoon vanilla extract
- 1 cup halved fresh strawberries
- 1 cup fresh blueberries
- 1 cup fresh raspberries
- 1 cup fresh blackberries
- 1 cup sliced fresh or frozen rhubarb
- ⅓ cup all-purpose flour
- 1 teaspoon ground allspice
- 1 teaspoon ground cinnamon
- 1½ cups plus 1 teaspoon sugar, divided
- 2 tablespoons butter
- 1 tablespoon 2% milk

1. In a large bowl, combine flour and salt; cut in shortening until crumbly. Gradually add water, tossing with a fork until dough forms a ball. Divide dough in half so that one portion is slightly larger than the other; wrap each in plastic wrap. Refrigerate 30 minutes or until easy to handle.
2. Preheat oven to 400°. On a lightly floured surface, roll out larger portion of dough to fit a 9-in. deep-dish pie plate. Transfer pastry to pie plate.
3. In a large bowl, toss the apples with the lemon juice and vanilla; add the berries and rhubarb. Combine the flour, allspice, cinnamon and 1½ cups sugar; add to the apple mixture and toss gently to coat. Spoon into the crust; dot with butter.

4. Roll out remaining pastry; make a lattice crust. Trim, seal and flute edges. Brush milk over lattice top. Sprinkle with remaining sugar.
5. Bake 15 minutes. Reduce the heat to 350°; bake pie 50-60 minutes longer or until the crust is golden brown and the filling is bubbly. Cover the edges with foil during the last 15 minutes to prevent overbrowning if necessary. Cool on a wire rack.
NOTE *If using frozen rhubarb, measure rhubarb while still frozen, then thaw completely. Drain in a colander, but do not press liquid out.*

Upside-Down Berry Cake

The batter for my upside-down cake soaks up the tangy juices from three different kinds of berries. Serve slices warm or cold and add a scoop of ice cream or a dollop of whipped cream.
—**CANDICE SCHOLL** WEST SUNBURY, PA

PREP: 20 MIN. • **BAKE:** 30 MIN. + COOLING • **MAKES:** 15 SERVINGS

- ½ cup chopped walnuts
- 1 cup fresh or frozen blueberries
- 1 cup fresh or frozen raspberries, halved
- 1 cup sliced fresh strawberries
- ¼ cup sugar
- 1 package (3 ounces) raspberry gelatin
- 1 package yellow cake mix (regular size)
- 2 eggs
- 1¼ cups water
- 2 tablespoons canola oil
- 1½ cups miniature marshmallows

1. In a well-greased 13x9x2-in. baking pan, layer walnuts and blueberries; sprinkle with sugar and raspberry gelatin. In a large bowl, combine the cake mix, eggs, water and oil; beat on low speed for 30 seconds. Beat on medium for 2 minutes. Fold in marshmallows. Pour over top.
2. Bake at 350° for 35-40 minutes or until a toothpick inserted near center comes out clean. Cool for 5 minutes before inverting onto a serving platter. Refrigerate leftovers.

White Chocolate Raspberry Torte

We grow our own raspberries, which I like to use in my cooking and baking. Whenever I make this torte, I hear oohs and aahs.

—**MARTHA SCHWARTZ** SARASOTA, FL

PREP: 1 HOUR • **BAKE:** 30 MIN. + COOLING • **MAKES:** 12 SERVINGS

- 1 cup butter-flavored shortening
- 2 cups sugar
- 4 eggs
- 1 cup white baking chips, melted and cooled
- 1 teaspoon vanilla extract
- 2½ cups cake flour
- 1 teaspoon baking powder
- ½ teaspoon baking soda
- 1 cup buttermilk

FILLING

- 2 cups fresh or frozen raspberries
- ¾ cup water
- ½ cup sugar
- 3 tablespoons cornstarch

FROSTING

- 1 package (8 ounces) cream cheese, softened
- 1 cup white baking chips, melted and cooled
- 1 carton (12 ounces) frozen whipped topping, thawed
  Fresh raspberries, optional

1. Preheat oven to 350°. Line two greased 9-in. round baking pans with waxed paper; grease paper and set aside.

2. In a large bowl, cream the shortening and sugar until light and fluffy. Add the eggs, one at a time, beating well after each addition. Beat in the melted white baking chips and vanilla. Combine the cake flour, baking powder and baking soda; add to the creamed mixture alternately with the buttermilk, beating well after each addition. Transfer to the prepared pans.

3. Bake 26-30 minutes or until a toothpick inserted near center comes out clean. Cool 10 minutes before removing from the pans to wire racks to cool completely; gently peel off waxed paper.

4. In a small saucepan, bring raspberries and water to a boil. Reduce heat; simmer 5 minutes. Remove from heat. Press raspberries through a sieve; discard seeds. Cool.

5. In the same pan, combine sugar and cornstarch; stir in the raspberry puree until smooth. Bring to a boil; cook and stir for 2 minutes or until thickened. Cool. Spread between cake layers.

6. In a large bowl, beat the cream cheese until fluffy. Beat in the melted white baking chips; fold in the whipped topping. Spread over the top and sides of cake. Pipe the frosting over the top edge of cake and garnish with raspberries if desired. Store in the refrigerator.

Brown Sugar Angel Food Cake

Angel food cake is extra-special when you sprinkle it with made-from-scratch toffee.

—JANET EVERETT WINFIELD, IA

PREP: 1 HOUR + CHILLING
BAKE: 25 MIN. + COOLING
MAKES: 16 SERVINGS

- 1½ **cups egg whites (about 10)**
- 1¾ **cups packed brown sugar, divided**
- 1 **cup cake flour**
- 1½ **teaspoons cream of tartar**
- 1½ **teaspoons vanilla extract**
- ½ **teaspoon salt**

TOFFEE/TOPPING

- 1 **teaspoon plus 1 cup butter, divided**
- 1½ **cups chopped pecans**
- 1½ **cups packed brown sugar**
- 1 **cup (6 ounces) semisweet chocolate chips**
- 1 **carton (12 ounces) frozen whipped topping, thawed**

1. Place the egg whites in a large bowl; let stand at room temperature 30 minutes. Sift 1 cup brown sugar and flour together twice; set aside.

2. Place oven rack in lowest position. Preheat oven to 350°. Add the cream of tartar, vanilla and salt to egg whites; beat on medium speed until soft peaks form. Gradually add the remaining brown sugar, about 2 tablespoons at a time, beating on high until stiff glossy peaks form and the sugar is dissolved. Gradually fold in the flour mixture, about ½ cup at a time.

3. Gently spoon into an ungreased 10-in. tube pan. Cut through the batter with a knife to remove the air pockets. Bake 25-30 minutes or until lightly browned and the entire top appears dry. Immediately invert the pan; cool completely, about 1 hour.

4. Run a knife around the side and center tube of pan. Remove the cake to a serving plate.

5. For toffee, line a 13x9x2-in. baking pan with foil; grease foil with 1 teaspoon butter. Sprinkle pecans into prepared pan; set aside.

6. In a small heavy saucepan over medium-low heat, bring brown sugar and remaining butter to a boil, stirring constantly. Cover and cook 2 minutes. Cook and stir with a clean spoon until a candy thermometer reads 300° (hard-crack stage). Immediately pour into the prepared pan. Sprinkle with chocolate chips; spread with a knife when melted. Refrigerate for about 1 hour or until set.

7. Frost cake with whipped topping. Finely chop half of the toffee; press onto cake. Serve with remaining toffee if desired. Store leftover toffee in an airtight container.

NOTE *We recommend that you test your candy thermometer before each use by bringing water to a boil; the thermometer should read 212°. Adjust your recipe temperature up or down based on your test.*

COOL RULE

If a foam cake baked in a tube pan is not cooled upside down in the pan, the cake will collapse and flatten. If you are using a tube pan with legs, simply invert the pan onto its legs. If you are using a tube pan without legs, invert the pan and place it over a funnel or the neck of a narrow bottle. Make sure the cake has cooled completely before you remove it from the pan.

Upside-Down Apple Pie

Here's a tried-and-true winner! The recipe has received eight ribbons at area fairs.
—**SUSAN FRISCH** GERMANSVILLE, PA

PREP: 30 MIN. + CHILLING
BAKE: 50 MIN. + COOLING
MAKES: 8 SERVINGS

- 2 **cups all-purpose flour**
- ½ **teaspoon salt**
- 6 **tablespoons shortening**
- 2 **tablespoons cold butter**
- 5 **to 7 tablespoons orange juice**

FILLING
- 6 **tablespoons butter, melted, divided**
- ½ **cup packed brown sugar**
- ½ **cup chopped pecans**
- 8 **cups thinly sliced peeled tart apples (about ⅛ inch thick)**
- 1 **cup sugar**
- ⅓ **cup all-purpose flour**
- ¾ **teaspoon ground cinnamon**
- ¼ **teaspoon ground nutmeg**

GLAZE
- ½ **cup confectioners' sugar**
- 2 **to 3 teaspoons orange juice**

1. In a large bowl, combine flour and salt; cut in shortening and butter until crumbly. Gradually add orange juice, tossing with a fork until dough forms a ball. Divide dough into two balls. Wrap in plastic wrap; refrigerate for at least 30 minutes.

2. Line a 9-in. deep-dish pie plate with heavy-duty foil, leaving 1½ in. beyond edge; coat the foil with cooking spray. Combine 4 tablespoons butter, brown sugar and pecans; spoon into prepared pie plate.

3. In a large bowl, combine the apples, sugar, flour, cinnamon, nutmeg and remaining butter; toss gently.

4. On waxed paper, roll out one ball of pastry to fit the pie plate. Place the pastry over the nut mixture, pressing firmly against mixture and sides of plate; trim to 1 in. beyond plate edge. Fill with apple mixture.

5. Roll out remaining pastry to fit top of pie; place over filling. Trim to ¼ in. beyond plate edge. Fold bottom pastry over top pastry; seal and flute edges. Cut four 1-in. slits in top pastry.

6. Bake at 375° for 50-55 minutes or until apples are tender and crust is golden brown (cover edges with foil during the last 20 minutes to prevent overbrowning if necessary).

7. Cool for 15 minutes on a wire rack. Invert onto a serving platter; carefully remove the foil. Combine the glaze ingredients; drizzle over pie.

Banana-Berry Pie

With a homemade crust, layer of fresh strawberries, and banana cream topping, this tempting pie will impress everyone.
—**JULIE GUNTZEL** BEMIDJI, MN

PREP: 30 MIN. + CHILLING
MAKES: 8 SERVINGS

- 1¼ **cups graham cracker crumbs**
- 5 **tablespoons butter, melted**
- 2 **tablespoons sugar**
- 1 **teaspoon ground ginger**

FILLING
- ¾ **cup sugar**
- 2 **tablespoons plus ¾ teaspoon cornstarch**
- 1 **tablespoon strawberry gelatin**
- ¾ **cup cold water**
- 2 **cups sliced fresh strawberries, divided**
- 1 **can (14 ounces) sweetened condensed milk**
- 1 **package (8 ounces) reduced-fat cream cheese**
- ¼ **cup cold 2% milk**
- 1 **package (3.4 ounces) instant banana cream pudding mix**

1. Combine the graham cracker crumbs, butter, sugar and ginger. Press onto bottom and up sides of an ungreased 9-in. pie plate. Bake at 350° for 8-10 minutes or until lightly browned. Cool on a wire rack.

2. For the filling, in a small saucepan, combine sugar, cornstarch and gelatin. Stir in cold water until smooth. Bring to a boil; cook and stir for 2 minutes or until thickened. Cool slightly. Arrange 1 cup berries over crust. Pour gelatin mixture over berries. Refrigerate for 2 hours or until set.

3. In a large bowl, beat the sweetened condensed milk, cream cheese, milk and pudding mix for 1 minute. Spread over top of pie. Refrigerate for 2 hours or until set. Garnish with remaining berries. Refrigerate leftovers.

Blueberry-Blackberry Rustic Tart

My dad would stop the car on the side of the road in Maine and say, "I smell blueberries." He had a pail ready for picking! Mom would bake the wild berries in a cornmeal crust.

—**PRISCILLA GILBERT** INDIAN HARBOUR BEACH, FL

PREP: 20 MIN. + CHILLING • **BAKE:** 55 MIN. • **MAKES:** 8 SERVINGS

- 2 cups all-purpose flour
- ⅓ cup sugar
- ¼ cup yellow cornmeal
- ⅔ cup cold butter, cubed
- ½ cup buttermilk

FILLING

- 4 cups fresh blueberries
- 2 cups fresh blackberries
- ⅔ cup sugar
- ⅓ cup all-purpose flour
- 2 tablespoons lemon juice
- 1 egg, beaten
- 2 tablespoons turbinado (washed raw) sugar or coarse sugar
  Whipped cream, optional

1. In a large bowl, mix the flour, sugar and cornmeal; cut in the butter until crumbly. Gradually add buttermilk, tossing with a fork until dough holds together when pressed. Shape into a disk; wrap in plastic wrap. Refrigerate 30 minutes or overnight.

2. Preheat oven to 375°. On a lightly floured surface, roll the dough into a 14-in. circle. Transfer to a parchment paper-lined baking sheet.

3. In a large bowl, combine berries, sugar, flour and lemon juice; spoon over pastry to within 2 in. of edges. Fold pastry edge over filling, leaving center uncovered. Brush folded pastry with beaten egg; sprinkle with turbinado sugar.

4. Bake 55-60 minutes or until crust is golden brown and filling is bubbly. Using parchment paper, slide tart onto a wire rack to cool. If desired, serve with whipped cream.

Dreamy S'more Pie

Broiling makes the marshmallows on top of this pie toasty and golden brown, just like in traditional s'mores treats.

—**KAREN BOWLDEN** BOISE, ID

PREP: 10 MIN. + CHILLING • **BROIL:** 5 MIN. • **MAKES:** 8 SERVINGS

- 1 package (8 ounces) cream cheese, softened
- 1¼ cups heavy whipping cream
- 1 jar (13 ounces) Nutella
- 1 graham cracker crust (9 inches)
- 3 cups miniature marshmallows

1. In a large bowl, beat cream cheese and cream until thickened. Add Nutella; beat just until combined. Spoon into crust. Cover and refrigerate for at least 3 hours.

2. Just before serving, top with marshmallows; press gently into filling. Broil 6 in. from the heat for 1-2 minutes or until marshmallows are golden brown.

Creamy Peanut Butter Pie

As a busy mother, I'm always on the lookout for recipes that are quick to fix and guaranteed to please. Everyone who likes peanut butter loves this cool, creamy dessert.

—**DAWN MOORE** WARREN, PA

PREP: 30 MIN. • **BAKE:** 10 MIN. + CHILLING • **MAKES:** 8 SERVINGS

- 24 Nutter Butter cookies, crushed
- ⅓ cup butter, melted
- 1 cup cold 2% milk
- 1 package (3.4 ounces) instant vanilla pudding mix
- 1 cup creamy peanut butter
- 4 ounces cream cheese, softened
- ½ cup sweetened condensed milk
- ¼ cup hot fudge ice cream topping, warmed
- 1 cup heavy whipping cream
- 2 tablespoons sugar
  Chocolate curls

1. Combine cookie crumbs and butter; press onto the bottom and up the sides of an ungreased 9-in. pie plate. Bake at 350° for 6-8 minutes or until the crust is lightly browned. Cool on a wire rack.

2. In a small bowl, whisk the milk and vanilla pudding mix for 2 minutes (mixture will be thick). In a large bowl, beat the peanut butter, cream cheese and condensed milk until smooth; stir in pudding. Set aside.

3. Gently spread ice cream topping into crust. In a large bowl, beat cream until it begins to thicken. Add sugar; beat until stiff peaks form. Fold 1½ cups into pudding mixture; pour into crust. Spread remaining whipped cream over top; garnish with chocolate curls. Refrigerate until serving.

Apple Upside-Down Cake

PREP: 25 MIN. • **BAKE:** 30 MIN. + COOLING
MAKES: 8 SERVINGS

- ⅓ cup butter, melted
- 1 cup packed brown sugar
- 3 medium tart apples, peeled and sliced
- ½ cup chopped walnuts

CAKE
- 3 tablespoons butter, softened
- ¾ cup sugar
- 2 eggs
- 1 cup all-purpose flour
- ¾ teaspoon baking powder
- ½ teaspoon baking soda
- ¼ teaspoon salt
- ¼ teaspoon ground cinnamon
- ½ cup buttermilk
- 3 tablespoons sour cream
- 1 teaspoon apple brandy or rum, optional

1. Pour the butter into an ungreased 9-in. round baking pan; sprinkle with ½ cup brown sugar. Arrange apples in a single layer over the brown sugar; layer with the walnuts and remaining brown sugar.

2. In a large bowl, cream the butter and sugar until light and fluffy. Add the eggs, one at a time, beating well after each addition. Combine flour, baking powder, baking soda, salt and cinnamon; add to creamed mixture alternately with the buttermilk and sour cream, beating well after each addition. Beat in brandy if desired.

3. Spoon batter over brown sugar layer. Bake at 350° for 30-35 minutes or until a toothpick inserted near the center comes out clean. Cool for 10 minutes before inverting onto a serving plate. Serve warm.

❝You'll flip for the crunchy, sweet, buttery fruit topping on each slice of Apple Upside-Down Cake. It's so good!❞

—**LINDA WETSCH** MANDAN, ND

GRAND PRIZE WINNER ★★★★

GRAND PRIZE

Chocolate Truffle Cake

Chocoholics—and everyone else—will get in line for a piece of this tantalizing dessert. A velvety ganache, a bittersweet filling...what's not to love?

—**JOANN KOERKENMEIER** DAMIANSVILLE, IL

PREP: 35 MIN. + CHILLING
BAKE: 25 MIN. + COOLING
MAKES: 16 SERVINGS

- 2½ cups 2% milk
- 1 cup butter, cubed
- 8 ounces semisweet chocolate, chopped
- 3 eggs
- 2 teaspoons vanilla extract
- 2⅔ cups all-purpose flour
- 2 cups sugar
- 1 teaspoon baking soda
- ½ teaspoon salt

FILLING
- 6 tablespoons butter, cubed
- 4 ounces bittersweet chocolate, chopped
- 2½ cups confectioners' sugar
- ½ cup heavy whipping cream

GANACHE
- 10 ounces semisweet chocolate, chopped
- ⅔ cup heavy whipping cream

1. In a large saucepan, cook the milk, butter and chocolate over low heat until melted. Remove from the heat; let stand for 10 minutes. Preheat oven to 325°. In a large bowl, beat the eggs and vanilla; stir in chocolate mixture until smooth. Combine flour, sugar, baking soda and salt; gradually add to chocolate mixture and mix well (batter will be thin).

2. Transfer cake batter to three greased and floured 9-in. round baking pans. Bake 25-30 minutes or until a toothpick inserted in center comes out clean. Cool 10 minutes before removing from pans to wire racks to cool completely.

3. For the filling, in a small saucepan, melt the butter and chocolate. Stir in the confectioners' sugar and cream until smooth.

4. For the ganache, place chocolate in a small bowl. In a small saucepan, bring cream just to a boil. Pour over chocolate; whisk until smooth. Cool, stirring occasionally, until ganache reaches a spreading consistency.

5. Place one cake layer on a serving plate; spread with half of the filling. Repeat layers. Top with remaining cake layer. Spread ganache over top and sides of cake. Store in refrigerator.

Chocolate-Strawberry Celebration Cake

Although I have some great from-scratch recipes, this one jazzes up a packaged mix with fabulous results. I decorate it with fresh berries and chocolate garnishes for an event-worthy presentation.

—**NORA FITZGERALD** SEVIERVILLE, TN

PREP: 30 MIN. • **BAKE:** 30 MIN. + COOLING
MAKES: 12 SERVINGS

- 1 package chocolate cake mix (regular size)
- 1 package (3.9 ounces) instant chocolate pudding mix
- 4 eggs
- 1 cup (8 ounces) sour cream
- ¾ cup water
- ¼ cup canola oil
- 4 ounces semisweet chocolate, melted

FROSTING
- 2 cups butter, softened
- 4 cups confectioners' sugar
- ¾ cup baking cocoa
- ½ cup 2% milk

GARNISHES
- 2 ounces semisweet chocolate, melted
- 1 pound fresh strawberries, hulled

GANACHE
- 4 ounces semisweet chocolate, chopped
- ½ cup heavy whipping cream

1. Combine the first seven ingredients; beat on low speed for 30 seconds. Beat on medium for 2 minutes. Transfer to two greased and floured 9-in. round baking pans.

2. Bake at 350° for 28-32 minutes or until a toothpick inserted near the center comes out clean. Cool for 10 minutes before removing from the pans to wire racks to cool completely.

3. In a large bowl, cream the butter, confectioners' sugar and cocoa until light and fluffy. Beat in the milk until smooth. Spread the frosting between layers and over top and sides of cake.

4. Pipe or spoon melted chocolate onto waxed paper in decorative designs; let stand until set.

5. For ganache, place chocolate in a small bowl. Heat cream just to a boil; pour over chocolate and whisk until smooth. Drizzle over the top of cake, allowing ganache to drape down the sides. Arrange strawberries on top of cake. Top with chocolate garnishes.

Caramel Banana Ice Cream Pie

Cool off on scorching summer days with a frosty delight from the freezer. Banana pudding, vanilla ice cream and just a few other ingredients are all you need.

—**APRIL TIMBOE** SILOAM SPRINGS, AR

PREP: 20 MIN. + FREEZING
MAKES: 8 SERVINGS

- ¼ cup plus 1 tablespoon caramel ice cream topping, divided
- 1 graham cracker crust (9 inches)
- 1 cup cold 2% milk
- 2 packages (3.4 ounces each) instant banana cream pudding mix
- 1 quart vanilla ice cream, softened
- 1¾ cups whipped topping
- 1 English toffee candy bar (1.4 ounces), chopped

1. Spread ¼ cup caramel topping into the crust. In a large bowl, beat the milk and banana cream pudding mix on low speed for 2 minutes. Add the vanilla ice cream; mix well.

2. Spoon into the prepared crust. Top with whipped topping. Drizzle with remaining caramel topping; sprinkle with chopped candy bar.

3. Cover and freeze for 2 hours or until firm. Remove from the freezer 15 minutes before serving.

Brittle Torte

When I was in high school, my mother often asked me to make this amazing dessert. The crunchy homemade brittle sprinkled over the frosting is such a special touch.

—**PHYLLIS MURPHEY** LOWER LAKE, CA

PREP: 50 MIN. • **BAKE:** 50 MIN. + COOLING • **MAKES:** 12 SERVINGS

- 8 **eggs, separated**
- 1½ **cups all-purpose flour**
- 1½ **cups sugar**
- 1 **teaspoon salt**
- ¼ **cup water**
- 1 **teaspoon lemon juice**
- 1 **teaspoon vanilla extract**
- 1 **teaspoon cream of tartar**

TOPPING
- 1½ **cups sugar**
- ¼ **cup light corn syrup**
- ¼ **cup water**
- ¼ **teaspoon instant coffee granules**
- 1 **teaspoon baking soda**

WHIPPED CREAM
- 2 **cups heavy whipping cream**
- 2 **tablespoons sugar**
- 2 **teaspoons vanilla extract**

1. Let eggs stand at room temperature 30 minutes.
2. Place oven rack in lowest position. Preheat oven to 325°. Combine the flour, sugar and salt. Whisk the egg yolks, water, lemon juice and vanilla; add to the flour mixture. Beat until blended.

3. Beat the egg whites and cream of tartar until soft peaks form; fold into batter. Spoon into an ungreased 10-in. tube pan. Cut through batter with a knife to remove air pockets. Bake 50-60 minutes or until the top springs back when touched. Immediately invert pan; cool completely.
4. For the topping, grease a 15x10x1-in. pan. In a heavy saucepan, combine the sugar, light corn syrup, water and instant coffee granules. Bring to a boil, stirring constantly. Cook, without stirring, until a candy thermometer reads 300° (hard-crack stage).
5. Remove from the heat; stir in baking soda. Immediately pour into the prepared pan. Stretch the brittle in the pan with two forks; cool. Break into pieces. In a large bowl, beat the cream until it begins to thicken. Add sugar and vanilla; beat until stiff peaks form.
6. Unmold cake; cut horizontally into four layers. Place bottom layer on a serving plate; top with ½ cup whipped cream. Repeat the layers twice; top with remaining layer. Frost top and sides of cake with remaining whipped cream. Sprinkle with brittle.

Chocolate Almond Silk Pie

Years ago, our local newspaper featured a silk pie recipe I clipped out to try. It was an instant hit with my husband and daughters. They loved the blend of rich chocolate and toasted almonds.

—**DIANE LARSON** ROLAND, IA

PREP: 20 MIN. • **COOK:** 30 MIN. + COOLING • **MAKES:** 8-10 SERVINGS

- ⅔ **cup all-purpose flour**
- ¼ **cup butter, softened**
- 3 **tablespoons finely chopped almonds, toasted**
- 2 **tablespoons confectioners' sugar**
- ⅛ **teaspoon vanilla extract**

FILLING
- ¾ **cup sugar**
- 3 **eggs**
- 3 **ounces unsweetened chocolate, coarsely chopped**
- ⅛ **teaspoon almond extract**
- ½ **cup butter, softened**
  Sweetened whipped cream and toasted sliced almonds, optional

1. In a small bowl, combine the first five ingredients. Beat on low speed until well combined, about 2-3 minutes. Press onto the bottom and up the sides of a greased 9-in. pie plate. Bake at 400° for 8-10 minutes or until golden. Cool on a wire rack.
2. For the filling, combine the sugar and eggs in a small saucepan until well blended. Cook over low heat, stirring constantly, until mixture coats the back of a metal spoon and reaches 160°. Remove from the heat. Stir in chocolate and almond extract until smooth. Cool to lukewarm (90°), stirring occasionally.
3. In a large bowl, cream the butter until light and fluffy. Add cooled egg mixture; beat on high speed for 5 minutes. Pour into cooled pie shell. Refrigerate for at least 6 hours before serving. Garnish with whipped cream and almonds if desired. Refrigerate leftovers.

Raspberry Chocolate Torte

Wow guests during the holiday season or anytime with this eye-catching torte. Boasting fresh raspberries and a creamy topping, it tastes just as good as it looks.

—AMY HELBIG MESA, AZ

PREP: 40 MIN. • **BAKE:** 20 MIN. + COOLING
MAKES: 12 SERVINGS

- 1 cup butter, softened
- 2 cups sugar
- 4 eggs
- 1 teaspoon vanilla extract
- 1½ cups all-purpose flour
- ⅓ cup baking cocoa

GLAZE

- ¼ cup boiling water
- 4 teaspoons raspberry gelatin
- 2 tablespoons seedless raspberry jam

TOPPING

- 2 cups (12 ounces) semisweet chocolate chips
- 2 cartons (8 ounces each) frozen whipped topping, thawed
- 2 cups fresh raspberries

1. Line a greased 15x10x1-in. baking pan with waxed paper; grease the paper. In a large bowl, cream butter and sugar until light and fluffy. Add the eggs, one at a time, beating well after each addition. Beat in vanilla. Combine flour and cocoa; gradually beat into creamed mixture. Transfer to prepared pan.

2. Bake at 350° for 20-25 minutes or until a toothpick inserted near center comes out clean. Cool for 5 minutes before inverting onto a wire rack to cool completely. Carefully remove the waxed paper.

3. For the glaze, stir the boiling water and raspberry gelatin until gelatin is dissolved. Stir in the jam. Brush evenly over the bottom of cake. Trim edges; cut cake widthwise into thirds.

4. For topping, in a microwave, melt chips; stir until smooth. Fold in half of the whipped topping until blended; fold in the remaining whipped topping (mixture will be thick).

5. Place one cake layer on a serving platter; spread with ¾ cup topping. Repeat layers; top with remaining cake. Frost and decorate with berries and remaining topping.

Chocolate Toffee Cake

I like getting together with relatives and friends for coffee, and they often request this treat. Now that I have grandchildren, I make it for their birthdays, too.
—**PENNY MCNEILL** KITCHENER, ON

PREP: 25 MIN. • **BAKE:** 55 MIN. + COOLING
MAKES: 12 SERVINGS

- 1 package (8 ounces) milk chocolate English toffee bits
- 1 cup (6 ounces) semisweet chocolate chips
- 2 tablespoons brown sugar

CAKE
- 1 cup butter, softened
- 1¼ cups packed brown sugar
- 4 eggs
- 1 teaspoon vanilla extract
- 3 cups all-purpose flour
- 1½ teaspoons baking powder
- ½ teaspoon salt
- ½ teaspoon baking soda
- 1¼ cups buttermilk

CARAMEL ICING
- ¼ cup butter, cubed
- 2 teaspoons all-purpose flour
- 1 can (5 ounces) evaporated milk
- 1 cup packed brown sugar

1. Combine the milk chocolate toffee bits, semisweet chocolate chips and brown sugar; set aside.
2. In a large bowl, cream the butter and brown sugar until light and fluffy. Add the eggs, one at a time, beating well after each addition (the mixture will appear curdled). Beat in vanilla. Combine flour, baking powder, salt and baking soda; add to the creamed mixture alternately with buttermilk, beating well after each addition.
3. Pour a third of cake batter into a greased and floured 10-in. fluted tube pan. Sprinkle with a third of the toffee mixture. Repeat the layers twice. Bake at 350° for 55-65 minutes or until a toothpick inserted near the center comes out clean.
4. Cool cake for 10 minutes before removing from the pan to a wire rack to cool completely. For the caramel icing, in a small saucepan, melt the butter. Stir in the flour until smooth; gradually add the evaporated milk and brown sugar. Bring to a boil; cook and stir for 4-5 minutes or until thickened. Cool. Drizzle over cake.

Chocolate Banana Cream Cake

One day when I was experimenting in the kitchen, I was inspired to try combining my dad's love for cake, my mom's love for chocolate and my love for bananas into one sweet sensation. Here is the result! It's become a favorite not only in our family, but also with guests.
—**SUSIE PATTISON** DUBLIN, OH

PREP: 30 MIN. • **BAKE:** 20 MIN. + COOLING
MAKES: 12 SERVINGS

- ½ cup butter, softened
- 1¼ cups sugar
- 2 eggs, separated
- 1½ cups mashed ripe bananas (about 3 medium)
- ¼ cup sour cream
- 2 teaspoons vanilla extract
- 1½ cups all-purpose flour
- 1 teaspoon baking soda
- ¼ teaspoon salt

FILLING/FROSTING
- 1½ cups cold 2% milk
- 1 package (3.4 ounces) instant banana cream pudding mix
- 1 can (16 ounces) chocolate frosting
- 2 medium firm bananas, sliced
- 3 tablespoons lemon juice

1. In a large bowl, cream the butter and sugar until light and fluffy. Beat in egg yolks. Beat in bananas, sour cream and vanilla. Combine the flour, baking soda and salt; add to creamed mixture and mix well.
2. In a small bowl, beat egg whites until stiff peaks form. Fold into the batter. Transfer to two greased and floured 9-in. round baking pans. Bake at 350° for 20-25 minutes or until a toothpick inserted near the center comes out clean. Cool for 10 minutes before removing from pans to wire racks to cool completely.
3. For filling, in a small bowl, whisk milk and pudding mix for 2 minutes. Let stand for 2 minutes or until soft-set. Cover; refrigerate until chilled.
4. In a small bowl, beat frosting until light and fluffy. Place the bananas in a small bowl; toss with lemon juice.
5. Place one cake layer on a serving plate; spread with 3 tablespoons frosting. Stir pudding; spread half over frosting. Top with half of the bananas and the remaining cake. Repeat frosting, filling and banana layers. Frost the sides and decorate top of cake with remaining frosting. Store in refrigerator.

Apple Praline Pie

Feel free to prepare this without the nuts—it's still scrumptious!

—NOELLE MYERS

GRAND FORKS, ND

PREP: 30 MIN. • **BAKE:** 1 HOUR + COOLING
MAKES: 8 SERVINGS

- 1¾ cups all-purpose flour
- 1 teaspoon sugar
- ½ teaspoon salt
- 1 cup cold butter, cubed
- 1 teaspoon cider vinegar
- 4 to 6 tablespoons cold water

FILLING

- 6 cups thinly sliced peeled tart apples
- 1 tablespoon ginger ale
- 1 teaspoon lemon juice
- 1 teaspoon vanilla extract
- ¾ cup sugar
- ¼ cup all-purpose flour
- 3 teaspoons ground cinnamon
- ¼ teaspoon ground nutmeg
- 2 tablespoons butter

TOPPING

- ¼ cup butter, cubed
- ½ cup packed brown sugar
- ⅔ cup pecan halves
- 2 tablespoons heavy whipping cream
- ½ teaspoon vanilla extract

1. In a large bowl, combine the flour, sugar and salt; cut in the butter until crumbly. Sprinkle with cider vinegar. Gradually add the cold water, tossing with a fork until the pastry dough forms a ball.

2. Divide the pastry dough in half so that one portion is slightly larger than the other. Roll out the larger portion to fit a 9-in. pie plate. Transfer pastry to the pie plate. Trim pastry even with the edge.

3. In a large bowl, toss the apples with the ginger ale, lemon juice and vanilla. Combine the sugar, flour, cinnamon and nutmeg; add to the apple mixture and toss to coat. Spoon into the crust; dot with butter.

4. Roll out remaining pastry to fit top of pie. Place over filling. Trim, seal and flute edges. Cut slits in pastry.

5. Bake at 400° for 55-65 minutes or until the crust is golden brown and the filling is bubbly. Cover edges with foil during the last 30 minutes to prevent overbrowning if necessary.

6. Meanwhile, in a small saucepan over medium heat, melt butter. Stir in brown sugar; cook and stir until mixture comes to a boil and sugar is dissolved. Stir in nuts; cook 1 minute longer. Remove from heat; stir in cream and vanilla. Immediately pour over pie. Bake 3-5 minutes longer or until topping is bubbly. Cool on a wire rack.

German Apple Pie

Our babysitter shared her apple pie recipe, and I've baked it countless times since.

—MRS. WOODROW TAYLOR

ADAMS CENTER, NY

PREP: 20 MIN. • **BAKE:** 65 MIN. + COOLING
MAKES: 8 SERVINGS

- 1½ cups all-purpose flour
- ½ teaspoon salt
- ½ cup shortening
- 1 teaspoon vanilla extract
- 2 to 3 tablespoons ice water

FILLING

- 1 cup sugar
- ¼ cup all-purpose flour
- 2 teaspoons ground cinnamon
- 6 cups sliced peeled tart apples
- 1 cup heavy whipping cream
  Whipped cream, optional

1. In a small bowl, combine flour and salt; cut in the shortening until crumbly. Add vanilla. Gradually add water, tossing with a fork until dough forms a ball. Roll out pastry to fit a 9-in. pie plate. Transfer pastry to pie plate. Trim pastry to ½ in. beyond edge of pie plate; flute edges.

2. For filling, combine the sugar, flour and cinnamon; sprinkle 3 tablespoons into crust. Layer with half of the apples; sprinkle with half of the remaining sugar mixture. Repeat layers. Pour cream over all.

3. Bake at 450° for 10 minutes. Reduce heat to 350° bake for 55-60 minutes or until apples are tender. Cool on a wire rack. Store in the refrigerator. Serve with whipped cream if desired.

Apricot Almond Torte

To save time when entertaining, I bake the layers of my apricot torte in advance and assemble it the day of serving.

—**TRISHA KRUSE** EAGLE, ID

PREP: 45 MIN. • **BAKE:** 25 MIN. + COOLING • **MAKES:** 12 SERVINGS

- 3 **eggs**
- 1½ **cups sugar**
- 1 **teaspoon vanilla extract**
- 1¾ **cups all-purpose flour**
- 1 **cup ground almonds, toasted**
- 2 **teaspoons baking powder**
- ½ **teaspoon salt**
- 1½ **cups heavy whipping cream, whipped**

FROSTING

- 1 **package (8 ounces) cream cheese, softened**
- 1 **cup sugar**
- ⅛ **teaspoon salt**
- 1 **teaspoon almond extract**
- 1½ **cups heavy whipping cream, whipped**
- 1 **jar (10 to 12 ounces) apricot preserves**
- ½ **cup slivered almonds, toasted**

1. Preheat oven to 350°. In a large bowl, beat eggs, sugar and vanilla on high speed until thick and lemon-colored. Combine flour, almonds, baking powder and salt; gradually fold into egg mixture alternately with the whipped cream.

2. Transfer to two greased and floured 9-in. round baking pans. Bake 22-28 minutes or until a toothpick inserted near center comes out clean. Cool 10 minutes before removing from pans to wire racks to cool completely.

3. In a large bowl, beat cream cheese, sugar and salt until smooth. Beat in extract. Fold in whipped cream.

4. Cut each cake horizontally into two layers. Place bottom layer on a serving plate; spread with 1 cup frosting. Top with another cake layer; spread with half the preserves. Repeat layers. Frost the sides of cake; decorate the top edge with remaining frosting. Sprinkle with almonds.

Give Me S'more Cake

Bring a campfire classic to your table! Kids of all ages will love the graham crackers, chocolate and marshmallow frosting.

—**KATIE LEMERY** CUDDEBACKVILLE, NY

PREP: 50 MIN. • **BAKE:** 20 MIN. + COOLING • **MAKES:** 12 SERVINGS

- ½ **cup shortening**
- ¼ **cup butter, softened**
- 1 **cup sugar**
- 3 **eggs**
- 1 **teaspoon vanilla extract**
- 2¾ **cups graham cracker crumbs**
- 3 **teaspoons baking powder**
- 1 **can (12 ounces) evaporated milk**

MARSHMALLOW FROSTING

- 4 **egg whites**
- 1 **cup sugar**
- ½ **teaspoon cream of tartar**
- 1½ **teaspoons vanilla extract**
- 1½ **cups miniature semisweet chocolate chips, divided**

1. Line bottoms of two greased 9-in. round baking pans with parchment paper; lightly coat paper with cooking spray. In a large bowl, cream shortening, butter and sugar until light and fluffy. Add eggs, one at a time, beating well after each addition. Beat in vanilla. Combine the crumbs and baking powder; add to creamed mixture alternately with milk, beating well after each addition.

2. Transfer the batter to prepared pans. Bake at 350° for 18-22 minutes or until a toothpick inserted near center comes out clean. Cool 10 minutes; remove from pans to wire racks to cool completely.

3. In a large heavy saucepan, combine the egg whites, sugar and cream of tartar over low heat. With hand mixer, beat on low speed 1 minute. Continue beating until frosting reaches 160°, about 8-10 minutes. Pour into a large bowl; add the vanilla. Beat on high until stiff peaks form, about 7 minutes.

4. Place a cake layer on a serving plate; spread with ⅔ cup frosting and sprinkle with half of the chocolate chips. Top with the remaining cake layer. Frost top and sides of cake; sprinkle with remaining chips.

Never-Miss Apple Cake

I always make this family-favorite dessert to usher in the fall season. Every slice has a rich ribbon of cream cheese, chunks of tart apples and a drizzle of praline icing.
—**JAMIE JONES** MADISON, GA

PREP: 40 MIN. • **BAKE:** 50 MIN. + COOLING • **MAKES:** 12 SERVINGS

- 1 package (8 ounces) cream cheese, softened
- 2 cups sugar, divided
- 4 eggs
- 1 cup canola oil
- 2 cups all-purpose flour
- 2 teaspoons baking powder
- 2 teaspoons ground cinnamon
- 1 teaspoon salt
- ¼ teaspoon baking soda
- 2 cups chopped peeled tart apples
- 1 cup shredded carrots
- ½ cup chopped pecans

PRALINE ICING

- ½ cup packed brown sugar
- ¼ cup butter, cubed
- 2 tablespoons 2% milk
- ½ cup confectioners' sugar
- ½ teaspoon vanilla extract
- ¼ cup chopped pecans, toasted

1. Preheat oven to 350°. In a small bowl, beat cream cheese and ¼ cup sugar until smooth. Beat in 1 egg; set aside.
2. In a large bowl, beat the oil with the remaining sugar and eggs until well blended. Combine the flour, baking powder, cinnamon, salt and baking soda; gradually beat into the oil mixture until blended. Stir in apples, carrots and pecans.
3. Transfer half of the apple batter to a greased and floured 10-in. fluted tube pan; layer with cream cheese mixture and remaining apple batter.
4. Bake at for 50-60 minutes or until a toothpick inserted near the center comes out clean. Cool 10 minutes before removing from pan to a wire rack to cool completely.

5. In a large saucepan, bring the brown sugar, butter and milk to a boil. Cook and stir 1 minute. Remove from heat; whisk in confectioners' sugar and vanilla until smooth. Drizzle over cake. Sprinkle with pecans.

Pumpkin Streusel Cupcakes

A spiced streusel filling and canned pumpkin really dress up these yummy cupcakes. No one will guess you used a boxed mix!
—**DONNA GISH** BLUE SPRINGS, MO

PREP: 25 MIN. • **BAKE:** 20 MIN. + COOLING • **MAKES:** 2 DOZEN

- 1 package spice cake mix (regular size)
- 1¼ cups water
- 3 eggs
- ½ cup canned pumpkin

STREUSEL

- ½ cup packed brown sugar
- ½ teaspoon ground cinnamon
- 1 tablespoon butter

FROSTING

- 1 package (8 ounces) cream cheese, softened
- 2 tablespoons butter
- 2 cups confectioners' sugar
- ½ teaspoon vanilla extract

1. In a large bowl, combine the cake mix, water, eggs and pumpkin. Beat on low speed just until moistened. Beat on medium for 2 minutes.
2. In a small bowl, combine brown sugar and cinnamon; cut in the butter until crumbly. Fill paper-lined muffin cups one-fourth full with the batter. Drop streusel by heaping teaspoonfuls into the center of each cupcake. Cover with remaining batter.
3. Bake at 350° for 18-20 minutes or until a toothpick inserted in the cake portion comes out clean. Cool for 10 minutes before removing from the pans to wire racks to cool completely.
4. In a small bowl, beat the cream cheese and butter until fluffy. Add the confectioners' sugar and vanilla; beat until smooth. Frost cupcakes. Store in the refrigerator.

Strawberry-Rhubarb Meringue Pie

PREP: 45 MIN. • **BAKE:** 50 MIN. + CHILLING
MAKES: 8 SERVINGS

- ½ cup all-purpose flour
- ¼ cup whole wheat pastry flour
- ¼ cup ground almonds
- ½ teaspoon salt
- ¼ cup cold butter, cubed
- 2 tablespoons cold water

FILLING

- 1 egg, lightly beaten
- ¾ cup sugar
- 2 tablespoons all-purpose flour
- ¼ teaspoon ground cinnamon
- 2 cups chopped fresh or frozen rhubarb, thawed
- 1½ cups sliced fresh strawberries

MERINGUE

- 3 egg whites
- ¼ teaspoon almond extract
- 6 tablespoons sugar

1. In a food processor, combine the all-purpose flour, pastry flour, almonds and salt; cover and pulse until blended. Add the butter; cover and pulse until mixture resembles coarse crumbs. While processing, gradually add cold water until the dough forms a ball.

2. Roll out the pastry to fit a 9-in. pie plate. Transfer the pastry to pie plate. Trim pastry to ½ in. beyond the edge of plate; flute edges.

3. In a large bowl, combine the egg, sugar, flour and cinnamon; stir in the rhubarb and strawberries. Transfer to the prepared crust. Bake at 375° for 35-40 minutes or until the filling is bubbly. Place pie on a wire rack; keep warm. Reduce heat to 350°.

4. In a large bowl, beat the egg whites and almond extract on medium speed until soft peaks form. Gradually beat in the sugar, 1 tablespoon at a time, on high until stiff peaks form. Spread the meringue over the hot filling, sealing the edges to the crust.

5. Bake for 15 minutes or until golden brown. Cool on a wire rack for 1 hour; refrigerate for 1-2 hours before serving.

Strawberry-Rhubarb Meringue Pie is a rite of spring in our house. I've served up slices to guests many times, and they always enjoy the sweet-tart flavor.
—**JESSIE GREARSON-SAPAT** FALMOUTH, ME

Sour Cream-Lemon Pie

At a local restaurant, I sampled a tangy lemon dessert. With one bite, I knew I wanted to make it at home! I started hunting around for a recipe and finally found a version that had the same smooth, luscious taste.

—MARTHA SORENSEN FALLON, NV

PREP: 20 MIN. + CHILLING
MAKES: 8 SERVINGS

Pastry for single-crust pie (9 inches)
1 cup sugar
3 tablespoons plus 1½ teaspoons cornstarch
1 cup milk
½ cup lemon juice
3 egg yolks, lightly beaten
¼ cup butter, cubed
1 tablespoon grated lemon peel
1 cup (8 ounces) sour cream
1 cup heavy whipping cream, whipped

1. Preheat oven to 450°. On a lightly floured surface, roll the pastry dough to a ⅛-in.-thick circle; transfer to a 9-in. pie plate. Trim the pastry to ½ in. beyond the rim of the pie plate; flute the edge.

2. Line the unpricked pastry with a double thickness of foil. Fill with pie weights, dried beans or uncooked rice. Bake 8 minutes or until the bottom is lightly browned. Remove the foil and weights; bake 5-7 minutes longer or until golden brown. Cool on wire rack.

3. In a large heavy saucepan, mix the sugar and cornstarch. Whisk in milk and lemon juice until smooth. Cook and stir over medium-high heat until thickened and bubbly. Reduce heat to low; cook and stir 2 minutes longer. Remove from heat.

4. In a small bowl, whisk a small amount of hot mixture into egg yolks; return all to pan, whisking constantly. Bring to a gentle boil; cook and stir 2 minutes. Remove from heat. Stir in butter and peel. Cool without stirring.

5. Stir in sour cream. Add the filling to the crust. Top with whipped cream. Store in the refrigerator.

Lemon-Rosemary Layer Cake

Flecks of fresh rosemary and citrus peel make for a delightful layer cake. Keep it in mind for bridal showers and other events.

—MARY FRASER SURPRISE, AZ

PREP: 20 MIN. • **BAKE:** 25 MIN. + COOLING
MAKES: 16 SERVINGS

1 cup plus 2 tablespoons butter, softened
2½ cups sugar
4 eggs
1 egg yolk
4 cups all-purpose flour
3 teaspoons baking powder
1½ teaspoons salt
¼ teaspoon plus ⅛ teaspoon baking soda
1½ cups (12 ounces) sour cream
6 tablespoons lemon juice
3 teaspoons grated lemon peel
3 teaspoons minced fresh rosemary
FROSTING
2 packages (8 ounces each) cream cheese, softened
8¼ cups confectioners' sugar
3 teaspoons grated lemon peel
2¼ teaspoons lemon juice

1. In a large bowl, cream butter and sugar until light and fluffy. Add eggs and yolk, one at a time, beating well after each addition. Combine flour, baking powder, salt and baking soda; add to creamed mixture alternately with sour cream, beating well after each addition. Beat in lemon juice, peel and rosemary.

2. Transfer to three greased and floured 9-in. round baking pans. Bake at 350° for 25-30 minutes or until the edges begin to brown. Cool for 10 minutes before removing from pans to wire racks to cool completely.

3. For frosting, in a large bowl, beat the cream cheese until fluffy. Add the confectioners' sugar, lemon peel and juice; beat until smooth.

4. Spread the frosting between the layers and over the top and sides of cake. Refrigerate leftovers.

GRAND PRIZE WINNER

Cranberry Buttermilk Sherbet, page 218

220

215

219

Just Desserts

What a treat! Delight all the sweet tooths you know with this chapter's **luscious assortment** of rich cheesecakes, comforting puddings, fruit-filled pastries, cookie pizzas and more.

Rhubarb Raspberry Crumble

Everyone enjoys the sweet-tart taste and nutty topping of this homey crumble. Plus, reduced-fat ingredients make it lighter.

—HEIDI FARNWORTH RIVERTON, UT

PREP: 20 MIN. • **BAKE:** 35 MIN. • **MAKES:** 8 SERVINGS

- 3 cups chopped fresh or frozen rhubarb, thawed
- 2 cups fresh raspberries
- 2 teaspoons lemon juice
- ½ cup sugar
- ½ cup reduced-fat plain yogurt
- ⅓ cup reduced-fat sour cream
- ¼ cup all-purpose flour
- 1 egg

TOPPING

- ½ cup quick-cooking oats
- ⅓ cup whole wheat flour
- ¼ cup flaked coconut
- ¼ cup packed brown sugar
- ½ teaspoon ground cinnamon
- 3 tablespoons cold butter
- 3 tablespoons thawed apple juice concentrate
- ¼ cup slivered almonds

1. In a large bowl, combine the rhubarb, raspberries and lemon juice. In a small bowl, combine the sugar, yogurt, sour cream, flour and egg. Pour over rhubarb mixture and stir gently to coat. Transfer to an 11x7-in. baking dish coated with cooking spray.

2. For the topping, place the oats, flour, coconut, brown sugar and cinnamon in a food processor; cover and process until combined. Add butter and apple juice concentrate; process until crumbly. Stir in the almonds; sprinkle over the fruit mixture.

3. Bake, uncovered, at 350° for 35-45 minutes or until bubbly. Serve warm.

NOTE *If using frozen rhubarb, measure rhubarb while still frozen, then thaw completely. Drain in a colander, but do not press liquid out.*

Praline Peach Cobbler

For an extra-special treat on a chilly day, serve scoops of cobbler warm from the oven with vanilla ice cream.

—MAITHEL MARTIN KANSAS CITY, MO

PREP: 30 MIN. • **BAKE:** 25 MIN. • **MAKES:** 12 SERVINGS

- 1½ cups plus 2 teaspoons sugar, divided
- 2 tablespoons cornstarch
- 1 teaspoon ground cinnamon
- 1 cup water
- 8 cups sliced peeled fresh peaches
- 2 cups self-rising flour
- ½ cup shortening
- ½ cup buttermilk
- 3 tablespoons butter, melted
- ¼ cup packed brown sugar
- 1 cup chopped pecans

1. In a large saucepan, mix 1½ cups sugar, cornstarch and cinnamon. Stir in water until smooth. Add peaches. Bring to a boil over medium heat; cook and stir for 2 minutes or until thickened. Pour into a lightly greased 13x9x2-in. baking dish; set aside.

2. In a bowl, combine flour and remaining sugar; cut in shortening until mixture resembles coarse crumbs. Add buttermilk and stir just until moistened. If needed, add additional buttermilk, 1 tablespoon at a time, until dough clings together. Turn onto a floured surface; knead gently 6 to 8 times. Roll into a 12x8-in. rectangle.

3. Combine butter, brown sugar and pecans; spread over the dough to within ½ in. of edges. Starting with a long side, roll up jelly-roll style. Cut into twelve 1-in. pieces. Place on top of the peach mixture. Bake, uncovered, at 400° for 25-30 minutes or until golden brown.

NOTE *If self-rising flour is not available, substitute 2 cups all-purpose flour, 1 tablespoon baking powder and 1 teaspoon salt.*

Pumpkin Cranberry Bread Pudding

Fall flavors really shine through in this bread pudding featuring pumpkin, cranberries and a rich vanilla sauce. Yum!

—**JUDITH BUCCIARELLI** NEWBURGH, NY

PREP: 15 MIN. • **COOK:** 3 HOURS
MAKES: 8 SERVINGS (1⅓ CUPS SAUCE)

- 8 slices cinnamon bread, cut into 1-inch cubes
- 4 eggs, beaten
- 2 cups 2% milk
- 1 cup canned pumpkin
- ¼ cup packed brown sugar
- ¼ cup butter, melted
- 1 teaspoon vanilla extract
- ½ teaspoon ground cinnamon
- ¼ teaspoon ground nutmeg
- ½ cup dried cranberries

SAUCE
- 1 cup sugar
- ⅔ cup water
- 1 cup heavy whipping cream
- 2 teaspoons vanilla extract

1. Place the bread in a greased 3- or 4-qt. slow cooker. In a large bowl, combine the eggs, milk, pumpkin, brown sugar, butter, vanilla, cinnamon and nutmeg; stir in cranberries. Pour over bread cubes. Cover and cook on low for 3-4 hours or until a knife inserted near the center comes out clean.
2. For sauce, in a large saucepan, bring sugar and water to a boil over medium heat. Cook until sugar is dissolved and mixture turns a golden amber color, about 20 minutes. Gradually stir in cream until smooth. Remove from the heat; stir in vanilla. Serve warm with bread pudding.

Apple Crisp Pizza

While visiting the bakery at a Wisconsin apple orchard, I sampled a scrumptious fruit dessert. I couldn't wait to create it at home! As the cinnamon-spiced pizza bakes, the enticing aroma spreads through our kitchen—and my family comes running.

—**NANCY PREUSSNER** DELHI, IA

PREP: 15 MIN. • **BAKE:** 35 MIN. • **MAKES:** 12 SERVINGS

- Pastry for a single-crust pie
- ⅔ cup sugar
- 3 tablespoons all-purpose flour
- 1 teaspoon ground cinnamon
- 4 medium baking apples, peeled and cut into ½-inch slices

TOPPING
- ½ cup all-purpose flour
- ⅓ cup packed brown sugar
- ⅓ cup rolled oats
- 1 teaspoon ground cinnamon
- ¼ cup butter, softened
- ¼ to ½ cup caramel ice cream topping or caramel apple dip
- Vanilla ice cream, optional

1. Roll pastry to fit a 12-in. pizza pan; fold under or flute the edges. Combine sugar, flour and cinnamon in a bowl. Add apples and toss. Arrange the apples in a single layer in a circular pattern to completely cover pastry. Combine the first five topping ingredients; sprinkle over apples.
2. Bake at 350° for 35-40 minutes or until the apples are tender. Remove from the oven and immediately drizzle with the caramel topping or dip. Serve warm with vanilla ice cream if desired.

Apple Kolaches

I received my recipe for kolaches from a fellow home economist, and it was a big hit in our family. My son, who usually isn't a fan of dessert, was disappointed when he came home one day and discovered his dad had eaten the last treat in the batch!

—**ANN JOHNSON** EVANSVILLE, IN

PREP: 30 MIN. + CHILLING • **BAKE:** 10 MIN. • **MAKES:** 2½ DOZEN

- 1 cup butter, softened
- 1 package (8 ounces) cream cheese, softened
- 2 cups all-purpose flour
- 1½ cups finely chopped peeled apples
- ¼ teaspoon ground cinnamon

ICING
- 1 cup confectioners' sugar
- 4½ teaspoons 2% milk
- ½ teaspoon vanilla extract

1. In a large bowl, beat butter and cream cheese until light and fluffy. Gradually add flour and mix well. Divide dough into two portions; cover and refrigerate for 2 hours or until easy to handle.

2. Preheat oven to 400°. In a small bowl, combine apples and cinnamon. On a lightly floured surface, roll one portion of the dough into a 15x9-in. rectangle; cut into 3-in. squares. Place a teaspoonful of apple mixture in the center of each square. Overlap two opposite corners of dough over filling; pinch tightly to seal.

3. Place 2 in. apart on ungreased baking sheets. Repeat with remaining dough and apple mixture. Bake 10-12 minutes or until the bottoms are lightly browned. Cool 1 minute before removing from the pans to wire racks. Combine the icing ingredients; drizzle over warm kolaches.

This beautiful dessert is sure to delight cheesecake and cranberry lovers. Try it at Christmastime.
—**TERI RASEY** CADILLAC, MI

Cranberry Celebration Cheesecake

PREP: 45 MIN. • **BAKE:** 1¾ HOURS + CHILLING • **MAKES:** 16 SERVINGS

- ½ cup dried cranberries
- 2 cups cake flour
- ½ cup ground almonds
- ¼ cup confectioners' sugar
- ½ cup cold butter, cubed

FILLING
- ¾ cup plus 1½ cups sugar, divided
- 2 tablespoons cornstarch
- ¼ cup cranberry juice
- 2 cups fresh or frozen cranberries
- 4 packages (8 ounces each) cream cheese, softened
- 1 teaspoon vanilla extract
- 4 eggs, lightly beaten

TOPPING
- 2 cups (16 ounces) sour cream
- ¼ cup sugar
- 2 teaspoons vanilla extract
- 1 cup heavy whipping cream
- ¼ cup ground almonds
- ¼ cup sliced almonds, toasted

1. In a food processor, finely chop the dried cranberries. Add the flour, almonds and confectioners' sugar; process until blended. Add butter; pulse just until crumbly.

2. Press onto bottom and 1½ in. up sides of a greased 10-in. springform pan. Place on a baking sheet. Bake at 350° for 10 minutes.

3. In a small saucepan, combine ¾ cup sugar and the cornstarch; stir in the cranberry juice until smooth. Add the cranberries. Cook and stir until thickened and bubbly. Set aside.

4. In a large bowl, beat cream cheese, vanilla and remaining sugar until smooth. Add the eggs; beat just until combined. Pour half of batter into crust. Carefully spoon ¾ cup berry mixture over batter; top with remaining batter.

5. Bake for 45 minutes. Reduce the heat to 250°. Bake 25-30 minutes longer or until the center is almost set. Combine the sour cream, sugar and vanilla; spread over top. Bake 20-30 minutes or until set. Cool on a wire rack for 10 minutes. Run a knife around edge of pan to loosen; cool 1 hour longer. Spread remaining berry mixture over the top. Refrigerate overnight.

6. Beat the cream until stiff peaks form; fold in ground almonds. Pipe around top edge of cheesecake; sprinkle with sliced almonds.

Chocolate Malt Desserts

When my mom gave me some malted milk powder, I created a smooth, chocolaty dessert. It looks extra-special garnished with whipped topping, chopped candy and cherries.

—LISA KEYS MIDDLEBURY, CT

PREP: 10 MIN. • **COOK:** 10 MIN. + CHILLING • **MAKES:** 6 SERVINGS

- ½ cup malted milk powder
- ¼ cup sugar
- 2 tablespoons baking cocoa
- 2 tablespoons cornstarch
- ½ teaspoon instant espresso powder
- 2 cups fat-free milk
- 2 ounces semisweet chocolate, finely chopped
- 1 teaspoon vanilla extract
- ¾ cup reduced-fat whipped topping
- 6 malted milk balls, chopped
- 6 maraschino cherries

1. In a small saucepan, combine the first five ingredients. Stir in milk until smooth. Cook and stir over medium heat until mixture comes to a boil; cook 1-2 minutes longer or until thickened. Remove from the heat; stir in chocolate and vanilla until smooth.

2. Transfer to six dessert dishes, about ⅓ cup in each. Cover and refrigerate for at least 2 hours before serving.

3. Garnish each serving with 2 tablespoons whipped topping, ½ teaspoon chopped malted milk balls and a maraschino cherry.

Peanut Butter Cheesecake Pizza

My grandchildren help me assemble this yummy cookie pizza. They love pressing the dough into the pan, sprinkling on the chips and nuts, and sampling the results!

—FANCHEON RESLER ALBION, IN

PREP: 25 MIN. • **BAKE:** 15 MIN. + COOLING • **MAKES:** 16 SLICES

- 1 tube (16½ ounces) refrigerated sugar cookie dough
- 1 package (8 ounces) cream cheese, softened
- 2 eggs
- ½ cup sugar
- 1 cup peanut butter chips
- 1 cup chopped unsalted peanuts
- 1 cup milk chocolate chips
- 1 teaspoon shortening

1. Press cookie dough onto an ungreased 14-in. pizza pan. Bake at 350° for 15-18 minutes or until deep golden brown.

2. In a small bowl, beat cream cheese until fluffy. Add eggs and sugar; beat until combined. Spread over crust. Sprinkle with peanut butter chips and peanuts.

3. Bake for 15-18 minutes or until the center is set. Cool for 15 minutes. Meanwhile, in a microwave, melt the chocolate chips and shortening; stir until smooth. Drizzle over pizza. Refrigerate leftovers.

Swedish Rice Ring

This traditional dessert from Sweden is a popular choice for get-togethers in Minnesota. I usually make two rice rings at once because they're so good! Lots of ruby-red strawberries piled in the center add a bright burst of color.

—**LORI JEANE SCHLECHT** WIMBLEDON, ND

PREP: 15 MIN. • **COOK:** 20 MIN. + CHILLING
MAKES: 12 SERVINGS

- 2 **envelopes unflavored gelatin**
- ¼ **cup cold water**
- 3 **cups whole milk**
- ½ **cup uncooked long-grain rice**
- ½ **cup sugar**
- ½ **teaspoon salt**
- 1 **cup heavy whipping cream**
  Fresh or thawed frozen sweetened strawberries

1. In a small bowl, sprinkle gelatin over cold water; set aside. In a small heavy saucepan, combine milk, rice, sugar and salt; bring to a boil, stirring occasionally. Reduce heat; simmer, covered, 15-20 minutes until the rice is tender. Remove from heat; stir in the gelatin mixture until completely dissolved. Refrigerate, covered, until partially set.

2. In a bowl, beat the heavy whipping cream until stiff peaks form. Fold into the chilled rice mixture. Spoon into a 6-cup ring mold coated with cooking spray; refrigerate until firm, about 3 hours. Unmold onto a serving platter. Serve with strawberries.

RICE ROUND-UP

White rice has had the hull and bran removed during the milling process. Long grain rice has a long, slender kernel, and it is separate, light and fluffy when cooked. Medium grain is shorter and wider than long grain. When cooked, it is moist and tender, and the individual grains cling together. Short grain has short, plump, almost round kernels. When cooked, the grains cling together and have a soft texture.

Cranberry Buttermilk Sherbet

Want something lighter for a Christmastime menu? Cranberry sherbet is refreshing after a rich meal, and the buttermilk adds a nice tang. Enjoy a scoop on a hot summer day, too.

—LISA SPEER PALM BEACH, FL

PREP: 25 MIN. • **PROCESS:** 20 MIN. + FREEZING
MAKES: ABOUT 1 QUART

- 1 cup fresh or frozen cranberries
- ¼ cup packed brown sugar
- ¼ cup orange juice
- ½ teaspoon grated lemon peel
- ½ teaspoon grated orange peel
- 1 cinnamon stick (3 inches)
- 2 cups buttermilk
- 1 cup sugar
- 1 cup light corn syrup
- ¼ cup lemon juice
  Dash salt

1. In a small saucepan, combine the first six ingredients; cook over medium heat until berries pop, about 15 minutes. Discard cinnamon stick. Mash berry mixture; chill.

2. In a large bowl, combine the buttermilk, sugar, corn syrup, lemon juice and salt; add the berry mixture. Pour into the cylinder of an ice cream freezer; freeze according to the manufacturer's directions. Transfer ice cream to freezer containers, allowing headspace for expansion. Freeze 2-4 hours or until firm.

Cinnamon-Toffee Croissant Bread Pudding

Ever since I sampled this for the first time, I've been a bread pudding buff. I think it's the ultimate comfort food! Sometimes I use almond extract in place of the vanilla.

—AMBER MASSEY ARGYLE, TX

PREP: 30 MIN. + STANDING • **BAKE:** 30 MIN.
MAKES: 12 SERVINGS (1¼ CUPS SAUCE)

- 3 eggs, beaten
- 4 cups 2% milk
- 2 cups sugar
- 4½ teaspoons vanilla extract
- 3 teaspoons ground cinnamon
- ½ teaspoon ground nutmeg
- 10 croissants, torn into pieces
- 1 cup toffee bits
- 1 cup chopped pecans, toasted
- 1 cup milk chocolate chips

SAUCE

- 1 cup sugar
- ½ cup half-and-half cream
- ¼ cup butter, cubed
- ½ teaspoon vanilla extract

1. In a large bowl, combine the eggs, milk, sugar, vanilla, cinnamon and nutmeg. Gently stir in the croissants, toffee bits, pecans and chips; let stand for 15 minutes or until the croissants are softened.

2. Transfer mixture to a greased 13x9x2-in. baking dish. Bake, uncovered, at 350° for 30-35 minutes or until a knife inserted near the center comes out clean.

3. For sauce, bring the sugar, cream and butter to a boil in a small saucepan. Reduce heat; simmer, uncovered, for 5 minutes. Remove from the heat; stir in vanilla. Serve with warm bread pudding.

Truffle Cake with Candy Cane Cream

One bite of this decadent chocolate dessert will get anyone into the holiday spirit! A pretty pink dollop of peppermint-flavored whipped cream is the festive finishing touch.

—CRISTI KIRKHAM WEST JORDAN, UT

PREP: 35 MIN. • **BAKE:** 40 MIN. + CHILLING • **MAKES:** 16 SERVINGS

- 1 cup graham cracker crumbs
- 1 cup chopped pecans, toasted and coarsely ground
- 2 tablespoons plus ¾ cup sugar, divided
- ¼ cup butter, melted
- 16 ounces semisweet chocolate, coarsely chopped
- 1 cup heavy whipping cream
- 6 eggs
- ⅓ cup all-purpose flour

CREAM

- 1 cup heavy whipping cream
- 2 tablespoons sugar
- 4 candy canes, finely ground
- ¼ to ½ teaspoon peppermint extract, optional

1. Combine graham cracker crumbs, pecans, 2 tablespoons sugar and butter; press onto the bottom and 1½ in. up the sides of a greased 9-in. springform pan. Place the pan on a baking sheet.

2. In a large saucepan, cook the chocolate and cream over low heat until the chocolate is melted. Cool. In a large bowl, beat the eggs, flour and remaining sugar on high speed until thick and lemon-colored, about 5 minutes. Gradually beat in chocolate mixture.

3. Pour batter into crust. Bake at 325° for 40-45 minutes or until center is almost set. Cool on wire rack for 10 minutes. Carefully run a knife around the edge of pan to loosen; cool 1 hour longer. Refrigerate for 4 hours or overnight.

4. Beat the cream and sugar until stiff peaks form; fold in ground candy and extract if desired. Serve with cake.

Dulce de Leche Rice Pudding

Give an old-fashioned favorite a modern, caramel-infused, sweet-and-salty twist with the taste of dulce de leche.

—CARLA CERVANTES-JAUREGUI MODESTO, CA

PREP: 15 MIN. • **COOK:** 50 MIN. • **MAKES:** 6 SERVINGS

- 2 cups water
- ½ cup uncooked brown rice
- ½ cup uncooked long grain rice
- ¼ cup sugar
- 1½ cinnamon sticks (3 inches)
- 1 tablespoon butter
  Dash salt
- 1 can (12 ounces) evaporated milk
- 8 caramels
- 1 tablespoon coarse sugar
- ⅛ teaspoon kosher salt

1. In a large saucepan, combine the first seven ingredients. Bring to a boil. Reduce the heat; simmer, uncovered, for 30 minutes or until water is absorbed.

2. Stir in the evaporated milk. Bring to a boil. Reduce heat; simmer, uncovered, for 12-16 minutes or until thick and creamy, stirring occasionally. Add caramels, stirring until melted. Discard cinnamon sticks.

3. Spoon into dishes. In a small bowl, combine coarse sugar and salt; sprinkle over pudding. Serve warm or cold.

Georgia Peach Ice Cream

We've been enjoying our state fruit in homemade ice cream for over 50 years.

—**MARGUERITE ETHRIDGE** AMERICUS, GA

PREP: 45 MIN. + CHILLING
PROCESS: 20 MIN./BATCH + FREEZING
MAKES: 3¾ QUARTS

- 4 **eggs**
- 1¼ **cups sugar, divided**
- ½ **teaspoon salt**
- 4 **cups whole milk**
- 2 **cans (14 ounces each) sweetened condensed milk**
- 1¾ **pounds fresh peaches, peeled and sliced**

1. In a large heavy saucepan, whisk eggs, 1 cup sugar and salt until blended; stir in milk. Cook over low heat until mixture is just thick enough to coat a spoon and a thermometer reads at least 160°, stirring constantly. Do not allow to boil. Remove from heat immediately.

2. Quickly transfer to a bowl; place bowl in a pan of ice water. Stir gently and occasionally for 2 minutes. Stir in condensed milk. Press plastic wrap onto surface of custard. Refrigerate several hours or overnight.

3. When ready to freeze, in a small bowl, mash the peaches with the remaining sugar; let stand 30 minutes. Fill the cylinder of ice cream freezer two-thirds full with custard, stirring in some of peaches; freeze according to manufacturers' directions. Refrigerate remaining mixture until ready to freeze.

4. Transfer the ice cream to freezer containers, allowing headspace for expansion. Freeze 2-4 hours or until firm. Repeat with remaining ice cream mixture and peaches.

GRAND PRIZE

Over-the-Top Blueberry Bread Pudding

This bread pudding recipe really lives up to its name! You could also use fresh mint and sweetened whipped cream as toppings in place of the sauce.

—**MARILYN HAYNES** SYLACAUGA, AL

PREP: 15 MIN. + STANDING • **BAKE:** 50 MIN.
MAKES: 12 SERVINGS

- 3 **eggs**
- 4 **cups heavy whipping cream**
- 2 **cups sugar**
- 3 **teaspoons vanilla extract**
- 2 **cups fresh or frozen blueberries**
- 1 **package (10 to 12 ounces) white baking chips**
- 1 **loaf (1 pound) French bread, cut into 1-inch cubes**

SAUCE

- 1 **package (10 to 12 ounces) white baking chips**
- 1 **cup heavy whipping cream**

1. Preheat oven to 350°. In a large bowl, combine eggs, cream, sugar and vanilla. Stir in blueberries and baking chips. Stir in the bread cubes; let stand 15 minutes or until bread is softened.

2. Transfer pudding mixture to a greased 13x9x2-in. baking dish. Bake, uncovered, 50-60 minutes or until a knife inserted near the center comes out clean. Let pudding stand 5 minutes before serving.

3. For the sauce, place baking chips in a small bowl. In a small saucepan, bring cream just to a boil. Pour over baking chips; whisk until smooth. Serve with pudding.

Magnolia Dream Cheesecake

Love cheesecake? Try the yummy flavor blend of peach and hazelnut.

—CHARLENE CHAMBERS
ORMOND BEACH, FL

PREP: 50 MIN. • **BAKE:** 1½ HOURS + CHILLING
MAKES: 16 SERVINGS

- 1 cup hazelnuts, toasted
- 12 whole graham crackers
- ¼ cup sugar
- 6 tablespoons unsalted butter, melted

FILLING

- 1½ pounds ricotta cheese
- 2 packages (8 ounces each) cream cheese, softened
- 2 cups (16 ounces) sour cream
- 1½ cups sugar
- 6 tablespoons all-purpose flour
- 4 tablespoons hazelnut liqueur, divided
- 6 eggs, lightly beaten
- 3 medium peaches, sliced

1. Place a greased 10-in. springform pan on a double thickness of heavy-duty foil (about 18 in. square). Securely wrap foil around pan.

2. Place hazelnuts in a food processor; cover and pulse until coarsely chopped. Set aside ¼ cup for garnish. Add the graham crackers and sugar to food processor; cover and process until finely chopped. Add butter; process until blended. Press onto the bottom and 1 in. up the sides of the prepared pan. Place the pan on a baking sheet. Bake at 325° for 10 minutes. Cool on a wire rack.

3. In a large bowl, beat the ricotta, cream cheese, sour cream and sugar until well blended. Beat in flour and 2 tablespoons liqueur. Add the eggs; beat on low speed just until combined. Pour into crust. Place springform pan in a large baking pan; add 1 in. of hot water to larger pan.

4. Bake at 325° for 1½ hours or until center is just set and top appears dull. Remove the springform pan from the water bath. Cool on a wire rack for 10 minutes. Carefully run a knife around edge of pan to loosen; cool 1 hour longer. Refrigerate overnight.

5. Toss peaches with the remaining liqueur; arrange over the top of the cheesecake. Sprinkle the reserved hazelnuts in the center. Remove the sides of the pan.

Lemon Panna Cotta with Berries

Cool and smooth, these personal-size Italian desserts shaped in ramekins are fancy enough for even the most elegant dinner party. For an extra flourish, garnish each serving with a little lemon zest.

—MARIELA PETROSKI HELENA, MT

PREP: 25 MIN. + CHILLING
MAKES: 7 SERVINGS

- 1 envelope unflavored gelatin
- 1⅓ cups half-and-half cream
- 2 cups heavy whipping cream
- ⅓ cup honey
- 1 teaspoon grated lemon peel
  Dash salt
- ⅔ cup each fresh blackberries, blueberries and raspberries
- 2 tablespoons sugar
- 2 tablespoons lemon juice
- 1 tablespoon Amaretto, optional

1. In a small saucepan, sprinkle the unflavored gelatin over half-and-half cream; let stand for 1 minute. Heat over low heat, stirring until the gelatin is completely dissolved. Stir in heavy whipping cream, honey, lemon peel and salt. Cook and stir until blended. Pour into seven 6-oz. ramekins or custard cups.

2. Cover and refrigerate for at least 5 hours or until set. In a small bowl, combine the berries, sugar, lemon juice and Amaretto if desired. Cover and refrigerate for at least 30 minutes. Unmold the panna cotta onto dessert plates; serve with berry mixture.

Luscious Almond Cheesecake

Almond flavor and cheesecakes are a match made in heaven. Here's proof! I spread sour cream on top and add a sprinkling of toasted nuts.

—BRENDA CLIFFORD OVERLAND PARK, KS

PREP: 15 MIN. • **BAKE:** 1 HOUR + CHILLING
MAKES: 14-16 SERVINGS

- 1¼ cups crushed vanilla wafers (about 40 wafers)
- ¾ cup finely chopped almonds
- ¼ cup sugar
- ⅓ cup butter, melted

FILLING

- 4 packages (8 ounces each) cream cheese, softened
- 1¼ cups sugar
- 4 eggs, lightly beaten
- 1½ teaspoons almond extract
- 1 teaspoon vanilla extract

TOPPING

- 2 cups (16 ounces) sour cream
- ¼ cup sugar
- 1 teaspoon vanilla extract
- ⅛ cup toasted sliced almonds

1. In a bowl, combine the wafer crumbs, almonds and sugar; stir in the butter and mix well. Press into the bottom of a greased 10-in. springform pan; set aside.

2. In a large bowl, beat cream cheese and sugar until smooth. Add eggs; beat on low speed just until combined. Stir in extracts. Pour into crust. Place on a baking sheet.

3. Bake at 350° for 50-55 minutes or until center is almost set. Remove from the oven; let stand for 5 minutes (leave oven on). Combine sour cream, sugar and vanilla. Spoon around the edge of cheesecake; carefully spread over the filling. Bake 5 minutes longer. Cool on a wire rack for 10 minutes. Carefully run a knife around the edge of the pan to loosen; cool 1 hour longer. Refrigerate overnight.

4. Just before serving, sprinkle with the almonds and remove sides of pan. Refrigerate leftovers.

Crunchy Lime & Berry Parfaits

When we want to make our parfaits a bit lighter, we use reduced-fat whipped topping for the lime layers.

—ELIZABETH HAYES BRAZIL, IN

START TO FINISH: 25 MIN.
MAKES: 8 SERVINGS

- 1 cup coarsely crushed pretzels
- ¼ cup sugar
- ¼ cup butter, melted
- 1 carton (8 ounces) frozen whipped topping, thawed
- ½ cup confectioners' sugar
- 2 tablespoons lime juice
- 1½ teaspoons grated lime peel
- 1⅓ cups sliced fresh strawberries
- 1⅓ cups fresh raspberries
- 1⅓ cups fresh blueberries

1. In a small bowl, combine crushed pretzels, sugar and butter; press into a greased 9-in. square baking pan. Bake, uncovered, at 350° for 8-10 minutes or until lightly browned. Set aside.

2. In a large bowl, combine whipped topping, confectioners' sugar, lime juice and lime peel. In another bowl, combine the berries. Break pretzel mixture into small pieces.

3. Spoon 2 tablespoons lime mixture into each of eight parfait glasses. Layer each with 1 tablespoon pretzel pieces and ½ cup berries. Top each with the remaining lime mixture and pretzel pieces. Serve immediately.

Freezer Raspberry Sauce

PREP: 20 MIN. + STANDING
MAKES: 4 PINTS

- 10 cups fresh raspberries, divided
- 3 cups sugar
- 1 cup light corn syrup
- 1 package (3 ounces) liquid fruit pectin
- 2 tablespoons lemon juice

1. Rinse four 1-pint plastic containers and lids with boiling water. Dry the containers and lids thoroughly. Thoroughly crush 6 cups raspberries, 1 cup at a time, to measure exactly 3 cups; transfer to a large bowl. Stir in the sugar and corn syrup; let stand 10 minutes, stirring occasionally.

2. In a small bowl, mix the liquid fruit pectin and lemon juice. Add to the raspberry mixture; stir constantly for 3 minutes to evenly distribute the liquid pectin. Stir in the remaining whole raspberries.

3. Immediately fill all containers to within ½ in. of the tops. Wipe off the top edges of the containers; immediately cover with the lids. Let stand at room temperature 24 hours or until partially set. Refrigerate the raspberry sauce up to 3 weeks or freeze up to 12 months.

4. Thaw frozen sauce in refrigerator before using.

❝Put fresh raspberries to wonderful use in this sauce. It's so good over sponge cake, shortcake, ice cream and even waffles.❞

—KATIE KOZIOLEK HARTLAND, MN

Heavenly Cherry Angel Food Trifle

Cherries are a major crop in New York. I submitted my trifle for a cherry recipe contest held in celebration of George Washington's birthday, and I won!

—**HYACINTH RIZZO** BUFFALO, NY

PREP: 20 MIN. + CHILLING
MAKES: 8-10 SERVINGS

- 5 cups angel food cake cubes
- ¼ cup cherry liqueur, optional
- 1 cup confectioners' sugar
- 1 package (3 ounces) cream cheese, softened
- 8 ounces frozen whipped topping, thawed, divided
- ½ cup toasted chopped pecans
- 1 can (21 ounces) cherry pie filling or topping

1. Place the angel food cake cubes in large bowl. Sprinkle with the liqueur if desired; let stand 30 minutes.
2. In a medium bowl, combine the confectioners' sugar and cream cheese; beat until blended. Reserve 2 tablespoons whipped topping; fold the remaining whipped topping into the cream cheese mixture. Stir the topping mixture and pecans into the cake cubes; mix well.
3. Spoon cake mixture into a trifle bowl or glass serving bowl; spread cherry filling evenly over top. Or, if desired, layer one-half cake mixture and cherry filling; repeat the layers.
4. Cover and refrigerate at least 3 hours. Garnish servings with the reserved whipped topping.

TRIFLE TIME

Have leftover brownies from a party...or extra pieces of coffee cake from breakfast? Use them to create an all-new treat for dinner. Simply cube the pieces and use them to create a trifle. Complete your dessert with instant pudding, fruit pie filling or other add-ins, using whatever flavors suit your family.

—**LOUY CASTONGUAY**
WEST FARMINGTON, ME

Key Lime Mousse Cups

Lovely and refreshing, these miniature tarts look and taste so special. No one realizes they're super-easy to fix using convenient purchased phyllo shells.

—**SUZANNE PAULEY** RENTON, WA

START TO FINISH: 20 MIN.
MAKES: 2½ DOZEN

- 4 ounces cream cheese, softened
- ⅔ cup sweetened condensed milk
- ¼ cup Key lime juice
- ½ cup heavy whipping cream, whipped
- 2 packages (1.9 ounces each) frozen miniature phyllo tart shells
  Fresh raspberries and lime wedges, optional

In a large bowl, beat the cream cheese, milk and juice until smooth; fold in the whipped cream. Pipe into tart shells. Garnish with raspberries and lime wedges if desired. Serve immediately.
PER SERVING 69 cal., 4 g fat (2 g sat. fat), 12 mg chol., 30 mg sodium, 6 g carb., trace fiber, 1 g pro. **Diabetic Exchanges:** 1 fat, ½ starch.

Sensational Tiramisu

If you're a fan of classic Italian tiramisu but not of all the fat and calories it usually contains, consider this delightfully lighter variation. Moist and pretty, it cuts well into layered squares and gets plenty of traditional flavor from coffee, Kahlua liqueur and cream cheese.

—MARY WALTERS WESTERVILLE, OH

PREP: 25 MIN. • **COOK:** 10 MIN. + CHILLING
MAKES: 12 SERVINGS

- 1 package (8 ounces) reduced-fat cream cheese
- ⅔ cup confectioners' sugar, divided
- 1½ cups reduced-fat whipped topping, divided
- ½ cup plus 1 tablespoon sugar
- 3 egg whites
- ¼ cup water
- 2 packages (3 ounces each) ladyfingers, split
- ½ cup boiling water
- 2 tablespoons coffee liqueur
- 1 tablespoon instant coffee granules
- ½ teaspoon baking cocoa

1. In a small bowl, beat the cream cheese and confectioners' sugar until smooth. Fold in 1 cup whipped topping; set aside.

2. Combine ½ cup sugar, the egg whites and water in a small heavy saucepan over low heat. With a hand mixer, beat on low speed for 1 minute. Continue beating on low over low heat until the mixture reaches 160°, about 8-10 minutes. Pour into a large bowl. Beat on high until stiff peaks form, about 7 minutes. Fold into cream cheese mixture.

3. Arrange half of ladyfingers in an ungreased 11x7-in. dish. Combine the boiling water, liqueur, coffee granules and remaining sugar; brush half of mixture over ladyfingers. Top with half of cream cheese mixture. Repeat layers. Spread remaining whipped topping over top; sprinkle with cocoa. Refrigerate for 2 hours before serving.
PER SERVING *223 cal., 7 g fat (4 g sat. fat), 62 mg chol., 127 mg sodium, 34 g carb., trace fiber, 5 g pro.* **Diabetic Exchanges:** *2 starch, 1 fat.*

Frozen Strawberry Delight

Here's a cool dessert to keep in mind for warm summer days. If you like, garnish it with both strawberries and blueberries for a patriotic presentation.

—BARBARA CHRISTENSEN

JACKSONVILLE, FL

PREP: 20 MIN + FREEZING
MAKES: 10 SERVINGS

- 1 can (14 ounces) sweetened condensed milk
- ¼ cup lemon juice
- 4 cups sliced fresh strawberries, divided
- 1 carton (8 ounces) frozen whipped topping, thawed and divided
- 8 Oreo cookies, crushed

1. Line an 8x4-in. loaf pan with foil, letting the edges of foil hang over the sides of pan; set aside.

2. In a large bowl, combine milk and lemon juice; fold in 2 cups berries and 2 cups whipped topping. Transfer half of mixture to prepared pan. Sprinkle with the cookie crumbs; top with the remaining berry mixture. Cover and freeze for 6 hours or overnight.

3. To serve, using foil, lift dessert out of the pan. Invert onto a serving plate; discard the foil. Spread the remaining whipped topping over top and sides of dessert; garnish with the remaining berries. Cut into slices.

Substitutions & Equivalents

EQUIVALENT MEASURES

3 teaspoons	= 1 tablespoon	16 tablespoons	= 1 cup
4 tablespoons	= ¼ cup	2 cups	= 1 pint
5⅓ tablespoons	= ⅓ cup	4 cups	= 1 quart
8 tablespoons	= ½ cup	4 quarts	= 1 gallon

FOOD EQUIVALENTS

GRAINS

Macaroni	1 cup (3½ ounces) uncooked	= 2½ cups cooked
Noodles, Medium	3 cups (4 ounces) uncooked	= 4 cups cooked
Popcorn	⅓ to ½ cup unpopped	= 8 cups popped
Rice, Long Grain	1 cup uncooked	= 3 cups cooked
Rice, Quick-Cooking	1 cup uncooked	= 2 cups cooked
Spaghetti	8 ounces uncooked	= 4 cups cooked

CRUMBS

Bread	1 slice	= ¾ cup soft crumbs, ¼ cup fine dry crumbs
Graham Crackers	7 squares	= ½ cup finely crushed
Buttery Round Crackers	12 crackers	= ½ cup finely crushed
Saltine Crackers	14 crackers	= ½ cup finely crushed

FRUITS

Bananas	1 medium	= ⅓ cup mashed
Lemons	1 medium	= 3 tablespoons juice, 2 teaspoons grated peel
Limes	1 medium	= 2 tablespoons juice, 1½ teaspoons grated peel
Oranges	1 medium	= ¼ to ⅓ cup juice, 4 teaspoons grated peel

VEGETABLES

Cabbage	1 head	= 5 cups shredded	Green Pepper	1 large	= 1 cup chopped
Carrots	1 pound	= 3 cups shredded	Mushrooms	½ pound	= 3 cups sliced
Celery	1 rib	= ½ cup chopped	Onions	1 medium	= ½ cup chopped
Corn	1 ear fresh	= ⅔ cup kernels	Potatoes	3 medium	= 2 cups cubed

NUTS

Almonds	1 pound	= 3 cups chopped	Pecan Halves	1 pound	= 4½ cups chopped
Ground Nuts	3¾ ounces	= 1 cup	Walnuts	1 pound	= 3¾ cups chopped

EASY SUBSTITUTIONS

WHEN YOU NEED...		USE...
Baking Powder	1 teaspoon	½ teaspoon cream of tartar + ¼ teaspoon baking soda
Buttermilk	1 cup	1 tablespoon lemon juice or vinegar + enough milk to measure 1 cup (let stand 5 minutes before using)
Cornstarch	1 tablespoon	2 tablespoons all-purpose flour
Honey	1 cup	1¼ cups sugar + ¼ cup water
Half-and-Half Cream	1 cup	1 tablespoon melted butter + enough whole milk to measure 1 cup
Onion	1 small, chopped (⅓ cup)	1 teaspoon onion powder or 1 tablespoon dried minced onion
Tomato Juice	1 cup	½ cup tomato sauce + ½ cup water
Tomato Sauce	2 cups	¾ cup tomato paste + 1 cup water
Unsweetened Chocolate	1 square (1 ounce)	3 tablespoons baking cocoa + 1 tablespoon shortening or oil
Whole Milk	1 cup	½ cup evaporated milk + ½ cup water

Guide to Cooking with Popular Herbs

HERB	APPETIZERS SALADS	BREADS/EGGS SAUCES/CHEESE	VEGETABLES PASTA	MEAT POULTRY	FISH SHELLFISH
BASIL	Green, Potato & Tomato Salads; Salad Dressings; Stewed Fruit	Breads, Fondue, Egg Dishes, Dips, Marinades, Sauces	Mushrooms, Tomatoes, Squash, Pasta, Bland Vegetables	Broiled, Roast Meats; Meat & Poultry Pies; Stews; Stuffing	Baked, Broiled & Poached Fish; Shellfish
BAY LEAF	Seafood Cocktail, Seafood Salad, Tomato Aspic, Stewed Fruit	Egg Dishes, Gravies, Marinades, Sauces	Dried Bean Dishes, Beets, Carrots, Onions, Potatoes, Rice, Squash	Corned Beef, Tongue Meat & Poultry Stews	Poached Fish, Shellfish, Fish Stews
CHIVES	Mixed Vegetable, Green, Potato & Tomato Salads; Salad Dressings	Egg & Cheese Dishes, Cream Cheese, Cottage Cheese, Gravies, Sauces	Hot Vegetables, Potatoes	Broiled Poultry, Poultry & Meat Pies, Stews, Casseroles	Baked Fish, Fish Casseroles, Fish Stews, Shellfish
DILL	Seafood Cocktail; Green, Potato & Tomato Salads; Salad Dressings	Breads, Egg & Cheese Dishes, Cream Cheese, Fish & Meat Sauces	Beans, Beets, Cabbage, Carrots, Cauliflower, Peas, Squash, Tomatoes	Beef, Veal Roasts, Lamb, Steaks, Chops, Stews, Roast & Creamed Poultry	Baked, Broiled, Poached & Stuffed Fish; Shellfish
GARLIC	All Salads, Salad Dressings	Fondue, Poultry Sauces, Fish & Meat Marinades	Beans, Eggplant, Potatoes, Rice, Tomatoes	Roast Meats, Meat & Poultry Pies, Hamburgers, Casseroles, Stews	Broiled Fish, Shellfish, Fish Stews, Casseroles
MARJORAM	Seafood Cocktail; Green, Poultry & Seafood Salads	Breads, Cheese Spreads, Egg & Cheese Dishes, Gravies, Sauces	Carrots, Eggplant, Peas, Onions, Potatoes, Dried Bean Dishes, Spinach	Roast Meats & Poultry, Meat & Poultry Pies, Stews & Casseroles	Baked, Broiled & Stuffed Fish; Shellfish
MUSTARD	Fresh Green Salads; Prepared Meat, Macaroni & Potato Salads; Salad Dressings	Biscuits, Egg & Cheese Dishes, Sauces	Baked Beans, Cabbage, Eggplant, Squash, Dried Beans, Mushrooms, Pasta	Chops, Steaks, Ham, Pork, Poultry, Cold Meats	Shellfish
OREGANO	Green, Poultry & Seafood Salads	Breads; Egg & Cheese Dishes; Meat, Poultry & Vegetable Sauces	Artichokes, Cabbage, Eggplant, Squash, Dried Beans, Mushrooms, Pasta	Broiled, Roast Meats; Meat & Poultry Pies; Stews; Casseroles	Baked, Broiled & Poached Fish; Shellfish
PARSLEY	Green, Potato, Seafood & Vegetable Salads	Biscuits, Breads, Egg & Cheese Dishes, Gravies, Sauces	Asparagus, Beets, Eggplant, Squash, Dried Beans, Mushrooms, Pasta	Meat Loaf, Meat & Poultry Pies, Stews, Casseroles, Stuffing	Fish Stews, Stuffed Fish
ROSEMARY	Fruit Cocktail, Fruit & Green Salads	Biscuits, Egg Dishes, Herb Butter, Cream Cheese, Marinades, Sauces	Beans, Broccoli, Peas, Cauliflower, Mushrooms, Baked Potatoes, Parsnips	Roast Meat, Poultry & Meat Pies, Stews, Casseroles, Stuffing	Stuffed Fish, Shellfish
SAGE		Breads, Fondue, Egg & Cheese Dishes, Spreads, Gravies, Sauces	Beans, Beets, Onions, Peas, Spinach, Squash, Tomatoes	Roast Meat, Poultry, Meat Loaf, Stews, Stuffing	Baked, Poached & Stuffed Fish
TARRAGON	Seafood Cocktail, Avocado Salads, Salad Dressings	Cheese Spreads, Marinades, Sauces, Egg Dishes	Asparagus, Beans, Beets, Carrots, Mushrooms, Peas, Squash, Spinach	Steaks, Poultry, Roast Meats, Casseroles, Stews	Baked, Broiled & Poached Fish; Shellfish
THYME	Seafood Cocktail; Green, Poultry, Seafood & Vegetable Salads	Biscuits, Breads, Egg & Cheese Dishes, Sauces, Spreads	Beets, Carrots, Mushrooms, Onions, Peas, Eggplant, Spinach, Potatoes	Roast Meat, Poultry & Meat Loaf, Meat & Poultry Pies, Stews, Casseroles	Baked, Broiled & Stuffed Fish; Shellfish, Fish Stews

COOKING TERMS

AL DENTE An Italian term meaning "to the tooth." Used to describe pasta that is cooked but still firm.

BASTE To moisten food with melted butter, pan drippings, marinades or other liquid to add flavor and juiciness.

BEAT To rapidly mix with a spoon, fork, wire whisk or electric mixer.

BLEND To combine ingredients until just mixed.

BOIL To heat liquids until bubbles form that cannot be "stirred down." In the case of water, the temperature will reach 212°.

BONE To remove all meat from the bone before cooking.

BROIL To cook foods about 4 to 6 inches from a heat source.

COMBINE To place several ingredients in a bowl or container and mix thoroughly.

CREAM To beat ingredients together to a smooth consistency, usually in the case of butter and sugar for baking.

CRISP-TENDER A stage of vegetable cooking where the vegetables are cooked until they are crunchy yet tender enough to be pierced with a fork.

CUT IN To break down and distribute cold butter, margarine or shortening into a flour mixture using a pastry blender or two knives.

DASH A measurement less than ⅛ teaspoon that is used for herbs, spices or hot pepper sauce. This is not an accurate measurement.

DREDGE To coat foods with flour or other dry ingredients. Most often done with pot roasts and stew meat before browning.

DRIPPINGS The juices and melted fat that collect in the bottom of the pan as meat is cooked. The juices and some of the fat from the drippings can be used in gravies and sauces.

DUST To lightly sprinkle with confectioners' sugar, baking cocoa or flour.

FLAKE To separate foods into small pieces. The term is frequently used when describing the doneness of fish.

FLUTE To make a V shape or scalloped edge on pie crust using your thumb and fingers.

FOLD To incorporate several ingredients by careful and gentle turning with a spatula. Used generally when mixing beaten egg whites or whipped cream into the rest of the ingredients to keep the batter light.

COOKING TERMS

JULIENNE To cut foods into long thin strips much like matchsticks. Most often used for salads and stir-fry dishes.

KNEAD To work dough by using a pressing and folding action to make it smooth and elastic.

MARINATE To tenderize and/or flavor foods, usually meat or raw vegetables, by placing in a liquid mixture of oil, vinegar, wine, lime or lemon juice, herbs and spices.

MINCE To cut into very fine pieces. Often used for garlic or fresh herbs.

PARBOIL To boil foods, usually vegetables, until partially cooked. Most often used when vegetables are finished using another cooking method or chilled for marinated salads or dips.

PARTIALLY SET Describes the consistency of gelatin after it has been chilled for a short amount of time. Mixture should resemble the consistency of egg whites.

PINCH A measurement less than ⅛ teaspoon of a seasoning or spice that is easily held between the thumb and index finger. This is not an accurate measurement.

PROCESS To combine, blend, chop or puree foods in a food processor or blender.

PULSE To process foods in a food processor or blender using short bursts of power. This is accomplished by quickly turning the machine on and off.

PUREE To mash solid foods into a smooth mixture using a food processor, food mill, blender or sieve.

SAUTE To fry quickly in a small amount of fat, stirring almost constantly. Most often done with onions, mushrooms and other chopped vegetables.

SIMMER To cook liquids alone or a combination of ingredients with liquid just under the boiling point (180° to 200°). The surface of the liquid will have some movement and there may be small bubbles around the side of the pan.

SOFT PEAKS The stage of beating egg whites or heavy whipping cream when the beater is lifted from the mixture and the points of the peaks curl over.

STEAM To cook foods covered on a rack or in a steamer basket over a small amount of boiling water. Most often used for vegetables.

STIFF PEAKS The stage of beating egg whites or heavy whipping cream when the beater is lifted from the mixture and the points of the peaks stand straight up.

STIR-FRY To cook meats and/or vegetables with a constant stirring motion in a small amount of oil in a wok or skillet over high heat.

WARM To hold foods at a low temperature, usually around 200°, without further cooking.

General Recipe Index

This handy index lists every recipe by food category, major ingredient and/or cooking method, so you can easily locate recipes to suit your needs.

⊘ RECIPES INCLUDE **NUTRITION FACTS** AND **DIABETIC EXCHANGES**

Alphabetical Recipe Index

This index lists every recipe in alphabetical order so you can easily find your favorite recipes.

⊘ RECIPES INCLUDE **NUTRITION FACTS** AND **DIABETIC EXCHANGES**